Deja,
May your li
be filled w
little bit of adv
Michelle Oucharek

BAREFOOT IN THE DIRT

MICHELLE OUCHAREK-DEO

BAREFOOT IN THE DIRT

MICHELLE OUCHAREK-DEO

The Vinho Verde Trilogy

A crisp green wine filled with surprises.

ঔ

Book II

LIVE AND GROW
PRESS
Port Coquitlam

For information regarding permission, contact liveandgrowpress@gmail.com

Oucharek-Deo, Michelle B. 1969-

Oucharek-Deo, Michelle, author
www.michelleoucharekdeo.com

Barefoot in the dirt/ Michelle Oucharek-Deo

ISBN
Paperback 978-1-988348-05-6
Electronic 978-1-988348-04-9
Hardcopy 978-1-988348-07-0

Printed in the USA
First edition 2021
Book Cover Design by Nada Orlic

To Jennifer B.
A kindred spirit who pushed, pulled, and puddle jumped with me through the darkest and brightest times, reminding me to use my superpowers every single day.

Table of Contents

Character Index:

The Wells Family, Friends, and Others

Maya Wells: Lived in Peachland. Traveled to Portugal as one of Netuno's contest winners after canceling her wedding.

Judith Wells: Maya's mom. Recovering from a clinical depression which plagued her most of her adult life.

Phillip Wells: Maya's father. Lawyer turned vineyard owner and back to lawyer again after having to sell the vineyard.

Jordan Wells: Maya's sister. Grumpy young woman. Resentful towards Maya and generally unpleasant.

Grandma Stella: Maya's grandmother. Kind, filled with wisdom, has a sharp tongue when she needs to use it.

Aunt Olive: Maya's great aunt. Wealthy and loves to create pockets of chaos whenever she can.

Beth: Maya's best friend. Elementary school teacher. Level headed, thoughtful and patient with Maya.

Steven: Maya's ex-fiancé. Engineer. Jilted the night before his wedding with Maya. Devastated by the breakup.

Lazaro Family, Friends, and Others

Cristiano Lazaro: International flight attendant. Lives in Lisbon. Musician, loves to surf. Difficult family history.

Avo: Cristiano's grandmother. Raised him after his parents died in a plane crash. The maker of special bread.

Rosa and Michel Lazaro: Cristiano's adoptive parents who died in a plane crash in Egypt. History professors.

Pierre: Old friend and colleague of Rosa and Michel. Lives in Paris. Works at the Louvre.

Mrs. Dutra: An old friend of Cristiano's adoptive parents. Gatekeeper of Cristiano's apartment in Lisbon.

Jack: Old surfer from Texas who lives on the beach in Portugal. Friends with both Cristiano and Marcos.

Marcos and Euphemia: Cristiano's biological parents who live in Porto with their other two children, Zeferino and Jacinta.

Silva: Flight attendant with Portugal air. Friend and colleague of Cristiano's.

Ammon: Old friend of Pierre's. Taxi driver. Lives in Egypt.

Netuno Family, Friends, and Others

Contest Winners:

    Josie: 65-year-old powerhouse. Divorced three times.

    Ellen: Mother of two children. Unhappy marriage.

    Dalley: Journalist. Complicated character and past.

    Petra: High powered ad executive. Works too hard.

    Sachi: Quiet, engineer. Wants to be a chef.

    Jade: Beautiful, viper, toxic. Daughter of Axel Axeline.

    Maggie: Widow and mother of twin sons CJ and Tim.

Puro: Manager of Netuno Wineries and Inn. Friend of Rosa and Michel. Watched out for Cristiano for years.

Carmo: Works at Netuno, daughter of Puro. In love with Bento.

Reinaldo and Mateus: Brothers who own Netuno. Reinaldo is the father of Bento.

Bento: Sole heir to Netuno. In love with Carmo.

Branca: Bento's mother, Reinaldo's disgruntled wife.

Gervais: Chef at Netuno from France. Photographer

Francesco: Limo driver and friend to all at Netuno.

Luca: Old friend of Carmo, Bento and Cristiano's. Portuguese police officer; International Crimes.

Prologue

Maya

As LONG AS I WAS moving, I was closer to him. Stride after stride, my feet pounded into the dirt, my pain fueling each step I took. Then out of nowhere, a car came up from behind. It all happened so fast. I heard the brakes screech and at the last second, the car swerved and barely missed me. I fell to the ground; filled with rage, my heart hammering in my chest as if it was going to explode.

The brake lights flashed and the car stopped.

"You picked the wrong person to run over tonight!" I screamed, trying to catch my breath. As I waited for the driver to get out of their car I heard a female voice yell, "Sorry!" from her open window.

Before I could even think, obscenities came tumbling from my lips. The car sped off leaving me sitting on the side of the road with only my soured tongue and wounded heart to keep me company. It was in that moment that my fury turned to hysteria. I had never told anyone to 'f off' before in my life, and it felt good—better than it should have.

As my breath slowed and I sought out the stillness of the evening, the calm returned. Being angry seemed far more productive, but anger took energy and I had nothing left.

There I was, barefoot and a long way from the inn, so I stood up knowing I could not sit there forever and started back. I had only walked a few minutes when I heard a car approaching from behind.

I was prepared for a fight, but when the window rolled down all I saw was a scruffy looking man smiling back at me. After a brief interaction, he realized I was not a local and asked if I needed a lift. I hesitated, distracted by his unruly black hair. He laughed like it was not the first time his hair had upstaged a conversation, then pulled it back in a ponytail, flashed me a badge, and shrugged good naturedly.

At that point, I threw caution to the wind and broke yet another life rule: I got into a car with a stranger. He carefully studied my face, glanced down at my dirty feet, and then without another word drove me back to Netuno and dropped me off at the inn.

1

Shards of Glass

Cristiano

I STOOD IN THE BLACKNESS of the night at the side of the road, not sure where to go or what to do. The only thing left of me was a tinder-dry shell. My heart raced and the muscles in my chest tightened like someone was knocking flint rock together. And then it happened. An unstoppable rage exploded in my heart; it was just the spark I was waiting for.

I never thought I could feel hate, but in that moment I hated everyone: Jack, for not telling me *my* truth when I was a teenager; Avo, for revealing my adoption in a letter twenty years too late; my birth parents, for giving me up; my mom and dad, for dying in the plane crash in Egypt; Maya, for making me think I was worthy of being loved.

Fire raged as I got back into the car and it was only when I arrived on Jack's beach in Setubal that I took a breath. It was like breathing in shards of glass. It reminded me of the pain I used to feel, almost like an old friend coming back for a surprise visit.

I started yelling his name as I ran down the darkened path. Then I tore open his flimsy door and roused him out of bed.

"Cristiano? Is that you? What the hell are you …?"

I didn't give him a chance to finish. I pulled back my fist and hit him. Jack was unconscious before he smashed through his cot.

I searched through his things like a mad man until I found his phone. I needed to find my birth parents, find out where I really came from. I combed through his contacts until I saw their names. Tavares. Marcos and Euphemia Tavares. Cristiano Tavares? Cristiano Lazaro? I had no idea who I really was, but I was not going to stop until I found out.

༜

The drive towards Porto, their hometown, was just a few hours away. I usually loved driving, but with my emotions raw and anxiety high, I slowed down to a snail's pace and broke into an unwinnable argument with myself.

"It's the middle of the night. What am I going to do? Knock on their door? I would never get a second chance with them if I descended on their home filled with this much anger. Marcos would call the police. I know I would. Besides, my brother and sister don't even know I exist. I'm just a stranger looking for answers. They would think I was crazy. Am I crazy? Look what I did to Jack. Oh my God, I knocked him out cold. He could be hurt."

I pulled into a service station in Aveiro. I had heard of the town before but had never been. People said it was like the Venice of Portugal. Maya would have loved it. Aveiro was beautiful just like her. My heart twisted, then sank when I thought about her. All I could see was her in *his* arms, but it didn't make sense. None of it made sense.

"Do you really believe I could be unfaithful to you?" I asked looking up into the sky. "Maybe I should call her? No! I can't. But I do need to talk to Jack."

I reached for my phone—it was gone. The last time I used it was just after I landed and listened to Maya's message while driving to Netuno. "She told me she loved me …"

The gas attendant sold me a pre-paid phone. I dialed my number. It rang once, then twice.

"Hello?" The voice sounded groggy, like the person on the other end had been sleeping.

"Jack? Is that you?" I asked hesitantly.

"It depends. Are you going to hit me again? I think you broke a tooth. You sucker punched me. I was right in the middle of the most awesome dream," Jack responded, sounding relatively unphased.

"That's all you have to say? I knocked you out, broke a tooth, tore your place apart, and you're mad at me because I disrupted your dream?"

"No, I'm not mad at you. I expected you to be upset—maybe not break-my-bed upset, but …"

"Yeah, I'm sorry about that Jack. I'll buy you a new one."

"No, it's okay, maybe I should sleep on the floor as punishment for not telling you about Marcos myself."

"Yeah, you do deserve to be punished, but you don't need to sleep on the floor," I sighed. "Why don't you go and stay at my place in Lisbon until you get a new bed? I won't be back for a while. I'll call Mrs. Dutra and let her know you're coming."

"I never said I was going to stay at your place."

"When have you ever turned down a free anything? Just go and have a good time in the city."

"What do you mean you won't be back for a while? Please tell me you're not going to do something more stupid than beating up your best friend."

"You're my best friend?"

"Yeah, at least I thought I was."

I paused. "Jack? What *were* you thinking? Why didn't you tell me about being adopted when you figured it out?" Then I had to ask, "Maya's letter—was it all true?"

"I don't know anything about a letter, but when I told her about Marcos, she was very upset and insisted you had to know the truth."

"I have two questions for you. Firstly, why didn't you tell Marcos about my parents' death when he came to see me surf that first day? And …" I paused, feeling my chest tighten and my eyes fill, "why didn't he stay?"

"I don't know why he didn't stay. And I thought I had a good reason not to tell him about your parents. But Cristiano, the stuff with Marcos happened a long time ago, there is nothing I can do to change things and truthfully … I don't think I would," he said defiantly. "When he came to see you and confirmed my suspicions about being your father, I thought briefly about telling him everything, but you were just starting to pull your life back together. I was worried about you." He paused. "In the end, everything worked out though. You have Maya and Avo and me," he laughed. "You have everything you've always wanted."

"Right, I have everything I've always wanted," I spat back painfully. Jack's words reignited the anger and I had to stop talking before I said something I would regret.

"What's going on Cristiano? What did you do? Is Maya okay? Cristiano? Where are you?" Jack asked with uncharacteristic concern breaking through.

"Jack, I have to sort some things out and I need to start at the beginning."

"And where is that Cristiano?"

"Your phone said my family lives in Porto. Sounds like a good place to start."

"Cristiano? Like I said, don't do anything stupid."

"Sure Jack, whatever you say because you know so much about being smart."

"You're a real jerk you know?" he said coolly.

I winced, knowing he was right but couldn't admit it. "Mrs. Dutra will have the key. I have to go."

"Cristiano?" Jack paused. "You know she loves you, right?"

"Mrs. Dutra?" I asked dryly.

"No, you idiot, Maya … Maya loves you."

2

Broken Pieces

Maya

WHEN I STEPPED BACK INTO the lobby, it was eerily quiet. No guests or party stragglers, not even a staff person at the front counter. I evidently knew how to clear a room—all it took was a strong right hook. With my next step, my toe caught on the edge of a tile and I tumbled forward, my heart half expecting Cristiano to catch me, but the reality of his absence was confirmed when I hit the cold, hard floor.

I lay motionless for a moment, closing my eyes, hoping for a different reality. When I opened them, all I saw were three empty wine bottles on the table and half a dozen dirty glasses, including one stained with the distinctive pink lipstick of my new friend Josie. I could only imagine how proud she was of me for punching Dalley. I flexed my fist, remembering my knuckles on her chin. She had gone down with one shot, but she deserved it.

Dalley had stolen my journal and published my personal life on her blog. She was no journalist. I thought we were friends, but a friend would never betray you like she did.

Crawling closer to the coffee table, I saw papers strewn across the wooden surface along with a black folder—Jade's black folder. I could only assume that the research Dalley had done on each of us before coming to Portugal had been discovered. Or maybe offered? I couldn't determine which. All I could piece together was that Jade, the demon model from Montreal, was being put under the microscope by the remaining members of our group. I wasn't sure how Jade fit into the whole story, but it appeared Dalley's blog had become Jade's opportunity to try to destroy my future with Cristiano.

A splash of bile shot up into my mouth when I thought of Jade. She hated me and I hated her just as much. I choked back the acid that still lingered on my tongue and then washed it down with the remains from an almost empty wine bottle.

Trembling, I picked myself up from the floor and trudged up the stairs towards my room.

My spirits lifted briefly when I saw a tea cart parked outside my door, but they sank again as I pulled the cart in and saw the destruction. The sheers had been torn from both bed frames and lay in tatters on the floor, keeping company with a plethora of empty mini liquor bottles and chocolate bar wrappers. Was Dalley celebrating? Or had the guilt of what she'd done driven her to drink everything in sight? I couldn't ask her because she was gone.

She had packed up almost everything except her boot box which she'd left on my bed. Looking at it, I silently asked, "How did my almost life of happiness get hijacked by the betrayal of a friend and a toxic waste dump of a woman on the other side of the world?"

Dalley and Jade had blown up my life and the pieces were scattered everywhere.

Then I opened the box. On the top was a haphazardly folded note ironically written on a page torn from my journal. I hastily opened the note, hoping for something that would make me feel better.

Maya,
Honestly, these look better on you than me ...

I stared down at the boots I had borrowed that liberating day in Évora—Dalley's boots.

That was some right hook. I didn't know you had it in you.
I didn't mean for things to turn out like this. I was not working with Jade like everyone thinks. There is no excuse for my role in any of this, but I will find a way to make things right.
I'm sorry Maya. I really am sorry.
Dalley

I stepped out onto the balcony, then proceeded to throw the note, the boots, and the remnants of our friendship out into the night.

"Dalley, you're going to have to do a hell of a lot better than that!" I croaked into the wind. The sound of the boots hitting the bushes below left me feeling strangely unsatisfied, but I pushed the feeling away and walked back into the room.

Rummaging through an open drawer, I looked for my box of Cream Earl Grey tea, pushing aside more chocolate bar wrappers left in Dalley's guilty wake. Luckily, I found what *I* was looking for.

I carefully measured out my loose tea and let the colorful leaves share their story with the hot water. The familiar scent drifted around me and through my room. I could almost see it making its way out to the balcony—then it stopped and hung in the air like an invitation.

So I graciously accepted and settled into the chair, searching for comfort and answers and preparing myself for a long night.

I pulled out my phone and typed in Price's Portugal. I needed to unravel the web of truth and lies that had been posted on Dalley's blog and figure out what the world thought they knew about me.

❧

So much had happened in such a short time, and for a moment a trickle of my past fears slipped down my cheek but were wiped away before they tainted my tea. I was not the same Maya from Peachland, but if I was not her, who was I?

The first image I saw on the blog was the one of Jade kissing Cristiano. I winced at the thought of her touching him and anger surged through my body again. She had set him up. She had taken advantage of the situation. He was there for me, for Athena, to take back what was mine. Athena was much more than just a pen, and Cristiano knew that. I ran into the room and grabbed Athena from the box, walked back onto the balcony and held her up in the moonlight. Her jewels glistened and it was as if Athena herself was telling me to fight, to wage war against the wrongs that had been done to me. I took a deep breath and embraced the creases that I knew had formed on my forehead.

Holding Athena was a concrete reminder of how much he loved me, understood me. With no further delay I dove into the blog, prepared for anything.

Some of what Dalley wrote made me angry; other parts made me smile. She had taken every aspect of my life and woven it into a story of truth and fable. I was the heroine and the evil queen, all in one. The latest set of comments appeared to seal my fate and that of Cristiano's in the eyes of the readers though. All they saw was that *he'd* cheated on me with Jade, and *I* lied to him about his family by not sharing the truth.

I read until my pot of tea was empty and my eyes ached from the print on the small screen. It was only then that I saw a dull haze starting to shift in the sky. Morning had arrived and somehow I'd made it through the night. Then with great effort I dragged myself back into the room and collapsed on my bed.

When my phone pinged, I fell trying to reach for it on the nightstand. My heart ricocheted against my ribs. The text was from him—or so I thought until Jack started text-yelling at me and I yelled back at him.

MAYA, THIS IS JACK. WHAT THE HELL IS GOING ON?

Where's Cristiano? WHY do you have his phone?

BECAUSE, he dropped it when he ripped my place apart. I just woke up from being knocked out by his angry fist and received a very cryptic phone call from him. Like I said, WHAT is going on?

I took a moment and gathered my thoughts. Yelling at Jack was not going to get me what I needed.

Things are more complicated than I can explain in a text. You said you talked to him.

Irrelevant.

Jack please don't be difficult, I haven't slept for 24 hours.

I'm not being difficult. Just explain it. Simplify. What exactly did you do to him? And what was in the letter?

The letter? You think this is all about the letter?

Maya, honestly I don't really know what any of this is about.

You sound like you're blaming this whole situation on me. Really Jack? Why don't you look in the mirror? Oh, wait you don't have a wall to hang a mirror on. Do you?

That was kind of mean Maya. What's the matter with the two of you?

If you want to know what's going on just look up the blog Price's Portugal. Oh, and don't believe everything you see. He did not cheat on me.

Of course, he didn't. What a stupid thing to say. He's not that kind of man. Besides, Avo would kill him. And I know he is crazy about you.

Yah, well then next time you talk to him why don't you ask him how he could just run away from someone he's crazy about … Jack do you know where he is?

Not exactly, but he did go through my phone before he left.

Your phone? What was he looking for?

There was a pause before the next text came through.

He was looking for his birth parents.

You have to stop him. He's not thinking straight. He's not himself.

I warned him not to be stupid. There's nothing else I can do. Besides, I think it's time they meet.

What's their last name? Where can I find them? Please Jack …

Jack never returned the last text.

I sat on the floor leaning up against my bed. After some time, I heard a little tap on the door. I got up and found Bento standing there with a fresh pot of hot water.

"Hi Maya, I took a chance. I thought you might need this." He handed me the teapot.

"Thanks Bento. I …"

"No need to say anything. It has been quite a weekend, so far."

"So far? There's more?" I asked almost afraid to hear his answer.

"Yes, unfortunately there's lots more. I'm not sure where I should start, but I guess the black folder is a good place. When Dalley left us the folder on Jade Axeline, we weren't sure of its relevance until my dad got a call from my mother, Branca. She was drunk and told my dad she wanted a divorce."

"I'm confused, but how are the Axelines and your mother connected?"

"Oh, we were all very confused until I got her talking. She was drunk and filled with spite and vengeance. She took great joy saying how she was going to hurt my father. In addition to asking for the divorce, she told us that as of Friday afternoon she had sold off all her Netuno shares to Axel Axeline. She was laughing at all of us. I tried to ask her a few more questions but she hung up. That's when Carmo insisted that I call my friend Luca. He is a detective with one of the Portuguese policing agencies. I wasn't sure if he could help but Carmo insisted I call him. You met him already. He's the fellow who drove you back to Netuno earlier this evening."

"The guy with the hair? Did he know who I was when he picked me up?"

"Yes, the guy with the hair. And no, he did not know who you were at the time, I just filled him in after he told me about his encounter with you.

Bento took a breath and steadied himself against the open door. I could see the strain showing on his face.

"What does all this mean, Bento?" I asked, trying to put the pieces together.

"It was all pretty confusing at first and we still don't understand how everything happened, but while my father and my uncle were freaking out Gervais and Sachi joined the discussion. After hearing about the situation Sachi spoke up and offered to help us by calling her father. She said he 'knew' some people that might be able to get us more information."

"After Sachi's call, we discovered that Jade's father, Axel, had been planning to take control of Netuno for some time. We only went public a few months ago, thanks to Branca. She was the one who convinced my dad last year that it was in the best interest of Netuno and would eventually give us the capital for the expansion plans we had been putting off since building the inn … she must really hate us … me."

"Oh Bento, I'm sure she doesn't hate you. It's more likely that she hates herself, or at least she will when she wakes up tomorrow and realizes what she has done."

Suddenly, I remembered Jade's acidic voice from that first day at Netuno.

"Bento, I think Jade was here for her father all along. I think that's what she meant on the first day when she told me she wasn't here for the same reason as everyone else. But how did she end up as a winner in the contest?" I asked feeling puzzled.

"Yes, I agree, the question is how, but with Branca involved, anything is possible."

"How many lives can that woman ruin?" I asked rhetorically.

"My mother or Jade?" Bento smiled ever so slightly.

I raised an eyebrow.

"Just a little humor to take the edge off."

"Bento, what is your family going to do?"

His smile faded. "My father and Puro called Branca back and are trying to find out more information. Although she and I haven't been close for some time, I can't believe she is trying to steal the ground from under my feet."

As he said the words, I was thrown back to the day I slammed into the *for sale* sign posted at the vineyard in Peachland. I rubbed the scar on my arm remembering how my father held the gash together as I fell apart. That was the last time I recall crying as a child.

"Maya? Maya are you alright?" Bento shook my shoulder.

"Yes, just a bad memory. Please let me know if there is anything I can do to help. I wish Cristiano were here."

"Thank you, Maya. Yes, I wish he were here too." Bento paused for a moment. "Maya, I am so sorry about Cristiano and all this blog business. I have known him for a long time. He is a good man. He would never do anything to hurt you."

I tried to smile but my face wouldn't bend in that direction. "See you when the sun finishes rising."

He looked at me. "Maya, none of this would have happened if there had never been a contest."

"Bento, if there had never been a contest, I would still be selling sprinkler systems back home. Neither of us can give up, can we?"

A broad smile opened on his lips.

"Thank you, Maya. You are exactly right! Neither of us can give up. Sorry, there's something I need to do."

I watched Bento as he ran down the hallway like a man on a mission.

Walking back into the room I saw a flutter of wings as a nightingale landed on the balcony railing. The bird was so close I could almost touch it. When I was a child, my Grandma Stella had read me a poem about a nightingale who was searching for his lost love. The bird sang every night for the rest of his days, but the song only reached his mate's ears on the last day of his life.

My tears welled as I thought about Cristiano and how much love we still had to give one another. I was not going to be the nightingale; somehow, I would find him before it was too late. I grabbed Athena hoping to borrow some of her strength and wisdom and held her tightly as I gave myself over to the exhaustion.

ᘒ

When I woke, the sun was up and there I was, curled up in a ball with Athena held tightly in my hand. I knew it was time to tell my story to Christopher, my journal. I pulled him out from under my pillow and then unscrewed Athena's lid.

The next few seconds were filled with a mixture of white noise and rage. Jade had gutted her, cracked her insides apart and drained her ink—Athena was empty.

Something shifted inside of me and I began to scream, cursing the ground Jade walked on.

3

What's in a Point?

Jade

"Jade, what's the matter with you?" Axel grunted with minimal fatherly concern as I stumbled over my feet and bumped into him.

"What do you care if I fall and crack my head open or have a heart attack? It would give you more time to yell at someone else."

"My yelling is for your own good. And you deserve it after leaving Netuno early and not finishing your job. I'll be lucky to close this deal without any further problems … and don't joke about having a heart attack."

I flinched as I remembered the day when I found my mother on the floor. I hoped he hadn't seen my reaction, but no luck.

"Don't be such a baby, Jade. She died years ago. Sometimes you're worse than *she* was. Thank God Marilyn was around to step in and be a mother to you."

I hated Marilyn. She had moved in three days after my mom died. I often wondered if they had planned the whole thing.

"God? What does God have to do with this? You can pretend like you cared about mom, but you were screwing Marilyn long before they pushed the button and turned Mom to ash. You didn't even come to her funeral, do you remember? You sent me with the nanny."

"Jade, relax. The past is the past. I only asked because it looked like someone just walked over your grave." He paused and then stared me straight in the eye. "Is there anything you need to tell me?"

"Oh, shut up, Axel." But my thoughts went straight to Maya. I couldn't help but smile. "Actually, Dad, everything is great."

"We're back to 'Dad,' are we? If you say so, Jade," he quipped, not believing me for a moment.

"Everything is fine. The deal is solid. Branca signed over her shares to you. They don't know what's coming—trust me." As we continued down the street another agonizing pain shot through my body. I held it close, not wincing until Axel turned and hailed a taxi.

"Get in Jade."

"No, I've got plans." I half-smiled.

"Okay then, I'll see you on Sunday—well, actually Monday morning to be exact. They are six hours ahead of us in Amsterdam. You need to be at the office at least an hour before trading starts. That's 2:00 a.m. our time Jade."

"2:00 a.m.!!" I spat at him.

"Grow up! We have work to do." He spat back at me. The perfect father daughter relationship covered in spit.

As he drove off, I let out a guttural cry, clutching at my chest then stomach and multiple points on my arm. I thought about going to the hospital, but my dad would think I was weak. I was a lot of things but weak was not one of them. I caught a taxi and went home. The stabbing pain continued to bother me until the third shot of tequila kicked in. Then I happily felt nothing at all.

Maya

I sharpened my pencil repeatedly and continued to use it like a weapon, forcing Christopher to take the brunt of my rage. At one point, I pushed so hard the pencil tore through to the other side of the page. When I finally finished, a sadness ripped through me for what I had done to Christopher. I thought about tearing out the shreds of paper that remained but couldn't. I never wanted to forget the feeling. I decided it was time to start being true to myself, even if the Maya I was discovering had a darker side. So, I turned the page and started fresh, embracing my new me.

> *Saturday morning, (Netuno)*
> *The day after everything.*
> *I never thought I could hate anything or anyone, but I hate Jade. Athena will never write again. I know it sounds stupid, but she's not just a pen, she's a part of me. Jade knew that ... SCREW YOU JADE!!!!!*
> *Enough about Jade though. I read Dalley's blog. What's there to say? It's my words and her words mixed in with my heart. A story about eight women coming together, starring Maya Wells.*
> *My insides are aching as I think about my part in all of this. I should have told him about his parents sooner, and he should have trusted me and not run away when he saw me in Steven's arms. What a pair of idiots.*
> *Oh, I am so mad at you Cristiano, what were you thinking?*

As I contemplated my next words, a gust of wind blew through the open door. The sky had taken a sudden turn and a cloud burst was on its way. A wave of relief washed over me as I thought about going for a walk in the rain, feeling the cool droplets on my face, and taking a breather from the past evening's events. As I looked around for my shoes, I remembered tearing them off in my frenzy the night before and throwing them to the side of the road. It was then that I saw Dalley's empty boot box beside the dresser and my heart lunged.

"The boots!" I screamed, as the first thunder cracked, and a deluge of raindrops began to fall.

I ran down to the lobby and out the door, jumping off the veranda steps and landing in a freshly formed puddle, covering myself in water and dirt.

My eyes darted around the garden looking for the boots. It did not take long before I saw them hanging from an ancient hedgerow. They really were spectacular and didn't deserve such a fate as death by rain. With an extraordinary balancing act, I slipped them onto my dirty feet, zipped them up, and headed back towards the inn, dripping and momentarily content.

When I walked through the doors I saw that Steven was checking out at the front desk. I thought about turning around, but it was too late.

"Maya!" He shouted my name as if I was ignoring him, which I was.

I stepped towards him leaving a trail of puddles in my wake. "Yes, Steven. How can I help you?" I asked, borrowing some confidence from the boots.

"A little walk in the rain?" he teased gingerly.

"Something like that," I answered shortly, wanting the conversation to be over.

"I just wanted to let you know I'm leaving today," he said moving his hand towards me, but stopped.

I stood up straight and pushed my bangs out of my eyes. "Have a safe flight." I paused. "You do understand I'm not coming back to Peachland, right?"

He let out a forced laugh. "Yes, I figured that out last night. You've changed Maya. You're not the same girl I fell in love with."

"No, Steven, I'm not. But that's okay. It's better for both of us this way." I saw him wince a little and my heart softened as I studied his puffy eyes.

"Beth told me not to come, but I had to. Over these past few months, I thought you might change your mind, that you would come back to me. I didn't want to let you go, but I guess there's nothing left to hang onto. You're not my Maya anymore."

"Steven, I'm not anyone's Maya anymore. I'm just me."

"The hair, the boots, the right hook last night? It suits you," he offered with a look of resignation.

I chuckled, then gave him a gentle kiss on the cheek, turned, and walked away.

4

Rally the Troops

Maya

As I HEADED DOWN THE hall, I saw a gathering of people outside my room.

"Maya, please come out!" Josie screeched while pounding on the door.

"Maya, I've got my lawyers on the case back home. My husband has spoken with your father. They are working together to try and fix this. Just answer the door," Petra pleaded.

"Wow, the way you guys are talking, that girl sounds like she's in real trouble," I offered with an inappropriate amount of sarcasm.

The knocking stopped. They turned and stared.

"See, I told you she was going to be fine," Josie piped up.

"You did not," Ellen jabbed back, then stepped towards me. "She was up all night worried about you; we all were."

"Petra, what was that you said about the lawyers and my father?" I asked with curiosity.

"Oh, they are trying to get an injunction to close Dalley's blog down, but no luck so far. Free speech and all that stuff."

She reached out and touched my arm, concern showing on her face.

We heard a noise and saw Carmo sprinting down the hall towards us.

"I heard Josie yelling from downstairs and figured you all must have found her," Carmo said with relief. "Maya, have you talked to your family or Beth yet? They called at least a half-dozen times each. Puro let them know you were doing the best you could—under the circumstances."

"Let's take this into my room," I offered.

When I opened the door, a collective gasp escaped from the group. I had forgotten about the mess Dalley had created and when the troops saw the chaos, they jumped to the conclusion that I had lost my mind and, in the process, had torn the room apart.

"Oh Maya, what did you do?" Ellen whispered.

"I told you we should have come back to see her right away," Josie snipped at the others with a tone of smugness.

"Stop! All of you. This …" I yelped, while waving my arms around, "wasn't me. When I came back last night, I found it like this. Dalley …" was all I needed to say.

There was a long silence, and a heaviness filled the air. I took a deep breath then sighed loudly, feeling the weight of everyone's fatigue and sadness, not to mention my own.

"Maya, have you eaten anything since yesterday?" Sachi asked, shifting the attention away from the destruction. "Gervais has breakfast ready for us downstairs, but if you want, I could have him bring it up to my room and we can all eat there?"

I sighed, trying to find the right words, but my mind went blank.

"Sachi?" Ellen spoke softly. "Breakfast in your room sounds like a good plan. I'll help Maya get cleaned up. She can stay in my room until we get this placed sorted. We shouldn't be too long."

Ellen walked out onto the balcony while I said goodbye to everyone else. After they left, she came back and held out her hand. When her fingertips touched my palm, I felt a beautiful warmth. She smiled, then sat me down on the floor, and pointed to the boots I was wearing.

She shook her head, "Yes, they are beautiful, but you need to forgive her before you can accept them and make them yours."

"You remember them?"

"Yes, I remember the encounter at the spa a couple of weeks ago between you and Dalley and the boots."

I wasn't sure what to say so I opted for silence, then I carefully unzipped them. She walked over to the bathroom, dampened a facecloth, and handed it to me. I cleaned the boots both inside and out, then placed them back in the box.

"That takes care of the boots. Now it is your turn. Go take a shower and wash the last two days off."

I paused for a moment feeling resistant to her directive. "What if I don't want to? What if I don't want to forget?"

"Don't worry, you won't forget. Those scrapes on your feet will be a good reminder."

I was in the shower when my cell phone rang, and I felt my chest seize. I jumped out and with my heart pounding, grabbed a towel and ran into the bedroom.

Ellen answered on the third ring.

"Hello?" she said cautiously. "No, this isn't Maya. Just a moment please."

"Who is it?" My body shook with nerves, "Cristiano?"

"No," Ellen said quietly, feeling my disappointment. "But the woman was very insistent that she speak with you immediately. I'll grab another towel."

I hesitantly took the phone. "Hello?"

"Hi, Maya, it's Mom." I froze trying to process the idea that my mom was on the other end of the receiver.

"Mom? What is it? It's the middle of the night your time. Are you okay? I'm so sorry about all of this. I'm constantly causing you and dad so much trouble. What's going on? Is he okay? Grandma Stella?"

"Maya, I …" she tried to get my attention. "Maya …"

"I'm okay right now, but I'm in the middle of something and will have to call you back. Oh, can I talk to Dad, please?"

"Maya!" She raised her voice. "Stop talking for a second. First, everyone is as good as they can be, and if you want to talk with your dad, you'll have to call him yourself, he's at the office trying to figure out a way to shut down the blog. I'm on my cell right now, at the airport. When you do talk to him though, could you please let him know I'll text him when I land—I'm so excited. I feel like I'm twenty again."

"Mom, where are you going?" I asked cautiously.

"Oh, sorry, I didn't mention that part? I'm coming to Portugal. I'll be there tomorrow. Not sure if that is your tomorrow or my tomorrow but the flight arrives around noon in Lisbon. I have a few connecting flights, but I promise you I'll be there."

"Here? You're coming here?" I was gobsmacked.

"Don't sound so surprised Maya. You're not the only one who has changed, and I heard about that blog situation. You need me right now and I need to be with you. No arguments. Just call your dad. I don't want him to worry, and no, just before you let your imagination get away from you—I'm not off my meds. I am more stable now than I have been in years. See you soon. Love you. My flight to London is boarding."

"I'll send someone to the airport to pick you up," I yelled into the receiver.

"Awesome!!" she squeaked back.

"Awesome?" I stood stunned.

Ellen handed me another towel. "I take it that was your mom. She's coming here?" Ellen asked with curiosity.

"Yes. Apparently, I need her," I said, feeling a little perturbed.

Ellen smiled, clearly pleased that my mother was coming to Netuno to see me.

"I need to call my dad."

Ellen nodded and turned towards the door. "I'll meet you down at Sachi's. Take your time. And Maya, I don't know the whole story with your mom, but please give her a chance. Sounds like she's really trying."

I hesitated a moment, then thanked her.

She gently smiled back at me, and when the door closed, I dialed the number to my father's office.

5

Time to Listen

Maya

"Hello? Wells and Associates."

"Dad, it's Maya."

"Oh, I'm so glad you called. How are you, my girl?"

"Truthfully, I'm not sure. I'm still trying to figure out everything that's going on. I heard you've been working with Petra's husband and had a conversation or two with Puro."

"Yes, everyone has been very helpful."

"Dad, I need to tell you something. I just got a call from Mom, she's at the airport—on her way here, to Portugal."

He paused for a moment then started to laugh.

"Dad, why are you laughing? How could she leave without saying goodbye to you? This is serious."

"Apparently so … hmm. When I left the house a couple of hours ago, she couldn't wait for me to leave. I was wondering what was going on with her."

"You're not upset? Worried?"

"No, Maya. Well, maybe a little," he chuckled. "But she's stable and has been for months. She's acting more like herself than I have seen in years. She used to be a real adventurer, sometimes even impulsive."

"Impulsive? Adventurer? Mom?" I found his description of her hard to believe.

"Yes, we did have a life before the depression you know. She wasn't always sad. I just forgot how much fun she could be. I'm sure she has already made a few friends. She can be quite resourceful when she puts her mind to it."

I started to feel annoyed by my dad but tried to push it off to the side. "Mom said she'd send a message when she lands. Dad, what happened when she was twenty?"

"You will have to ask her. How are you doing? You sound a little hoarse. Are you getting sick?"

"It was a rough night as you know and I haven't slept very much," I responded with irritation.

"Yes, there is a lot of that going on." He said picking up my tone but choosing to ignore it. "I talked with Puro and he filled me in about the Cristiano situation. Maya, this whole thing is a little over the top don't you think?"

"I'm not sure what you want me to say. I'm sorry for causing so much trouble again," I barked shortly. But then my voice began to shake. "I have to find him Dad—I have to find Cristiano."

I could feel the anger rising. I knew I should try to stop it, but I didn't want to. It was like my blood began to heat in my veins and the hotter it got the faster it coursed through my body. I could feel everything. I tried feebly to push it back, to do the right thing, but in the end the anger won out. "What was he thinking? How could he just run off and leave me?" I yelled into the receiver. "And Steven, why the hell would Steven come here? He ruined everything. I came here to start over, and this is the do-over I was given? God must really hate me. And why is mom coming here? She was never there for me when I was growing up. She's just going to make things worse," I shouted at him, unleashing all my frustration.

"Maya!" he yelled my name curtly into the phone. "You are acting like a spoiled brat right now. Don't you dare lay any of what's happened to you at your mother's or Steven's feet. They haven't done anything to hurt you. All they have ever done is love you. Maybe you need to take some time and think about that!" He said punctuating his comment. "Honestly, Maya, you're being quite selfish right now."

"Selfish?" I asked feeling confounded.

"Maya, I'm sorry. I didn't mean that," he tried to back track.

"Yes, you did, all of it," I whispered.

"Maya. I'm not going to try and pretend I understand what is happening over there, but you just met this young man. I read through the blog, your journal entries, and …"

"I wish you hadn't, no one was supposed to read that, especially you. You're my dad, you're not supposed to know what's going on in my head and my heart," My anger flipping to sadness and utter irritation.

"I know it's embarrassing, but, Maya …"

"Embarrassing? You think I'm embarrassed?" I said gritting my teeth and commanding the tears to stay where they were. "Dad, I thought you understood, but you clearly don't get it. I love him. I would do anything for him. Cristiano didn't do anything wrong," I shouted defending him.

"I know, I know, Puro explained. But, Maya, is he worth all of this?"

"I can't believe you're asking me that. Yes, he's worth it, and I'm worth it too. You of all people should understand. You gave up everything for mom when she needed you."

"Maya, that was different, she was my wife."

"No, not different. You loved her, I love him. I'm going to find him no matter what it takes, and I don't care what you or anyone else thinks." At that point, my breath started to hitch. The tears were inevitable.

"Settle down Maya. Having a panic attack right now is not going to help you."

"I'm not having a panic attack!" I barked back.

"Maya, it's just that we are up against a situation."

"You think I don't know that?"

"I think this social media thing is way out of control."

"It's just a blog Dad."

"No, it's not just a blog, it's Twitter too. Your sister tells me Jade is trending."

"Twitter? Are you kidding me?" My anger was reignited and incinerated the rising panic.

"No, I'm not. Jordan texted me and let me know. She's following her now."

"Seriously? Jordan is following Jade. Well, they can both go to hell."

"Maya!" he shouted chastising me.

"What, Dad? I don't have the time or energy to care what she or anyone else thinks. I have to go. I'll have Mom text you when she arrives in Portugal."

"Maya, call Beth, she's worried about you too."

I had to take a few deep breaths to calm down, but he was right, I did need to speak with Beth.

❧

The phone hadn't even finish ringing when I heard Beth's panicked voice on the line.

"Maya! What is going on?"

"Oh, do you mean my online fame? Or everything else that has happened since?"

"How about last night?" she said sounding less worried and more annoyed.

"Well, let's see. I punched someone, threw my shoes into the bushes, and drove in a car with a stranger—a stranger with a badge mind you."

"Wait, you punched someone? Who? Speak up, I can hardly hear you."

"Dalley Price, that's who," I said while trying to clear my throat.

"Where is she? I'll finish her off," Beth snapped with an unfamiliar bitter tone.

"No need, she's gone."

"Hopefully for good."

"I don't know. I kind of wish I could speak with her."

"What the hell for?" Beth bit back at me.

"Things here are complicated. In some way, I think she might be able to help."

"Help? Help with what? Maya, are you crazy? This is all her fault."

"No, it's not, not all of it anyways. I can't explain everything right now."

"Please be serious."

The unfamiliar condescension I heard in her voice triggered a response that neither of us was ready for.

"Serious, you want serious.?" I cleared my throat and my heart filled with fire again. "Okay, let's try this …" I spat back, "Last night the man I love left me standing in the middle of a dirt road because he saw me in the arms of another man, who caught me when I fainted after I saw a doctored picture of the man *I* love in the arms of another woman. Cristiano thought I believed the garbage picture that was posted on the crazy blog written by a lying journalist who claimed to be my friend and who stole my journal and splayed it out to the world. Cristiano thinks I don't love or trust him and that I would just fall back into another man's arms. Wait, it gets better. The big secret that I had discovered about Cristiano and wrote about in my journal was published and is now all over the Internet. He found out online that his biological parents are together, and he has a brother and a sister. Now he knows I didn't tell him about his family, and he thinks I betrayed him with Steven. So, did he leave because of Steven or my untold secret? It's irrelevant because either way he left!"

When I finished yelling, all that remained were charred memories of the last twenty-four hours. "I broke his heart Beth. I love him, but does he love me? I don't have any idea where he is or how I can find him or even if he wants to be found."

A few tears slipped out, but I pushed on. "And he can't answer my texts or my calls because he lost his phone after beating up his best friend, and on top of this I just had my first fight with my dad; not to mention that my mother, who has not left Peachland in over two decades, is on an airplane right now, on her way to Netuno to help me. Help me? She didn't know how to help me my whole life. What am I supposed to do with her here? Beth, I don't know what to do."

The pause on the line was brief but intentional.

"Shh, Maya," she whispered. "Stop. I don't think he ran because of you. I think you might be giving yourself too much credit."

My breath stalled, "That's kind of harsh, don't you think?" I let out a little laugh.

"No, not really. From what you've told me about him, he sounds like an emotional soul, not a vengeful one. I'm guessing he'll want to find out more. More about his family and where he came from, and how you fit into all of it. He may need to put himself first for a little while. Maya? I think you both may need a couple of days just to figure things out. Is there anything I can do?"

"Come and run interference for me with my mother? You've always known just what to say to her. She likes you better than me."

"No, she doesn't … well, maybe a little," she laughed. "You'll be alright, you'll see. Just let her be a mother."

I sighed and cleared my scratchy throat unsuccessfully.

"Maya? Are you sick? You sound like you're getting sick."

"I don't know. Let's hope not."

"Are you sure he's worth all of this?" Beth asked quietly.

"Why do people keep asking me that?" I whispered.

"Because we love you. Oh, and don't go getting into any more cars with strangers, even those with badges."

As I walked down the hall to Sachi's, I thought about my conversations with my mom, dad, and Beth. I was resolute in my decision that he was worth it. He was worth everything.

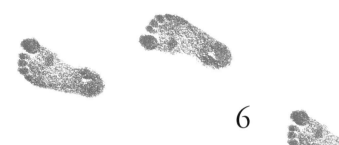

6

The Loud Breakfast

Maya

WHEN I ARRIVED, BREAKFAST HAD been delivered and everyone had gotten started. The food was beautiful. Gervais had outdone himself once again, but my stomach was sour, and even the warm croissant I nibbled on made me feel unwell.

"Maya, I'm not sure if you are aware but things are more complicated than just the blog situation," Petra began.

I put my croissant down on the table and tried to respond, to let her know I knew about the Axelines and the shares, but the only sound that exited my mouth was a push of forced air. It was as if my voice had gotten lost somewhere in the hallway.

"I told you we should have waited, she's speechless," Josie quipped with frustration.

Sachi, Petra, and Ellen threw her a glance.

I opened my mouth again, but there was no sound. My mind whirled and I grabbed my throat, fear being eclipsed by frustration.

Ellen paused then stared into my eyes. "She's more than speechless Josie, she's voiceless."

The ladies crowded around me.

"Call the doctor!" several people yelled.

"Maya? Is there anything we can do?" Sachi asked.

I took a breath and motioned for a piece of paper to write on. Someone gave me a postcard and a pen.

I don't know. It doesn't hurt. Please keep talking, distract me. Last night Bento told me a little about what was happening. I know about Branca, the divorce, the selling of the shares, oh, and that Jade has taken to Twitter.

"Okay, so that's something *we* didn't know," Josie blurted with a head shake. "That girl is a piece of work."

"I might have a few other words to describe her," Ellen added uncharacteristically.

Petra smiled, then looked over at me. "So Maya, we found out a little more about how our contest came to be. Do you want me to explain?"

I nodded my head.

"It appears that the whole thing got started at a gallery opening last November in Italy. Branca met Axel Axeline while he was trying to acquire a new painting. They hit it off. She got drunk and then, from what we understand, went on about Netuno and how much she hated it. She told him way more about the business than she should have. By the end of the night, they had hatched a plan for him to take over Netuno. The contest was just part of the plan—a way for Axel to get someone on site because he wanted to see what he was potentially buying, even if it was just through Jade's eyes," Petra scoffed. "So, Branca took Reinaldo's retreat idea and decided to exploit it with the contest scheme, which allowed her to do whatever she wanted, no questions asked.

"The situation is very tense and there are several unknowns for the brothers, but Axel is going to be caught off guard when we strike back on Monday morning."

Strike back?

"Oh, yes, we have a plan. When the markets closed in Amsterdam yesterday, the brothers were still in control of Netuno. Although the Axelines privately purchased Branca's shares, they had to contact the stock registrar to inform them of the transfer. We were able to get a hold of the information and confirmed that the transfer had been completed, but they have no idea that we know. Axel has to wait until Monday morning now to buy enough shares if he has any hope of tipping the majority in his favor. As a bonus he doesn't know that Branca imploded and told Bento and Reinaldo everything."

The worry on my face came through as the thought of the Axelines owning Netuno made me sick.

"I know it sounds risky, but I saved the best for last. Thanks to Sachi, we might actually have a chance."

????

"Yes, you heard me right," Petra said. "The brothers don't have enough capital or the technical resources to do this on their own, but Sachi and her family do. The plan is for her to purchase a large number of shares on Monday morning. That way, Sachi and the brothers would have a controlling interest even if the Axelines owned a large part. Early this morning, Sachi took the lead and called her father."

I looked at Sachi. She was uncomfortable with all the eyes on her but eventually took a breath and was ready to speak. "Let me explain," Sachi responded with a deep sigh. "Last night, when everything started to come to light, there was some concern that if we did not start putting a bigger plan into place for Monday, we would have no chance of stopping the takeover. Luca, Carmo's and Bento's police friend, explained that as far as he knew the Axelines had not broken any laws and so he could not do anything. Gervais, Puro, Bento, and the brothers were beside themselves. They could literally lose everything, and I couldn't let that happen. So, I called my father." She looked at me. "Yes, I know, but I had no choice. In the end whatever power and influence that Axel Axeline thought he might have in the financial world I can assure you my father's reach is far more powerful and influential. Axel is a big fish in a small pond. My father, on the other hand, basically runs the ocean."

My eyes welled up for Sachi as I could not imagine what she had to agree to to secure that kind of support from her father.

She surveyed my inquiring face. "Oh Maya, don't worry, we're working it out. I'm negotiating my terms with him as we speak," she smiled politely ending any further conversation on the topic.

"The brothers are nervous, but Bento and Carmo convinced them it was the only way. Truthfully though, I'll be happy when I can go back to the kitchen and things are normal again, but until then …"

✒

The doctor came at the end of our meal and examined my throat. He found no medical reason for the loss of my voice. He told me just to be patient and that it should come back within a couple of days, maybe a week.

Carmo joined us after the doctor left. Although she tried to hide it at first, the edges of her beautiful smile popped up creating a moment of curiosity and reprieve from a tense conversation.

"Well, I guess I could never be a poker player. Bento wanted me to keep it quiet for a bit but the whole evening didn't go as badly as it could have," she said with growing excitement.

We all looked at her with anticipation. But she didn't need to say a word. All it took was an extended left hand showing off the most beautiful engagement ring I had ever seen. Bento must have had it made for her and was keeping it for just the right moment.

"Oh my God Carmo, that is quite the ring," Josie exclaimed.

"Yes, I know," she blushed. "It happened early this morning while we were in the middle of everything. He came running down the stairs after bringing Maya a pot of hot water."

She looked over at me and raised an eyebrow.

"What did you say to him?"

I shrugged my shoulders.

"Then he took my hand and led me out into the olive groves. The moon was low in the sky, but I could see he had tears in his eyes. I thought they were tears of sadness, but I was wrong. He launched into the most amazing proposal a girl could ever ask for." She paused. We were hanging on every word at that point.

"So?" Josie screeched. "Tell us, how did he do it? What did he say?"

"'My dear Carmo, as we stand amongst these olive trees we planted together as children, I am humbled by your dedication and the love you have shown to Netuno, my family, and to me. I grew up never seeing true love between my mother and father and envied you and the love your mother and Puro shared before she died. It was so true, something you could hang on to. Even after she died, their love stayed all around the two of you. When the sun rises on Monday morning, all this could be gone. Netuno could be lost and I would have nothing. Could you still love me? Could you marry a man with only an olive branch to offer you?'

"I was so taken aback I froze for a moment. Then he froze because I did too. We stood in the moonlight searching, staring into one another's hearts until I reached out to take the olive branch that he held in his hand. Then I saw the ring, sparkling in a shaft of moonlight. He carefully removed it, then took my trembling hand and placed the ring on my finger, reassuring me that no matter what happened we would marry during the harvest, in just a few weeks' time."

7

Change is Good

Judith

"WELL THAT WENT BETTER THAN anticipated," I chirped, slipping my phone back into my bag.

"Pardon me, ma'am, you're next," the flight attendant said as her beautiful accent gently brought me back to my place in line.

"Sorry, I was just speaking to my daughter Maya. She's in Portugal right now. That's my destination. I was going to surprise her, but I thought she had had enough surprises in the past twenty-four hours, so I called to let her know I was on my way."

"Does she live in Portugal?" the attendant asked kindly while holding out her hand for my passport and boarding pass.

"No, not right now, but I think she wants to move there. She's fallen in love, but there was some drama that happened with the young man and the winery she is staying at. I'm going there to help her—if I can, I hope."

"You're an amazing mother to fly all the way to Portugal to be with her."

"Hmm, honestly I haven't been—but I want to be."

A voice came from close behind me in line. "Are you Maya Wells' mom?"

"Excuse me?" I turned around almost bumping into two young ladies who stood uncomfortably close. I stepped back instinctively and collided with the flight attendant, then whirled around, "Oh, I am so sorry," I offered to the woman.

"I am fine." She bent down to pick up my boarding pass which had fallen from her hands when I bumped her. "Do you know those ladies?"

"No, I have never met them before in my life."

One of the girls stepped in closer to me again, "Portugal, wineries, drama? It's all the talk online right now. Jade is tweeting constantly. Please tell me. Did Cristiano really cheat on Maya with Jade?"

I turned away from the girl, horrified to hear what she was implying.

"Of course, he did," her friend responded. "Did you see those pictures? Her hand was in his pocket! Eeww." She looked at me with her head cocked to the side and a smug smile to support my impression that she was taking some pleasure in Maya's unfortunate situation. "I'm sorry to tell you this Maya's mother, but I think your daughter deserved it. She should have told him the truth about his family. I'm rooting for Cristiano, but the rest of my friends think Maya is better off without him."

I really had no idea what she was talking about, but there was one thing I learned from being married to a lawyer for so long was: never let them see your vulnerabilities. I took a few deep breaths and launched in.

"Everything is not always as it seems ladies. Maybe you should spend a little more time reading the classics instead of the latest Twitter drama." My comment only stung the duo briefly, and then one of them looked me square in the eyes and raised her voice.

"Hey Leah, you wouldn't believe who we ran into. It's *Maya Wells'* mom," she yelled out, informing the rest of the passengers.

Three more people broke the line and rushed forward with phones in hand snapping pictures of me. My little sprinkle of courage was gone, and I felt a surge of panic, but before it could take hold, another attendant stepped in front of me creating a barrier with her arms while the first shouted into the phone. Within a minute, a security guard arrived and escorted me onto the plane. He then handed me over to a third attendant who led me up a flight of stairs to a seat that was not in economy class.

"Mrs. Wells? Are you alright? You look a little flushed. Why don't you sit down?" the lovely woman offered.

"Thank you so much. What's happening? I asked in quieter tones. "Why am I here? Am I in trouble?"

"Oh, no, Silva just wanted to make sure you were okay and that no one else bothered you on your trip. The truth is Cristiano is a colleague of ours. He and Silva are old friends."

"Well imagine that." I shook my head and sat down in the seat offered.

"Would you like something to drink? We have time before we take off."

"A cup of tea would be nice if you can manage it," I responded with a smile and a sigh.

"Are you sure you wouldn't like something a little stronger? I heard you had to fight off a crowd down at the gate."

I smirked. "No, thank you, a cup of tea should do the trick." My phone rang. "Please excuse me."

"No problem, I'll be back in a few minutes."

I saw the screen, and to my surprise, it was Phillip. "Oh, hello dear."

"I couldn't wait for your call." He paused. "Is everything alright? Your voice sounds strained."

"Yes, I'm fine. I'm in Vancouver. Nothing to worry about. I just had to climb some stairs. Please remind me to add more cardio to my exercises when I get home."

"And when will that be? One, two, three weeks?"

"That sounds about right. Not sure yet. Can you believe it?"

"Believe what? That you are on your way to Portugal?" Phillip asked with hesitation.

"No, not that. They bumped me up to first class dear."

"First class? How did you manage that Judith?" he sounded slightly suspicious.

"Oh Phillip, no need to worry. There was a little kerfuffle in the line at the gate. A few people discovered I was Maya Wells' mom and they started asking me questions and taking pictures."

"Pictures?" he asked with a hint of hidden anxiety in his tone.

"Yes Phillip, I'm fine. I did what any good lawyer's wife would do."

"And what would that be?" he queried with some curiosity.

"I didn't let them rattle me—or at least didn't let them see it."

"And did they?"

"Only a little, but no big deal. Silva and the security guard took care of everything. Looks like I've made some new friends already."

"Silva? Security guard? Do you need me to meet you in London?"

"No, Phillip, no rescuing needed, not this time. Anyway, to answer your other questions, Silva is a flight attendant who knows Cristiano and she called the security guard to escort me onto the plane. No big deal."

"Yes, you've already said that once. Please don't be so nonchalant about this. There is a lot going on right now and this is the first time you've traveled on your own in over two decades."

"Oh, Phillip, I know it has been a long time. But I'm better now. Besides, our daughter needs me, and I must do this on my own. Please don't worry." I paused. "I wish you would have shared a little more information about what was going on with Maya."

"I'm sorry Judith, I didn't anticipate you hopping a plane in the wee hours of the morning and needing a briefing ahead of time. I was just trying to protect you," Phillip relented with a sigh.

"I'm sorry Phillip. Truthfully, I didn't know I was going either until I heard Jordan on the phone with Steven. It was clear he was on his way home, alone, and I just had a feeling: I needed to be with her. I should have said something to you before you left for the office. I'm sorry." I paused. "So, you talked to Maya. Did she say anything about me coming?" Phillip's pause answered my question.

"You don't need to protect me anymore. I'll be alright Phillip. You are the greatest husband in the whole world."

"I'm proud of you Judith, but that doesn't mean I might not worry just a little bit."

⌘

"Hello, Mrs. Wells, we met downstairs at the gate. I see you're settling in. No one else is bothering you I hope?"

"Oh Silva, I cannot thank you enough for helping me back there. What a strange situation that was."

"Those girls were just looking to cause trouble. I love the way you stood up to them. I have them sitting by the bathrooms in economy. They won't be bothering you on your flight. I will make sure of that."

"Silva, the other attendant mentioned you've known Cristiano for a long time?"

"Yes, Cristiano and I have worked together for many years."

"Forgive me for my bluntness, but how well do you know one another?"

Silva smiled. "I'm a widow. Cristiano has only ever been a good friend to me. He is one of the kindest men I have ever known." She knelt beside me and whispered into my ear. "Whatever you have read about him it is not true. He would never do anything to harm your daughter. He loves her with all his heart."

"That blog must be something else," I shrugged my shoulders.

"I'm sorry Mrs. Wells. I just presumed you read the story and that was why you were on your way to Portugal to meet Maya."

"I know about it, but my husband strongly suggested I not read it. You've piqued my curiosity though."

Silva looked uncomfortable but continued, "Some of it is quite shocking, but you deserve to know what is being said. Then you can make up your own mind on what is truth and what is fiction."

"Yes, you're right. I do need to know more about the situation. Let's start with Cristiano."

"Oh, you want *me* to tell you?"

"Yes, who better than an old friend?"

"I'll try my best. I only have a few minutes though before I must get back to work. First, he never dated any flight attendants, not that most of the single girls didn't try. He has a charisma that draws people in, but he rarely gets close with others. He is kind but guarded. He *had* clear rules about everything in his life, but I remember the day when he met Maya. Meeting her flustered him. I had never seen him like that before. At first, I thought he was ill, but then I saw him with her, and I knew. He didn't know which way to turn. The truth is, love sometimes just happens. It offers itself to you, invites you in. I think Maya and Cristiano were just meant to be together." She paused, falling briefly into her thoughts. "I wanted you to know that at some point when you do read the blog— know that he would never do anything purposefully to hurt her. I don't understand everything that is going on, but I know him, and I know he loves her."

"I don't think I want to read it, at least not yet. You've told me everything I need to know."

"If you need anything during your flight, just push the call button."

"I hope I don't run into any more people like those girls."

"I can help with that, but it might be best that you do not tell anyone else who you are. I would suggest you stay on the plane while we are refueling in Montreal. I'm sorry to be the first to tell you, but your photo has already been posted on the blog and Twitter. By the time we land, I would imagine you could be all over social media."

"Social media? Oh, my goodness. Who would care about me? I am just the mom."

"No, you are the mom of two young lovers, ripped apart by circumstance and betrayal. People are vultures and will want to know everything about you and your family."

"Did you meet Maya?" I asked trying to understand as much as I could.

"Yes, we met briefly when she flew to Portugal and then I saw her again last week on her way back from Paris."

"Paris? She was in Paris? With Cristiano?"

Silva smiled gently, looking a little uncomfortable "Yes, but Cristiano could not fly back with her as he got called in to work an international flight. Truthfully, I don't think she even remembered seeing me that evening. She looked rather distracted after Cristiano dropped her at the gate and while on the flight, she borrowed some paper from one of the attendants and spent most her time writing."

"Well, it sounds like … I'm just glad that I'll see her soon."

Silva changed the subject, telling me more about Cristiano's life and how, after his parents died, his grandmother looked after him. My heart broke for all he had gone through and I started to understand what might have drawn Maya and Cristiano together.

"I know," Silva responded looking at my face. "It is an incredibly sad story, and now all of this. He doesn't deserve any of what is happening to him Mrs. Wells."

"Thank you for sharing, Silva."

"Oh, it's no problem. I hope it helped. I'll check on you later," she noted as she touched my hand and went back to work.

I smiled as the flight leveled out and the seatbelt sign went off. I could hardly believe I was on my way to Portugal with a layover in England; what more could I ask for? I missed London and looked forward to being in the city, even if it was just for one night.

The next few hours were spent in a whirlwind of memories about Phillip and I and how we met.

Our love wasn't so different from Cristiano and Maya's. Fate brought us together in the most colorful way.

❧

He was a law student on vacation in London for two weeks and I was a stressed-out fashion design student from the Royal College of Art. I was taking a break at the local pub when in walked Phillip. I knew he was from home—the Canadian flag on his backpack gave him away. I waved and invited him over. He was bold and handsome and accepted my invitation without hesitation. He and I soon discovered that British Columbia was home for both of us. He grew up in the quaint town of Peachland and me, well I was stationed in one too many small towns with my father, the policeman, who could never say no to the most remote postings the province had to offer. I think I was ten the first time I refused to unpack my boxes. I lived out of cardboard for about a year. I finally relented, and six months later we moved again.

That first night we met, I took Phillip back to the design studio at school. I'm not sure what came over me. All I knew was that I couldn't say goodbye. He sat with me while I cut and clipped and sewed. I listened to his stories, and what should have taken me three hours to complete took me six. But neither of us minded. We went for breakfast the next morning and each morning after that for thirteen days. He shared his dream of completing law school and one day having his own vineyard. I later found out he had canceled the rest of his trip with his friends and booked himself into a local hostel, spending the mornings with me before class, wandering around London in the afternoons, and then nightly bringing me supper so I could stay at the studio and work on my designs.

The more he talked of his vineyard and the life he saw for himself, the more I knew I wanted to be part of that dream. He went back to Canada and took my heart with him. I had one year of school left, but my plans to work in the fashion houses of Europe had shifted and all I wanted was to be with him.

Phillip and I married soon after I moved back to Canada. He had graduated from law school and had been offered a job at a small firm in his hometown of Peachland. I started working at a little boutique in the center of town. It was a quiet shop, which allowed me the time to sketch and dream about all the amazing designs I wanted to create. The owner even let me put a few of my creations out. It was an amazing time in my life. I felt so free and loved; it was a perfect mixture of the two. Then one day we found out we were pregnant, and everything changed. My sketches gave way to the lists of things I needed to do to get ready for the baby. I wasn't sad about the pregnancy, but strangely, I wasn't happy either. I remember being scared. I was afraid that I couldn't be a good mom, that I didn't have the confidence to make the right decisions like my mom always did.

She was one of those amazing people that everyone loved. She always had the right answer. She was a "supermom." As Maya's birth got closer, my nerves worsened. I kept wondering what kind of mother I was going to be and perseverated on all the things I didn't know how to do.

When Maya was born, I felt instantly lost, and within hours of her birth all my worst fears were solidified. I felt so alone. When I looked at her, I knew how I was supposed to feel but it wasn't there. I wanted to love her, to fawn over her, to hold her like she was the love of my life, but I couldn't. I was a terrible mother and I had not even gotten started.

I think Phillip knew something wasn't right from the beginning, but he never asked and I never talked about it. Maya and I lived in a secret world of sadness for the first year. Then one day I heard Maya laugh and I started laughing with her. After that, day by day, things started getting better. It was perfect when she laughed, but when she cried I got nervous, so Phillip stepped in and took over. He made it easier.

Then I got pregnant again. I was excited for a moment. Maya would have a sibling, something I never had. I would be a better mom, stronger. I told myself I knew what I needed to do. However, when Jordan was born, the sadness that hit me was like a crashing wave. I felt suffocated. It was even worse than the first time. I could hardly breathe, let alone take care of two small children. Phillip struggled to hold our household together. Then one day a phone call came that resulted in an unexpected inheritance. He cut his practice down to two days a week, and we bought the vineyard he had always dreamed about. He thought that the move would do us all good. He loved me so much. I saw how my depression was tearing him apart, but he wouldn't give in and he never let me give up. So off we went. Things got better for a time. I was able to look after Jordan while Phillip and Maya wandered around the vineyard. Maya became my adventurer and would head out to the little peach orchard at the back of our property every day. I longed to be able to climb a tree with her, but I couldn't. Things had shifted again and some days just getting out of bed to make her lunch took everything I had.

The depression wasn't getting better and Phillip couldn't manage everything on his own, so he gave up his dream, sold the vineyard, and we returned to town. Maya was never the same, but she was quiet and easy and took care of Jordan when we needed.

It took years to dig myself out of the depression, but no matter what, Phillip was my constant, my grounding tool. During my last hospital stay, when Maya was in her senior year in high school, I asked him to leave. Leave the hospital, leave me, and never come back. The next day he showed up with my sewing machine and my sketch book and told me to get to work. He started bringing me breakfast every day and would bring fabric to the hospital in the evenings. I had so much stuff there that the hospital finally relented and gave me my own space to work. I started to come alive again.

"Mrs. Wells?"

"Oh, hello Silva," I said wiping the tears from my eyes.

"We will be landing in Montreal soon. Can I get you anything? Are you okay?"

"I am perfectly content. Just reminiscing, thank you."

Silva tilted her head to the side, "You and Maya look so much alike when you smile."

"Thank you." I looked out the window at the clouds. There I was, soaring on the edge of another journey, Maya at the center again. But I was ready this time, ready to become the mother I knew I could be. The question was, would she let me?

8

Truth be Told

Maya

As HAPPY AS I WAS for Carmo about the engagement, I knew I needed to be alone. Although Ellen offered to let me stay in her room, I didn't want to be around anyone. I was exhausted. My insides ached and I just wanted to curl up into a ball, but when I got into my room and crawled under the duvet, Christopher poked me, reminding me that avoiding my feelings was what got me into my mess in the first place. I had to feel it. I had to feel everything.

I picked up the pencil that lay beside my broken Athena. I couldn't cry out, but I could write. I opened Christopher and began:

> *Saturday morning 11:00 am*
> *My room is a disaster.*
> *I want to scream but I can't. I want to run, but I don't trust my legs to carry me. I tried to hide but you and Athena wouldn't let me. Thank you. There is nowhere to hide from my thoughts, from the scene that continues to play out in my mind from last night. I am*

surrounded by my friends, but my heart feels empty. Where could he be?

Cristiano, where are you? I cannot imagine what you are going through right now. You need to know that I love you, only you. I sent Steven home. He came because he thought he was trying to protect me, save me. But he never understood me.

I don't need protecting. I need someone to walk with me, stand strong, help me, challenge me. I need you. Cristiano, we have only just begun. There is so much more we need to learn about one another. I know nothing happened with Jade. Puro gave me the box. I know why you were there—Athena.

Where are you? You need to come home. But I keep asking myself: Did you run because of me? Was it the letter? Your family? Please let me know. You do not have to do this alone. Cristiano??

The dam broke and the sobs flowed until my pillow was soaked. Then a soft breeze whistled through the room and demanded for me to stop. I turned my head and caught the scent of the fresh freesia that lay withering on my bedside table.

I didn't know a scent could make you listen so hard. My inner voice began to perseverate on one single thought. I needed to find him and the only path I could think of sounded irrational. People would think I was crazy.

I pulled out my phone and typed in Price's Portugal. Frustration and aggravation soon took over as I fell down the rabbit hole of reading one too many comments on what an awful person I was.

When I stepped into the lobby, Puro was standing behind the desk, but his mind was somewhere else. His usually serene face looked wrinkled with worry and I could see the strain around the edges of his eyes.

I knocked on the counter to get his attention.

"Oh, Maya! You startled me. Sorry, I was somewhere else." He smiled slightly and studied my face carefully before he spoke again.

"I heard you lost your voice. Are you alright? Does it hurt?"

I shook my head, then reached out for him to give me a pen and paper.

No, it doesn't hurt. At least not the voice … I paused, trying to smile.

Have you heard from him? Anything? I haven't. I got a text from Jack though, he told me Cristiano came to see him and that he left in a hurry. Jack said Cristiano was angry. He thinks Cristiano went to meet his biological parents. Jack wouldn't tell me anything else. Puro what am I going to do? This is all Jack's fault, if he had just told someone, something …

"He did. He told you. This is not Jack's fault and you know that. He kept the secret for all those years because of how much he cares about Cristiano, and he told you about all of this for the same reason. Anyway, Jack knows that when Cristiano is ready, he will come back like the first time.

Yes, the first time, in high school, but I don't know what really happened.

"Cristiano was in his final year of school and disappeared for about six weeks. Two weeks into his disappearance Jack contacted us with news that Cristiano was with him. Four weeks later he came home. He was different though, even quieter than before. During the week he went to school, and on the weekends he worked here at the vineyard without complaining. That's when I started to get really worried; the only time he smiled was when he played his guitar. Carmo told me he talked to a few people at school, like Luca, but she and Bento were his closest friends.

It was a difficult time for all of us as we watched him retreat farther into himself every day.

"When he finished school, he started working full time at Netuno. It was a very dry season and we all had to work extra hours to save the new vines and to make sure we had a harvest to collect. Once the worst was over, and we knew that Netuno was going to be okay, I started to see shimmers of change in him. I'm not sure if it was being part of something bigger than himself, or if he just got better at pretending that he was happier, but I took it as a sign of hope that he was finally moving forward, accepting his parents' death, and finding his own way.

"A week or so before harvest, he announced he had been accepted into school and was leaving. Everyone was excited at first, and then he told us where he was going to school. He had decided to become a flight attendant. Now you must understand, he had never flown before as Avo wouldn't allow him on a plane. We were skeptical about his choice and wondered if Avo would even allow it, but when any of us tried to talk to him about it he told us it was just something he had to do. He had made up his mind. When he left, I wondered if we would ever see him again.

"He did come back to visit, and, in some ways, he was better. His travels opened his eyes to the world. He left as a wounded boy and came back as a man appearing to have stitched himself back together, but he still looked lost to me."

I steadied myself at the front desk, as I discovered yet another layer of truth in Cristiano's story. I could almost feel his hand on my shoulder trying to comfort me. My body shivered, but I waved at Puro to continue.

"Rumors floated around Netuno about him. You know, there aren't too many male flight attendants who work for Portugal Air, so he became the topic of many conversations, but I paid them no mind. I was just content to hear that he was managing and hoped that somehow, in all of his travels, he would find what he was looking for—and then he met you and everything changed."

My heart skipped.

Me?

"Yes, you. What you did for him and how meeting you gave him an opportunity to change. But I don't think he had enough time to start believing that it could be true. Learning about the adoption, his biological family, Dalley's blog, and then seeing you with Steven. It was …"

Too much. His leaving; it was all my fault, wasn't it?

"No, Maya, the truth came out for a reason. It's not about fault. You spilled your tea, Avo wrote the letter, Jack told you Cristiano's story, and yes, even Dalley's part in writing the blog will have meaning in the end. Mind you, I think we could have done without the Jade and Steven situations, but we will deal with them too. Honestly, as painful and overwhelming as all of this is, he has to work through it."

I held the pen in my hand ready to respond but stopped. Avo danced through my thoughts like she was thinking about me too and then I was hit with a wave of sadness that almost knocked me off my feet.

"Maya, what is it?" Puro asked running around the desk to help steady me.

How is Avo going to deal with this? I scribbled on the paper.

"Honestly, I'm not sure. We all thought he was home for good when you came into his life."

I'll go out to see her. She needs to know what's happening.

"Maya, are you sure you should go? Carmo and I can …"
I interrupted him with a hand slap on the counter.

I have to be the one to tell her! I scrawled on the paper.

He looked shocked at my behavior and a part of me was too, but I just didn't have time to be polite.

Puro, could you call Francesco and have him pick my mother up at the airport tomorrow?

"Your mother?"

Yes, she's decided she needs to be with me.

"I spoke with your father last night and he didn't mention anything about her coming."

He didn't know. Right now, she is on a flight to London and will arrive here around noon tomorrow.

"I'll book the car for her. Is there anything special I need to do to prep for her arrival?"

I honestly don't know. How horrible is that? I have no idea what she likes and doesn't like, except a cup of tea, like me.

"Well, I guess that is a good place to start." There was an awkward moment between the two of us, but he finally jumped back into the conversation. "Do you want a ride over to Avo's?"

No, I'll walk. I need time to figure out how I am going to tell her.

Puro smiled. "If there's one thing I know about Avo, you won't have to say much to her. She'll understand," he said.

I nodded, knowing there was no easy way to get through this situation. As I walked towards the door, I turned back briefly, staring at Puro, aching to ask the question. He read my face like an open book.

"I don't know, Maya. He's a man who believes his heart has been broken. He's always had trouble trusting himself and others, so I would imagine he is very confused right now, questioning everything and everyone in his life."

My chest seized. I turned and walked away. I knew I wouldn't be able to breathe deeply again until his heart had been put back together.

I thought I had left all my fears behind when I boarded the plane to Portugal. But I had been naïve to imagine all my fears grew from the same root. This fear of losing Cristiano was new, and it wound around me like an invasive plant.

9

Avo, Mom, and Me

Maya

As I neared her cottage gate, I could smell the bread baking. Avo was in the garden removing a loaf from the outdoor oven when she saw me. Her smile faded as she read my face and saw my sagging shoulders.

She placed the loaf she was holding on the old wooden table and walked out to Cristiano's tree, sat down, and closed her eyes.

Puro was right. It didn't matter that I had no voice, for no words could express the pain and sadness that weighed heavily on both our hearts while we sat under his tree together.

Some time later, when she opened her eyes, Avo stood and offered me her hand. We walked back to the cottage leaning on one another. As we got closer, I could smell the bread burning in the oven and I tried to break away to save what I could, but she held my arm tightly and shook her head. Then, to my surprise, she made me watch as each smoldering loaf broke into colorful flames and turned to ash. It was painful. I wanted it to stop. When the loaf pans cooled, we removed the charred remains, she still not uttering a word and me not able to. She pointed to the pans and then out into the field. I picked them up carefully at first, trying to avoid the inevitable, but finally gave in to stacking them against my chest and covering myself in sadness and ash. I walked out behind the cottage, and there I found a series of blackened and rusted out memories carefully placed side by side on the ground.

When the task was complete, she pulled me inside and took out the grain mill. I didn't want to bake but she insisted. As we began to grind and sift the grain, she started to hum. She looked at me and raised her hand as if she expected me to join her. I pointed to my throat to show her I could not make a sound, but she continued to push me. I closed my eyes at her insistence and listened to her tone. She placed one hand on my throat and the other on my heart, and then began to sing. Before I knew it, the next sound I heard was coming from me. I was humming along with her, feeling more alive and at peace than I had felt in days. After finishing the song, she looked fragile, her eyes heavy. She walked to her room and shut the door.

I cried. For her, for Cristiano, for me, and then I stopped. I knew my voice was back, but it didn't feel like mine and I didn't feel like I deserved it. Feeling sorry for myself was getting me nowhere though. So, I decided to bake.

I baked into the night and chose silence as my song. I was afraid of the sound of my new voice; afraid of what she had given up for me. I didn't know how to explain it, but I was different.

I found a pen and paper at an old writing desk and took them outside. I knew I could slip the paper between Christopher's pages when I got back to Netuno.

Sunday Morning
I don't think I slept for more than a couple of hours last night between the risings. And when those loaves were done baking I started again. So here I am. The sun

is barely casting a glow in the sky and I'm hoping that when I'm finished, I will have created my own magic bread. Maybe a different kind of magic than Avo's but magical all the same. I'm not sure what I believe in anymore, but I do know that I have to believe in something. And the closest thing to my heart right now is Cristiano.

I believe in my love for Cristiano.

You are not alone. I am with you.

The wood just cracked in the oven. It's time to bake again.

Maya

As the sun finished its own rising, I pulled out the last of the loaves, letting them cool under a blanket of morning stillness. I walked into the cottage and tapped quietly on Avo's door. She said my name ever so softly, giving me permission to enter. I brought with me a loaf for us to share then broke off two small pieces and whispered in her ear, "For love, for hope, for finding lost things."

She then took the smallest bite and stared at me, appearing to savor the bread like it was a piece of chocolate cake. She tore another piece off the loaf and held it close to her heart.

"Magic? For me?" She looked slightly confused, then smiled and sighed. "*Obrigado.*"

I wasn't sure what to say. So, I tasted the bread just as she had. It was lovely, but it was nothing like the loaf she had given to me in the market. I rolled the idea around in my mind that maybe, somehow in my baking, I made my own magic.

Avo ate and drank little that morning, but she would not put her loaf of bread down. I was nervous about leaving the cottage and going back to Netuno, but my mom was to arrive in just a few hours. I texted Puro to let him know what was happening and he said he would send Carmo down immediately.

Before I left, I took Avo out to the garden. As we waited for Carmo to arrive, I got up and started washing the loaf pans from my evening of baking.

I was just finishing the last pan when I could feel something shift in the garden. I hadn't heard the vehicle on the gravel, but I heard the car door slam and thought Carmo arrived. I turned to Avo and then followed her eyes as she watched someone approach the gate. I could not see the visitor's face at first because the sun was in my eyes, but when she took two more steps, I saw that it was my mother. She ran into the garden, arms open, wanting a hug. Offering a hug? I wasn't sure which.

"Maya? Is that you? You look so different," my mom remarked with surprise.

"Yes, Mom, it's me. It's only been three weeks since I've seen you. I haven't changed that much, have I? What are you doing here? I thought you weren't landing for a few hours."

"I couldn't wait! I had to see you. So, I called my new friend Silva at the airline and had her book me on an earlier flight this morning. She called Francesco and, well, here I am. I came straight from the airport."

I gave up asking why, let my guard down, and allowed her to hug me. Surprising myself, I hugged her back. When we finally relaxed our embrace, she reached out to hold my hand. I wasn't sure what to do, so I took it. It felt awkward at first, but slowly a level of comfort settled over me.

"Francesco, thank you for picking my mom up at the airport. I hope it was not too inconvenient for you."

"No, not at all. We had a wonderful time, didn't we, Judith?" he said, waving his hands around.

"Yes, it was lovely and very informative," Judith smiled genuinely at Francesco.

"Maya," Francesco said gently, "I spoke with Puro and let him know that I picked your mom up early from the airport. He said that Carmo will be here soon, but Puro is worried about Avo and wants her at Netuno where he can keep an eye on her."

"Yes, that makes sense, but I don't know if she'll go," I whispered back.

"He asked if you could pack her things. He thinks Carmo can help convince her if she gets stubborn."

"I'll take care of that right now. Thank you for everything, Francesco."

I walked over to Avo and touched her on the shoulder.

"Avo, Puro has invited you to come stay for a few days at Netuno."

She nodded her head and smiled weakly showing no resistance. It was then that my worry set in.

"Mom, can you sit with Avo while I pack her things?"

"Yes, of course, Maya. Anything you need sweetheart."

My mother's assurance that she could help left me feeling confused, but I could not focus on that in the moment.

Avo stared out towards Cristiano's tree like she was willing him to appear. She may have been magical, but she was no magician.

As I walked towards the cottage, my mom sat down with Avo and began to chat. She held her hand just like I used to hold hers when I was a child.

"Hello, Avo. Can I call you Avo? I don't know your first name. Oh my, what an adventure it was getting here, but everyone has been so kind. I met all these lovely ladies who know your grandson very well. They spoke so highly of him. I feel like I know him ..."

I could hear my mom's voice until I entered the cottage, then everything fell silent. The room felt small and dark with a dash of sorrow. I stepped into Avo's bedroom, not wanting to touch or move anything, but then I saw it: a shelf of pure love. Images of Cristiano, Avo, and his parents. Their smiles could have lit up the world, and I imagine while they were alive, they did. My eyes were drawn to a simple frame that lovingly held a photo of a six-year-old Cristiano, sitting in his favorite tree in the garden. Sharing the shelf was a sealed jar that appeared to be empty, but the label read *Special Laughter: Cristiano, 6-years-old.*

The tears that fell were neither efficient nor quiet. I held two fingers over my lips, hoping I could keep the sobs inside, but there was no stopping the sadness. I grabbed the picture frame and crumpled onto the floor, holding it tightly to my chest, praying that I could find him and that he would want to come back. I heard a light knock and looked up. There in the doorway stood my mother. As she entered, she held me in her eyes, walked slowly towards me, then sat down. I never knew how much I needed a mother—my mother—until that moment. She held me until the sobs relented.

"Oh mom, what am I going to do? I love him so much. He is my whole heart. I don't know how, or why, but he is."

She smiled and moved the hair from my eyes.

"Then go and find him and don't stop until you do. Carmo just arrived. Why don't you join them outside while I finish packing Avo's things?"

I took the picture of Cristiano out of the frame and slipped it into my pocket. When I stepped outside, the morning sun was warming the garden, and Carmo sat holding hands with Avo. Carmo nodded for me to take over. She looked at my non-glamorous, puffy red eyes and smiled back. I nodded my head, took a deep breath, and led Avo towards the car. The scent in the garden tapped me on the shoulder as we walked towards the gate. I paused.

"Carmo, can you take Avo? I have to pack up one last thing."

"Maya, your voice—it's back!"

"Yes, it seems that I may have a few more things to say."

"Well thank goodness. We need you well if we are going to get through the next couple of days."

I smiled, then walked back into the garden and wrapped up the loaves I had baked throughout the night. I was not going to leave them there and let our hope go stale.

My mom walked out of the cottage with Avo's bag and shut the door. She was strong, filled with resolution. Seeing my hands were full, she grabbed the two remaining loaves and closed the garden gate behind us.

"I never knew you could bake, Maya?"

"I never knew I could either."

My mom's smile spoke volumes without saying a single word: she was proud of me.

10

Home Base

Puro

I SAT ON THE VERANDA drinking my coffee and allowed myself a moment to think about my upcoming trip to Vancouver to see Maggie.

I never thought it was possible to imagine myself with anyone else after my wife's death, but Maggie was different—and different was just what I needed. When she arrived at Netuno for the contest, we blended together like a perfect *rosé*, just waiting to be opened. We had walked the same path of losing our spouses and raising our families without the one we loved. I had Carmo and Netuno to keep me busy, and she her twin boys, CJ and Tim.

Thinking of her was comforting, and it was a pleasant distraction from all that was going on at Netuno with the Axelines' and Branca's deception.

❧

I saw the puff of dust on the road before I heard the crunch of gravel under the wheels of the car. My two newest guests would soon arrive: Judith and Avo.

When they stepped out of the car, Judith was arm in arm with Avo, while Carmo and Maya gathered up a full stock of fresh bread.

"You and Avo must have been baking all night," I stated with some concern.

Maya smiled and quietly responded, "No, it was just me."

"Your voice—it's back!!" I spontaneously ran over and hugged her, thrilled to have some good news.

"Yes, it's back," she said quietly, "but I think my night of bread making has caught up with me. I need to have a rest. Can you take care of my mom please?" she said in a whisper.

"Oh, no need for that," Judith chimed in. "I am going to be just fine." Judith leaned in and gave her daughter a little side hug. Although no one else appeared to see it, Maya stiffened for a second, then tried to relax, but didn't say a word.

At that moment, the rest of the ladies stepped out onto the veranda and jumped into the conversation.

"Oh my God, Maya, your voice is back! You can talk again," Josie yelled over everyone else.

"Yes, it's back, thanks to Avo," she said taking a breath. "Oh dear, I just remembered my room is a disaster. Where are we going to stay?" Maya asked, looking distressed.

"I'll be fine, Maya. I don't need to stay anywhere special," Judith said.

Ellen stepped over to Maya and took her hand. "Oh Maya, that's already taken care of. Carmo, Netuno's other resident miracle worker, had your room fixed up and it's ready for you."

"Oh, I don't know what to say."

Judith was quick to respond to Maya's hesitancy.

"Maya, I'm not sure it's such a good idea we stay together," Judith shared with some insistence.

Maya looked confused.

"What are you talking about? Of course, you're staying with me," she responded quickly, but I could see a little relief in her eyes.

"No, I think it's best if I don't," Judith said, firm in her decision.

Ellen read the situation and stepped in. "Maya, I think what your mom is saying is that you've been through so much over the last few days, it might be good for you to have a couple of nights on your own." Ellen looked over at Judith. "If you want, I have a spare bed in my room."

"Ellen is it? That sounds perfect." Judith accepted without giving Maya a chance to say anything else.

"Oh good," Ellen said with relief. "I've been a little lonely since Maggie left."

"Yes, I heard about what happened to Maggie," Judith said. "So terrible."

An awkward moment of silence fell over the group but was broken when Avo shuffled up behind Maya, squeezed her arm, and then gave her a nudge towards the grapevines.

"The chapel," Avo said with a hoarse voice.

"Chapel? You have a chapel here on the grounds?" Judith asked, looking to me.

"Yes, it was built many years ago. Maya, maybe you can take your mom while she is here." Maya's face went pale. It was obvious that Judith and Maya's relationship was strained, but Judith was trying her best not to push her.

"Oh yes, that would be lovely," Judith said, "But for today I'll just stay here and unpack."

Maya looked relieved and distressed at the same time. "Off you go, Maya," I said waving her away. "The ladies will help get your mom settled."

Maya nodded, then looked at her mother questioningly.

"I'll be fine, I promise. Come join me when you get back," Judith offered lovingly.

Maya handed the loaves off to Sachi and Ellen, then disappeared into the vines.

"Should someone go with her?" asked Petra. "She doesn't look herself."

"No," Judith stated. "Being outdoors by herself is just what she needs, trust me." Judith's eyes filled with tears when she said the last phrase. Then she took a deep breath and formally introduced herself.

"Hello, everyone, I'm Judith Wells, Maya's mom."

❧

With the future of Netuno hanging in the balance, and everyone entrenched in sadness and worry, I decided a change of pace was in order—at least for a few hours. We needed to celebrate something, and what could be better than Carmo and Bento's engagement. So, the wine began to flow, and for a brief time, we let the worries of the weekend stand anchored while we danced around them.

Avo smiled when I offered her a glass of wine, but she waved it off and asked if she could lie down. She looked tired, and I saw an unfamiliar weariness in her demeanor. It was as if she had aged a decade since I'd seen her last.

I settled Avo in her room, only leaving her side once she closed her eyes. While she rested I went onto her balcony and sat quietly, enjoying the stillness.

Her room faced the back of the property where the new grape vines had been planted four years ago. We were expecting our first commercial harvest from the crop, and I could smell the scent of the nearly ripened grapes. My heart sank at the thought of possibly losing Netuno, my home. I heard a stirring behind me and knew Avo had woken from her rest. She came out onto the balcony, sat down, and held my hand like she did when I was a child. Then she asked the inevitable question.

"What happened? Where did he go?" she asked with a deep sadness.

"Oh, Avo. He ran off again. I tried to stop him, but it was too much. Between the adoption, his birth parents, his siblings, and the situation with Maya, I think he was just overwhelmed."

Avo tilted her head just enough to indicate she wanted to know more. She sat in deep concentration after I shared the whole story with her. Then she spoke.

"Hmm, Euphemia was a beautiful girl. Oh, and Marcos, he could sing. Cristiano asked me when he was young from whom he had gotten his voice, as he didn't remember either of his parents singing, I told him it was from God. Maybe the letter was not the best idea. I should have told him a different way."

"No, Avo. You did what you thought was best. What a secret to keep for so many years. I can't believe I didn't put the pieces together myself."

Avo looked out into the fields. Her eyes glistened as she formulated her thoughts and then she spoke again, "I was going to tell him when he was ten, then twelve, and I tried again at fourteen, but I never seemed to find the right words. And then he turned eighteen and he left.

"He came and went a few times over the last ten years, but never long enough. It wasn't until a few weeks ago that I had a feeling. It was so strong. He needed me, he needed the truth, and so I wrote the letter. When I saw him, I knew he had read it, but he didn't ask me any questions about the adoption. His mind was focused on one thing, one person: Maya. He was so enchanted with her. I think I knew he had fallen in love even before he did."

She stopped and held her breath, holding her tears, then slowly let them out.

"There is no easy way through this, Avo. No way but together."
We sat quietly for some time until the stillness was disturbed by several
workers in the field discussing Netuno's latest problems.

Avo looked at me with raised eyebrows, questioning the conversation
which she heard.

"Puro, what is going on with Netuno? Is it in trouble?"

"Yes, it is—we are. Branca did something unbelievably bad."

"What? What could she have done that would put Netuno at risk?"

"She sold all her shares to a man who wants to take over."

A flash of anger erupted in her eyes. She and Branca had never
gotten along. Avo knew from the beginning Branca could never fit in at
the vineyard.

"How bad is it?" she asked simply.

"We won't know until tomorrow morning, but it is serious. We could
lose the vineyard and the inn—everything."

Avo gazed out into the fields and then stood up and turned to me,
"What can I do?"

"Avo, you're not well. Don't worry yourself about this."

"Worry is to be shared by family, not to be held selfishly," she said
shaking her finger at me.

"You are right, of course. You're always right."

Avo smiled, "No. Not always, but in *this* case, yes."

"Prayers, that's what we need. We need some divine intervention and
a little bit of luck."

"Ah, you know what I think about luck."

"Yes, I remember your lectures from when Michel and I were children. You always said it was up to us to make our own luck."

"Exactly," she laughed, "but I still have some pull when it comes to
divine intervention."

"Maybe you should save that for Cristiano."

"I have enough prayers for both, don't you worry."

Avo sat down and crossed her arms and closed her eyes.

ॐ

When I returned to the dining room, everyone was laughing and enjoying themselves. The wine had continued to flow, and everyone was in the middle of a joyful reprieve.

Maya had slipped back in from her walk and joined the group. The visit to the chapel appeared to have lightened her heart briefly until she saw her mom holding a wine glass.

"Mom, you're not supposed to be *drinking!*" She barked with reproach.

Judith smiled with embarrassment. "Maya, I've been doing this for a long time. I know when I can and cannot drink—but it's just some soda water and cranberry juice. There's no need to worry about me," she said, standing up for herself.

Maya's body tensed and she walked away.

"I'm sorry, Puro. Maya wasn't expecting my arrival here at Netuno. She's not herself with all that is going on. Anyway, how is Avo feeling?" she asked, trying to step away from her discomfort.

"Avo is managing. She is worried about Cristiano but has faith he will find his way home somehow."

We stood for a moment looking at one another. Then I saw her glance over at Maya.

"Judith, it's going to be okay. She'll find her way too."

"My being here seems to be causing her more stress. I had hoped I could help, but now that I'm here, I don't know what I can do."

"I am sure she appreciates you coming all this way," I said as I touched her shoulder. "It doesn't matter how old your children are, you always want the best for them."

As Judith melted back into the crowd my attention was drawn to the front of the room where the brothers were about to make a toast to Carmo and Bento. Our worries were suspended as we raised our glasses, but like all moments, that one passed, and the celebration quieted down.

Bento stood at the front of the room with my daughter. I saw the way she looked at him and I knew that no matter what happened they would be okay. Then he began to speak.

"Thank you, everyone. What a beautiful way to celebrate our engagement and all that Netuno means to us. Netuno is our history, our present, and our future and I will not let our home be taken from us without a fight." Bento looked around and invited Sachi to stand with him. "Sachi, have you heard from your father yet?"

Sachi joined him and the room quieted down. "Yes, but I am waiting for one more call. Most of his people are in place. We are just finalizing the details."

Bento looked out at the crowd and saw many questions popping up on their faces. "Sachi, maybe you can fill everyone in with our plan to save Netuno."

Sachi pulled her shoulders back and spoke with unexpected assertion. "For those of you who don't know, on Friday afternoon we discovered that Branca sold her Netuno shares to the Axeline Corporation. We believe that on Monday morning, Axel Axeline is planning on buying enough shares to take control of the company. We discovered their plans and have put some countermeasures in place. Bento and his family have agreed that my father's company and I will be covering the financial transactions in order that people other than the Axelines would become the majority shareholders. If all goes as planned, at the end of the trading day, Reinaldo, Mateus, and I will together hold majority shares in Netuno."

A small gasp escaped from the room, but Sachi continued. She looked over at the brothers. "This will only be temporary, and when you and your family are ready, you can buy my shares and I can get back to the kitchen."

Sachi's phone rang and she stepped away from the group. I could only assume it was her father as she began speaking in Japanese. She was calm for the first part of the conversation, then her face went gray. She looked towards the kitchen door where Gervais stood rigidly. I saw a flash of understanding flow between them and Sachi shook her head, as if answering his question. Gervais then turned on his heels and crashed through the kitchen doors, almost ripping them off the hinges.

Asking for help always has a price, and it appeared Sachi's privately negotiated terms for her father to help save Netuno had just been presented to her.

11

Mac and Cheese

Maya

"Excuse me! Excuse me." Puro tapped on his wine glass, drawing attention away from the two dramatic exits.

Then I heard her voice, but I couldn't understand why she was talking. "Hello, everyone!" My mother spoke up, trying to get people's attention, "Puro's trying to talk."

I gritted my teeth as she spoke. My mother's presence was increasingly irritating me, and although a part of me appreciated her being there, a bigger part in *that* moment did not.

Puro smiled at my mother politely and then began: "I wanted to chat with you all about a few things. Firstly, for now, the inn and the vineyard are to operate as usual. But truthfully, I am not sure what to do about the final week of the contest. Everyone has worked so hard over the last three weeks, and it would be a shame to close it down now. I just don't know what to do."

Josie's sharp tone snapped everyone to attention. "Puro, are you kidding me? There is no way we are giving up," she blurted out defiantly.

"That's right, we are just getting started. Did you taste my stew on Friday night?" Petra said, rallying behind Josie. "I've made a lot of progress."

Everyone let out a chuckle, but Ellen's was a little reserved.

"Ellen? You think I haven't made progress?" Petra feigned indignation.

Ellen paused. "I guess this is as good a time as any to let you all know, I'm going home on Tuesday. This whole situation has made me think about what's important in my life right now. My kids need me, and I need them," she said, smiling. Ellen's statement was resolute, leaving no room for comments on the subject.

Puro sighed. Then he led his curious and anxious staff out into the lobby to answer more questions. Within minutes, the dining room was empty except for our group and my mother. We sat together in silence, not sure what to do next as the wine could no longer mask all the different emotions in the space.

"So, what is our theme going to be?" Petra asked our group.

"I don't know," Josie said dejectedly.

No one said anything for a few minutes, then my mother piped in. "Family?" she offered. "I know I'm not part of the group, but it might be a good theme."

"It is a beautiful idea, Judith, and of course you are part of the group," Ellen reassured her.

I rearranged myself in my chair, feeling restless and hoping for a distraction.

Josie laughed. "Thank you, Judith, and you're right, Ellen, it is a lovely idea. No need to decide right now, but I do have a great idea. I don't know about you, but I can't just sit around here and worry about what's going to happen tomorrow. Let's go make some mischief in Gervais' kitchen. I haven't had mac and cheese in forever, and *I* make the best macaroni and cheese in the world!"

No one could ignore the challenge Josie presented. Even I was a little intrigued.

"You think so?" Petra bantered back. "Really, Josie? I can't cook, but I know I can make better mac and cheese than you."

"You're on," Josie squealed.

"My kids have told me I am the queen of mac and cheese," Ellen added quickly.

And without missing a beat, my mom piped up with a chuckle, "Well don't leave me out. Maya can confirm that mac and cheese was the only thing I *ever* cooked when she was growing up."

I hesitated, as there wasn't anything funny about my childhood, but as I looked over, I saw her watching me. She ached for me to let go, to find a way beyond the past. She was right, of course, so I took a deep breath and added, "Mom, I don't think they have mac and cheese in a box here."

Everyone roared with laughter, including myself.

When we entered the kitchen, Gervais was standing by one of the windows. His eyes were red and puffy, but in grand Gervais style, as soon as his kitchen was filled with crazy cooks, he went into action.

"*Bonjour, mes amies.* So, what are we making today?"

"Macaroni and cheese," we all chimed in.

"Would you like to join our challenge?" Ellen asked.

"Yes, I think I would," he said with some levity in his voice. Then without even saying go, he ran over to the fridge yelling something in French about *fromage bleu.*

"Blue cheese? You can have it all," I responded with a head shake.

Next thing I knew, Petra had pulled out her phone and a small Bluetooth speaker. With the music on and everyone dancing around, I placed my worries on a nearby shelf and fell into the moment. As "We are a Family" blasted out, I laughed. I hadn't heard that song since I was a kid. Everyone started to sing along, including my mom. There she was, on the other side of the kitchen, singing her heart out. Momentarily, I was taken back to just a few weeks prior, to the afternoon of pie baking with Maggie. I wished she could have been there with us—with me—making mac and cheese. I realized that I needed to talk to her, to see her.

❧

The phone rang once, then again. One more ring and a green icon appeared, indicating the video call had connected. In a moment, Maggie's face appeared on the screen . She looked tired, but tried to mask it with a small smile.

"Maya? Oh, what a surprise. It is so good to see you. Is everything alright?"

"Yes and no," I answered, feeling instantly overwhelmed when I saw her and heard her voice.

She immediately jumped into helper mode, avoiding any chance of me asking how she was doing. "Did you see him? I got him on the plane as soon as I could. He loves you. He would never do anything to hurt you. Jade is such a bitch."

"Maggie!" I responded with shock.

"Well, it's true," she stated matter-of-factly.

"I know, I just didn't expect you to say it," I smirked.

"I'm not perfect Maya," she responded with a hint of defensiveness in her tone.

"I know," I said, worried that somehow I had hurt her feelings.

"Anyways, sometimes people are just who they are. I don't have anything nice to say about her at all."

"I agree. So, let's not talk about her."

I avoided answering her question about what had happened with Cristiano and launched into memories about our day of pie-making. I was sure Puro would fill her in shortly about what had happened on Friday, and I really did not want to go over it again.

"Oh Maggie, I miss you so much."

"I miss you too, Maya, but enough of that. I see you're in the kitchen. What's going on there?"

"We are having a mac-and-cheese off!"

"Sounds like fun!"

"Maya, who are you talking to?" Josie yelled from across the room.

"Is that Josie?" Maggie asked.

"Yes, she is as loud and wonderful as ever."

Josie came running across the kitchen to see who was on the phone. When she saw Maggie's face, her whole body shifted.

"Can I talk to her, please?" she asked with a soft and concerned voice.

"Of course, Josie."

"Maggie, Josie wants to talk to you. I wish you could be here with us."

Maggie smiled but didn't say anything.

"Maya, give me the phone. I can't wait all day," Josie said, tapping her foot impatiently.

Maggie chuckled, "Oh, and Maya, don't forget to sprinkle a little love into the cheese sauce."

Josie took the phone before I could say anything else and left the kitchen.

As fun as the music was, and as much as I wanted to leave all my worries on the shelf, I couldn't. Maggie had mentioned his name, and thoughts of him whirled around me again. Visions of Cristiano meeting his birth mother flashed through my mind. I wondered if he'd found her.

I imagined the look on her face, seeing her adult son after giving him up. Would she recognize him? Would she know? My wandering thoughts did not go unnoticed.

Only when I felt a hand on my shoulder did I realize that I had become frozen with a block of cheese in one hand and a grater in the other.

"Maya? Would you like some help?" my mom asked gently.

I turned to the unfamiliar hands and I hesitated. I had waited my whole life for a moment like that, and there it was.

"Sure, what kind of cheese do *you* want to use today?"

She took the block I had in my hand.

"This one smells delicious."

I was cooking with my mom, something I had only dreamed of.

"Maya? Are you okay?"

"Yeah, I was thinking about Cristiano meeting his mother, and hoping he is going to be alright."

"Well, if he isn't at first, he will be. I spent a good deal of time chatting with Silva on the flight over here and she told me a lot about him. He seems like a wonderful young man. But it sounds like he is going to need some time to figure things out."

I smiled awkwardly, as accepting parental advice from her still seemed odd.

"I'm not sure *figuring things out* quite describes what he is going through, Mom—I just wish I could be there with him."

"Maya, there are some things a person just has to do alone."

"I know, but is this one of them?" My agitation spiked.

"Maya, you have to let him find his way back to you. You can't go chasing after him."

Something shifted and I wasn't having fun anymore.

"I wouldn't be chasing him. I would be finding him. You're the one who told me just a couple of hours ago to not stop until I did."

"I know, and maybe I spoke too quickly. But I've been where he is, in a way."

"What the hell are you talking about mom? You know nothing about him or me," I bit back at her, causing a shock to filter through the room.

"You're right, you're right. I don't know anything. I've upset you. I'm sorry, Maya. You must do what you think is best."

She tried to placate me, and for everyone else's sake, I stayed for the remainder of the afternoon. But my heart wasn't in the kitchen. It was far away, somewhere with Cristiano.

When everyone had finished cooking, the kitchen was a mess and Gervais shooed us back into the dining room to taste our late afternoon snack.

As we settled into our comfort food, fragments of story bombs from Friday night landed like little explosions into our conversation. No one meant any harm in the retelling of the tale and, truthfully, the story was quite salacious if I had not been at the center of it.

"Mom," I whispered quietly into her ear. "I am heading back to my room to take a bath. I'm sorry about snapping at you." She nodded and gave me a little hug.

"Thanks for hanging in there today. I am proud of you. Give me a second and I'll create an opportunity for you to slip out."

"Josie, I think you had the best mac and cheese of everyone," my mom announced.

"Now you're talking. Someone who appreciates the finer things in life," Josie declared.

"Are you kidding me, Judith? I think you must be jet lagged," Petra lobbed back.

Mom winked at me and I slipped out while they engaged in a full-scale conversation about jet lag remedies. As I passed by the front desk, Carmo was sitting quietly, staring off into space.

"Carmo? Are you alright?"

"Oh, as good as I can be. This whole situation has unnerved me. Maya, I'm not sure if you realize but Netuno has been my whole life. I was born here, raised here, my mom died here. This is the only home I know. If I lost it … I don't know what I would do. Listen to me complaining though. I have Bento, and that is all I really need." I winced as her last words struck me hard, and then it was me whose sadness could not be hidden.

"Maya, how selfish of me. I'm so sorry."

"No, don't worry. I am trying to figure out a plan to find him. I'm just not sure where to start."

"Maybe with the blog? Maybe he made a comment or something?"

"Yeah, maybe. Can I borrow your laptop? I'm finding my phone a little hard to read from."

"Sure, no problem," she offered with a smile.

Carmo handed me her computer bag and I walked back to my room. Once settled, I ran the water for the tub, opened the computer, and typed in Price's Portugal.

My stomach dropped as I saw the number of people who had read the blog and jumped inside my life, what made it worse was that someone had posted a picture of my mom when she was at the airport and added some stupid tag. The comments had grown, and factions had been established. The readers wanted more. I thought about how odd it was that we lived in a world where one blog and the comments from a thousand keyboards could become a person's entertainment, but I couldn't let that get in my way. I wanted my life back, and the only way I could do that was to take it.

❧

I looked through the comments and found nothing from Cristiano. The only thing I did find was all the horrible things people were saying about him, me, and Netuno. I had to post something else, so I went into Carmo's picture files and found a series of beautiful shots of Netuno. I wanted people to see how amazing it was and to set a few things straight with some of the readers.

Maya: *Yes, this is the real Maya, and this is Netuno. It is one of the most beautiful places on the planet. Don't believe anything Jade has told you.*

I hesitated briefly, questioning my decision to add something to the blog. Then I pushed those thoughts off to the side and dove back in.

Maya: *Spectacular isn't it? But what has happened to me over the last three weeks since Dalley published my journal without my permission hasn't been. It has been a nightmare. I'll spare you the details but let's just say in addition to Dalley using my journal as her own writings, Jade attempted to tear my life apart. It looked like it was working but the truth is . . . well I guess that is the question. Do you really want to know the truth or just other people's versions of it?*

I pressed the comment button and closed the computer. Then I quickly got up and turned off the water. My mind was whirling, and when I dipped my hand in the bath, I almost scalded myself. The water was too hot even for me, so I had to wait. In the meantime, I walked downstairs and returned the laptop.

"Carmo, thank you so much."

"Oh sure, anytime. Did you find anything?"

"No, nothing from him. Just lots of stuff from other people about us. Some people are quite horrible."

"Yes, they are, aren't they? Maya, I just picked up the strangest voicemail a few minutes ago. It was a text to landline message for *you*. The automated voice said: *Please give this message to Maya Wells. Just read your comment. Maybe it's you who is the real blogger. If you want, my username to the blog is dalleypresspage and the password is milehighclub. It's yours to do with what you want. I'm sorry. D*"

Carmo slowly handed me the note. "Maya? Is that who I think it is?" she asked with irritation in her voice.

"Yes, it's from Dalley," I responded, quickly realizing that she was upset.

"What did she mean, 'your comment?' Maya, you didn't add something to the blog, did you?" Carmo sounded distressed now.

On hearing the tone in her voice, I looked away, feeling embarrassed. I knew exactly what Dalley's message was about.

"Did you?" she asked again, this time with a level of frustration and anger slipping through.

She spoke again before I could answer her question.

"I know you need to find him, and it feels like Jade and Dalley have ruined everything for you, but this isn't just about you. This is about Netuno, my dad, Bento, and his family. This is our home—my home. What were you thinking? We have one chance to get things right tomorrow. I—I can't believe you!" her voice quivered.

I felt sick. I hadn't even thought about how Carmo might feel.

"I wasn't … I wasn't thinking about you," I answered her simply.

"I have to go," she whispered then disappeared out the front door of the inn holding her laptop bag close to her chest.

I stood in the lobby, alone and feeling stupid. I had never intended to hurt Carmo, my mom, Cristiano, but I had.

The phone behind the desk began to ring, and since I had driven off the only person in the lobby, I stepped behind the counter to answer it.

A little while later, I saw my mother step out of the dining room.

"Hi, Maya, I thought you were going upstairs."

"Long story. Mom? I'm sorry."

She smiled and touched my hand. "I can't tell you how excited I am to be here with you and your friends. Truth is, I miss having friends. It has been so long. I forgot what it was like," she said more to herself than to me. "The depression robbed me of *almost* everything and I want it all back. I'm sorry if I'm making things more difficult for you."

I swallowed hard as she looked at me. She was right, she had lost almost everything, including me. But something about her had changed. She was different and so was I.

I placed my hand over hers, neither of us having to say another word on the topic.

"I'm going to bed Maya. Can you call your father and let him know I am settling in? I called him earlier and left a message, but I know he will still be worried until he hears my voice. I'm sure hearing yours will take care of it equally."

"Sure, I'll do that right now. Mom, I am glad that you're here."

As I watched her walk away, she didn't look back but just hopped up the stairs with purpose.

❦

"Judith?" he asked hoping to hear my mom's voice.

"Hi Dad, sorry to disappoint, but it's only me."

"Oh Maya, don't be silly." His tone changed. "Is everything okay with her?"

"Yes, but I have to admit having her here has been odd for me."

"I know. Please forgive her if she's trying too hard. When we spoke earlier, I could tell she was nervous about seeing you."

"Yes, she is trying hard, but more than that, I'm just trying to catch up to the idea that she is here and doing well. It's overwhelming, especially with everything else going on. Dad, I guess this is as good a time as any— and I don't want you to overreact—but I've decided to get a job here."

"So, it's official. You're staying?" he said with a hint of disbelief.

I ignored the tone in his response.

"Yes, I am. I have no reason to come home. I must find Cristiano and set things right. I'm not sure what's going to happen with him, but I have to try. I know he would do the same for me. So yes, I'm staying."

"Oh, so that's it then? No discussion."

"No, I'm an adult. It's my decision to make. I have some savings available. I'll use that until I get on my feet. And Dad? Can you please contact Petra's husband? I need you to stop trying to shut down the blog.

"Maya? What are you talking about? That blog has been the source of all your troubles. As we speak, Petra's husband has a team of lawyers working on it. After everything you have been through, why would you *not* want it taken down?"

"Dad, this is my decision to make. Please respect it."

The pause in the conversation was long enough to show that he was concerned about my judgment, but he didn't want to say it out loud.

"Okay," was all he could say on the topic. "Please send my love to your mother," he added curtly.

"I'm sorry if I've disappointed you," I added as a last thought.

"Let's be honest Maya, no you're not. Just remember—all decisions have consequences."

"That was uncalled for, don't you think?"

"Who am I to say, I'm only your dad," he said, and then hung up.

12

Singing Stones

Cristiano

As I DROVE AROUND PORTO trying to navigate the hills and roads, I finally entered the neighborhood of Póvoa de Varzim. I climbed the hill towards their family home, and with every turn of the wheel, my heart raced a little faster and my stomach soured.

What if they don't want to see me? What if I scare my brother and sister? They probably don't even know I exist. The thoughts whirled in my head as I inched closer.

And then I found it, their home. It was beautiful. A woman was standing on an upper balcony, leaning on the railing. Her hair dark and wavy; it looked like mine.

Moments later, a man came out and placed a shawl around her shoulders. They stood for several minutes, not talking, just staring out into the night. That must be them, Marcos and Euphemia, my parents. Minutes later, he kissed her cheek gently and guided her back into the house and turned out the lights.

I sat for a long time watching the shadowy dream that could have been my life, trying to figure out what to do next.

The last thought I had before my eyelids betrayed me with exhaustion was the image from Avo's letter of my two mothers holding me, crying over me, and Euphemia letting me go. She loved me; they both did.

When the sun rose that morning, I was covered in dew and stiff as hell. But there she was again, standing outside on the balcony, leaning against the railing. Soon two teenagers, a boy and a girl, came out and gave her a hug. I smiled. Euphemia hugged them back and waved goodbye. Marcos came out and kissed her, and then she was alone. That was my chance.

I decided to call her on the disposable phone I'd picked up. The phone rang once, then twice. She didn't move.

"Just go and pick it up," I said to her impatiently while sitting in the car. "I know you're there; I see you." I hung up and tried again. This time she went inside. I had no idea what I was going to say.

"Ola?"

"Um, yes, I was wondering if your house is for sale. I am looking for properties in the area."

"Oh, no thank you. My husband built our home. My family would never sell, but thank you."

I didn't know what else to say. "Have a good day. *Obrigado.*"

"Your voice, have we met?" she asked in an odd whisper.

"No, I am not from around here."

"Oh, *ciao.*" She hung up.

I watched her as she walked back on to the balcony with the phone still in her hand looking puzzled. When I heard the gentle sobs coming from her direction I knew it was time to go.

I started my car and slowly began to back down the steep hill trying to find somewhere to turn around. The movement on the road must have caught her eye because she stepped to the railing and began to wave. I wanted to wave back, but I couldn't. My hands were frozen to the steering wheel. I found a place to turn and sped off down the road, watching her in my rear-view mirror until she was too small to see.

"That's not my life, it could have been, but it isn't," I gasped, fighting back the tears.

I picked a road and started to drive, not knowing where I was going but needing to get away from everyone. After crossing the border into Spain, I drove for a couple more hours before landing in the little town of El Escorial.

It was afternoon and the people were out in droves enjoying the summer, smiling and laughing as if one of the worst days of my life was a joke. I could neither laugh nor smile as I searched for a place to eat and rest for a few hours. I had no idea where I was going or what I was doing next. I was lost.

I walked around the streets, not sure what I was looking for. A group of schoolgirls saw me and started to giggle. Before, my ego would have been flattered, but on that day I just wanted to run. Run away from everyone. So I did. I started running, turning right and left until I stumbled and fell up a set of stairs on a rather deserted street. I scraped my palms and, from the feel of it, my knees too. With my head in my hands, the tears that I had been holding back flowed like when I was a child. When I looked up again, there was someone sitting beside me. She looked like a little elf dressed in a traditional nun's habit. She had to have been at least eighty-five years old.

"I'm so sorry for intruding on your property," I offered wearily.

"Why?" she asked innocently.

I stammered, "Well, for making such a scene on your stairs."

"No scene, just some tears. I cry too," she said with a matter-of-fact tone while patting my arm.

"Oh, well, thank you," I responded awkwardly. "I'll be on my way."

"No, come in. You are supposed to be here. That is how it works. You are our gift today."

"Your gift?" I asked hesitantly.

I had heard about little nunneries tucked away in some of these towns but had never been to one. From the way this one was disguised, I wondered if anyone was supposed to ever find it.

I was too tired to argue with an elderly nun, so I allowed her to take my scraped hand and hold it gently in hers and walk me to the front door. When we stepped into the hallway, four other little nuns came buzzing around me like bumble bees.

We walked into the kitchen and they invited me to join them at the table. They gave thanks and then offered me a bowl of broth—it was perfect.

"After you eat, you rest. Then we pray."

"Oh, I don't really pray anymore."

"Yes, you do—or, you will," one nun laughed, like she knew something I didn't.

There was not an ounce of resistance left within me, so I did what they said. I ate, then they showed me to a little room. The only things there were a bed, a sink, and a cross on the wall. I washed the dirt from my hands and my face, and fell into bed staring up at the cross, not sure what to say or do.

When I woke, it was dark outside. It must have been early Sunday morning. I heard some movement outside my door and looked out into the hall where I saw two little nuns struggling to carry a large bag of grain.

"Can I help you with that?" I offered.

They stopped and nodded their heads in unison. When I took the grain, they sighed and waved for me to follow them, leading me back to the kitchen. When we entered, it was like stepping back in time. Lit by candles, the room glowed with warmth and love. It felt like home.

"Can I help you with something?" They looked at one another.

"*Pao? Pan?* Bread?" they asked.

"Yes, I know how." They looked relieved, like someone had just taken a weight off their shoulders. I had not seen these two nuns when I arrived. They looked in their late fifties, younger than the others.

And so, after a lifetime of baking with Avo, there I was somewhere in Spain baking bread for a house full of nuns. We ground the flour and prepared the dough for the first rising. One nun went to turn on the oven, but the other stopped her and nodded her head towards the door. Shrugging her shoulders like a teenager, she led me out to the garden where I found an old outdoor oven that had not been used for many years. They pushed me towards it. It was still in decent shape, but needed some care and attention.

"I can try. My Avo bakes bread every day outdoors. I've prepped the fires in an oven like this all my life."

My two friends sat beside me while I finished cleaning the oven. They offered to help but I was already covered in soot and grime. It felt good.

The duo looked at one another, and one ran inside. On her return she handed me a damp cloth.

"Thank you very much. Where would I find the firewood?" I asked.

They pointed to the other side of the garden and walked with me to where we found a store of dried logs just waiting to be used. No words were spoken as they worked along side me gathering the wood for the next part of our bread adventure.

While the raging flames heated the clay oven, we went inside to continue working.

After the first rising had finished, I invited them to join me in punching down the dough. We all broke free and laughed as we formed our fists and enjoyed the action of letting everything go, at least for the moment. Next, we cut pieces and shaped them into loaves and placed them in the pans for the last rising. Then, quite naturally, my baking ritual kicked in.

With all the candles lit, the room became still, I felt Avo's prayer flow from me to ensure each loaf was filled with spirit and hope. It felt so peaceful.

When a bread pan slipped from the nun's hands and crashed onto the floor my heart leapt backwards in time. My thoughts threw me back to Friday night. I saw Maya in another man's arms and heard Puro yelling my name as I ran away.

"I'm sorry," I cried. "Why didn't I stay and fight for her, for us?" I asked myself. "I will never be worthy of her. I'm just a cast off. I was fooling myself to think she could really love me. Hell, how could she even like me? I don't like me."

"I like you," one of the little nuns piped up while bending down to pick up the pan.

"Thank you," I answered, trying to figure out a way to minimize my embarrassment.

"You're welcome. Come help me with the bread," she said, gently tugging at my arm and doing half of the work for me by not asking what I was talking about.

We gathered the bread pans and placed them on a table near the oven. She took my hand and walked me over to a bench that was placed under the oldest olive tree I had ever seen. The branches gently touched my head as I sat, and when I leaned back against the trunk, the stillness returned.

"That tree has been living in our garden long before you were born and will be here long after you die. Let it help you find the peace you seek," the nun said.

"Is it possible to find peace after so much heartache?"

"Anything is possible, you just have to believe."

"Is it that simple?"

She smiled. "Simple isn't always easy."

The fire was soon quiet, and the oven was ready. I stood up and wrapped one arm around myself, feeling the need to embrace the stillness I had been given. Then I invited my new friends to help me place the pans into the welcoming heat.

As the bread began to bake, I started to walk around the garden, studying it with great interest. Every pot and container was filled with herbs and flowers. I had never seen or smelt anything like it. Multi-sized stones covered the ground, creating a series of intersecting paths that looked like a labyrinth, but this maze had no beginning nor end. You had to decide to step onto the path before being able to follow the enchanting patterns within the stones.

While I knelt to pick a sprig of aromatic rosemary, an older nun I had not seen the night before came out from the house and hopped onto the path in her bare feet. The playful movement and her bare toes caught my eye, but she quickly settled into a prayerful walk. Then she began to sing. At first, all I could hear was a single tone being sung again and again like the ringing of a bell. It was not long before her call was heard, and more nuns arrived in their shoeless feet, hopping onto the path, adding their own tones to the chant.

They each sang a different note, releasing it into the wind and letting it bounce off the stone walls. Time was suspended; the result was all encompassing. Harmony and perfect dissonance rang out and the music whirled around me. It was neither stillness nor chaos. It was a mixture of pain and peace. It felt like the music was reaching inside and resetting my broken heart. I wasn't sure if I was ready to heal, but at least it felt like it was possible.

My experience was interrupted by the gentle scent of bread that was finished baking. I walked to the oven and carefully removed the pans, placing them side by side on the old wooden table just as Avo had taught me when I was a child. The nuns continued to sing as the bread cooled. Then, one by one, they sprung off the path like children who had just finished playing their favorite game. Each then took hold of a warm loaf and carried it inside.

The music resonated around me like it had been caught in the stone walls. I wasn't sure what was happening, but I knew it was important. My two nun friends approached me quietly, each taking one of my hands. Their skin was rough like it had faced hardship, but when I looked into their eyes, I saw only peace.

As they squeezed my hand, I felt a shift in my space and images flashed in front of me like a series of old photos tossed in my direction. I saw Euphemia, my birth mother; Avo; Maya; and Rosa, my forever mom. Confusion filled my heart, as I did not know what any of it meant. I pulled my hands away from the nuns and the faces of the women I loved disappeared. The nuns smiled with sadness, then walked out of the garden, leaving me by myself—or so I thought. I staggered over to the bench and collapsed, straining to hear the last of the music bouncing off the walls, but it was gone. I was alone.

"You're not alone," I heard her say. When I looked around there was no one there, and all I saw was an open door to the outside world. I looked back into the garden and eyed a single loaf of bread left on the table. I grabbed it and ran.

❧

When I crossed into France, the border guard glanced casually at my passport but became interested when he saw the half-eaten loaf of bread ripped apart on my passenger seat. I started my explanation with a story about baking bread with some nuns and ended with a tale about heart-ache. The French knew all about heartache and would let almost anything go if it were connected to love, even a suspicious Portuguese man whose car was covered in breadcrumbs and tissues.

As I sped along the road, not sure how or why I landed in France, thoughts of Maya flashed in front of me. Before my mind had a chance to torment me any further, I stuffed my face with more bread and slammed the accelerator into the floorboards.

13

I Love You

Maya

THE TALK WITH MY DAD left me sad and irritated.

"Who is he to judge me?" I asked the universe while opening Christopher to my last journal entry. "I'm an adult, and if I want to start a new life here that's up to me!"

> *Sunday*
>
> *My dad makes me so mad. He doesn't know Cristiano. And he obviously doesn't know me either. All I want is a chance at happiness, I thought he understood that. I know your life didn't quite turn out the way you planned, Dad, but that doesn't mean mine won't.*
>
> *I'm going to fight for him, or at least fight until I know if he still wants me. I miss him.*
>
> *I miss you Cristiano. I love you. I know it must feel like you are all alone right now, but you're not. You're not alone, do you hear me?*
>
> *You are not alone. I love you I love you I love you I love you I love you I love you I love you I*

love you I love you I love you I love you I love you I
love you I love you I love you I love you I love you I
love you I love you I love you I love you I love you I
love you I love ...

I wrote until my hand ached and a fierce wind drove me off the balcony and back into the bedroom. It was at that point I remembered my bath. The scorching water had cooled and now become a tepid pool of disappointment. As I slipped in and shimmied down, my muscles screamed at me to get out, but I refused to listen. I screamed back, then immersed every part of me except for my nose.

I lay submerged until my fingers pruned and I started to tremble. My body ached as I emerged from my self-imposed penance. And when my stomach grumbled, I remembered I had not eaten for hours. I wrapped myself in a towel and phoned down to the desk.

"Hello? How can I help you?" Puro answered with less joy than usual.

"Puro. It's Maya."

"Yes, Maya, what can I do for you?" he sounded cold.

"Uhm, ah, could you have the kitchen send something up to my room?" I paused. "Puro, I didn't think you were working tonight."

"Yes, well, I gave everyone else the evening off," he said abruptly.

"Carmo told you what happened didn't she?"

"She told me enough to know that you are not thinking about anyone but yourself right now, Maya."

I was taken aback, "Puro, I am so sorry. I didn't mean to upset her. I just felt so desperate. I needed to do something to try and find Cristiano."

"Maya, you're not the only one who cares about Cristiano. We all love him, too, but we have to deal with this situation at Netuno first, and you going onto that blog didn't help anyone."

"I'm sorry," I said, feeling embarrassed and not having anything else to offer.

Puro

"Maya?" But she had already hung up. I sighed deeply, not feeling like myself and knowing I should have done things differently.

"Hi, Dad," Carmo said, startling me from behind.

"Carmo, I thought you were back at the house with Bento."

"No, he is still in a meeting with Sachi. They are on a video conference call with her dad in Japan." She paused for a moment. "Dad, I'm embarrassed about the way I treated Maya earlier. I jumped to conclusions before I had even read what she wrote on the blog. I had a chance to read her comment when I got back to the house, and it was all about letting people know the truth—the truth about her and Netuno."

I shook my head, thinking about the things that I said to Maya. "Hmm, so maybe you and I both have apologies to make?"

"Yes, it looks that way doesn't it?" Carmo said giving me a hug.

"I feel terrible, Carmo. Ever since Maggie left and this whole situation with Cristiano and the Axelines occurred, I am not myself. I can't believe what I said to Maya. Maybe I can bring her something to eat?"

"Yes, mom would say that is a good place to start."

"Hey, can you—"

"Watch the front? Yes, of course. I was supposed to be working anyway. Besides, I don't think Bento and I will be going back to the house. We'll just crash here. No one's really going to get much sleep tonight, are they?"

"Yes, I agree with you," I said as I walked down the hall towards the kitchen.

❧

It took three knocks on the door before Maya answered. But when she finally did, I wheeled in the cart and she smiled with a sense of relief, then walked out to the balcony. She rewrapped herself in a quilt and sat down. Graciously, she accepted a cup of my tea and a slice of fresh bread layered in a thin coat of honey.

The two of us sat in silent conversation throughout the night, nursing our teacups and listening to the vineyard. Our sequestering was over when Carmo knocked on the door, letting us know the Amsterdam markets would be opening soon.

14

The Deal

Axel

"God, I love *this* day."

"What day is that, Mr. Axeline?" Jennie asked while leaning over my desk and grabbing the pen I had casually dropped on the carpet.

I had needed a new assistant and when Jennie applied last month, she was the perfect candidate: she was smart and had a great ass. What more could I ask for?

"The day I get everything I want." I answered her question enthusiastically.

"Don't you already have everything you want, sir?"

I laughed. "What a funny question. Maybe today, but not tomorrow. I'll never have everything I want. That is what makes this so exciting. The market opens in Amsterdam shortly. Are all the links ready?" I paused, briefly distracted by the empty desk on the other side of my room. When Jade came to work for me, I set up her desk in my office. I did this for one reason only: I wanted to keep an eye on her.

"What is it, Mr. Axeline?"

"Why isn't Jade here yet? I told her she'd better be on time. I told her 2:00 a.m. sharp, that is when I wanted her here. Amsterdam is six hours ahead. I've spent a lot of money and energy orchestrating this whole deal, and had to put up with that garish Branca woman for almost a year. She must have really hated that place to have sold out her family. Good for me, not so good for her husband," I laughed.

"What place is that?" Jennie asked.

"It's why we're here so freaking early in the morning. It's all about a family vineyard in Portugal that I will be acquiring tonight."

"Morning," she said, correcting me ever so carefully.

"Yes, you're right," I laughed at her. "Coffee, get me a decent cup of coffee, Jennie."

"Yes, of course," she responded with hesitation.

"What? It's been a month and you don't do coffee now?" I shot back at her.

"No, Mr. Axeline, I … I do, but …"

"But, what?"

"Portugal … that's weird."

"What's weird?" I yelled to her as she walked down the hall into the break room. When she returned, she was holding a triple espresso. I shot it back.

"That was perfect. I won't have to sleep until tonight. What's weird about Portugal? Have you heard from Jade yet?"

"No sign of Jade. Um, Mr. Axeline, may I ask you the name of the vineyard?"

"Of course you can, Jennie. The question is, will I tell you?"

She looked a little irritated, so I decided to give my new assistant a break. I liked her.

"Why not, Jennie? You've earned my trust. You'll know all the details shortly anyway. Today we are taking over Netuno."

"Netuno?" she looked like she had something to add, but stopped short.

"Yes, Netuno. Why?" I could feel the hairs on the back of my neck stand up and the blood rush to my ears. "Jennie?" my voice was now strained.

"Oh, it must be a coincidence," she choked out, looking flushed.

"I don't believe in coincidences. Spit it out girl."

"I think it's better if I show you."

She pulled out her laptop typed in Price's Portugal. It took about five seconds for me to find my words.

"What the hell is this? Why is my vineyard all over the internet? What the hell is going on, Jennie? And why is there a picture of Jade on the blog with some guy?"

"That's not some guy, it's *the* guy that everyone is talking about online. When you say Jade, are you meaning *your* Jade?" Jennie asked, taking a step back.

I was running out of patience with the conversation.

"Jennie!" I said sharply.

"Mr. Axeline, I've never actually met her, and you don't have any pictures of her around the office. I didn't know it was her," she responded with some sassiness in her tone. But she bravely kept going. "On Friday, a friend of mine sent me the link to this blog. I didn't put the pieces together until now." She swallowed hard.

"You better tell me what you do know, because in about twelve minutes, I am supposed to spend millions of dollars. And if I spend even one more dollar on this project and there is a problem, someone's career is going to come crashing down. The question is, will it be yours? I like my deals well executed with no fall out. Explain."

She took a breath. "Then you better read fast. Jade appears to have created quite a situation for you. Basically, it's anything but clean and simple. Dalley Price, a US-based journalist who was with Jade at Netuno, started writing a blog."

"Jennie, stop. Just stop. Please bottom line this for me in one minute."

"Three weeks ago, nobody knew what or where Netuno was. Dalley's blog was about a young couple who were falling in love, and the blog gained a little traction, but nothing significant. Then, five days ago, Jade posted some rather compromising images on the site and the traffic went crazy. By Friday night, I had heard that several networks in Europe went down. Jade's additions were not only trending on Price's Portugal, but also on Twitter, as she had started an account just for that reason alone. Done."

"Eight seconds left. Not bad, Jennie, I knew you had it in you. See if you can find Jade—now."

Jennie left the room. My broker had been on the other line during the whole conversation.

"Richard, what do you think?"

"I think we are too exposed."

"I need you to find out what the hell is going on and if the deal is still viable with all this media."

"I don't think we have time, Axel. Everything is in place. The markets open in just a few minutes. You'll have to decide in the moment. It's risky. Is it worth it?"

I ignored Richard's question.

"On Friday, were there any shares purchased besides the sale from Branca to us?"

"No nothing out of the ordinary. Maybe a little upswing, but consid ering the blog and the number of people following her, nothing I would worry about."

"You don't sound sure. You're always sure. I don't pay you to have doubts."

"Yeah, you pay me to stay up in the middle of the night to help you close deals. Right now, you own almost half of Netuno's shares, so we are close. If you decide to go ahead, as soon as the market opens, we will buy every share available and Netuno will be yours. But if something is happening that I don't know about … the deal could fall apart."

I walked over to the window and then back to the computer. "Something is wrong. Jade, what the hell have you done?" I scrolled quickly through the blog, looking at the comments. One name kept popping up: Maya. I read through the last post and the comments that followed. And there she was again: Maya, The Real Maya.

Jennie came running into the room slightly out of breath and holding a phone.

"Mr. Axeline, six minutes until the markets open. And I have Jade on your private line," Jennie said, trying to hand me the phone.

"I don't have enough hands to hold on to the phone right now," I snapped back at her.

"Jade, it's Jennie. You're on speakerphone now with your father."

"Speakerphone? I'm Jade Axeline. Nobody puts me on speakerphone."

"Too late," Jennie smiled.

"Dad, why do you have that bitch working for you?"

"Oh, shut up, Jade and don't call me Dad. Axel would be more appropriate right now."

"What the hell is your problem?" Jade spat back at me.

"My problem? Well let's see. Maybe because you are supposed to be here right now, and maybe because of Price's Portugal? And maybe because the whole world knows about Netuno and you neglected to tell me you created a colossal mess of things again."

"Oh Axel, is that really necessary? You don't think you can really talk to me like that, do you?" she said, attempting to stand up to me.

"Jade, I can, and I will. You screwed up. I warned you, didn't I? Just admit it." I asked, seeing if she would bend to me.

"It wasn't my blog. Not my fault. Besides, it was just a stupid blog anyway. There's no way it could have any effect on the takeover," she said, feigning confidence. I could smell her fear over the phone. She needed to work on that.

"Relax, Axel," Jade continued. "Those people are so clueless. They have no idea what we are about to do to them." I loved the venom in her voice; it reminded me of me, but business is business.

"Stop talking, Jade, and stay on the line. Jennie, get everyone up on Zoom. We have five minutes to make some decisions."

Two more minutes ticked away as Jennie did her magic.

Jade was surprisingly quiet, but I knew it would not last for long.

"Jennie, you ready?" She was like a miracle worker—suddenly, everyone was on screen.

"We have about three minutes before the market opens. Richard? What do you think?"

"Go with your instinct, Axel," he said bluntly.

Then Jade broke in. "Dad, Axel. Listen to me. This really wasn't my fault." Desperation leaked out in her tone. I was so ashamed of her.

"They were all crazy and then there was this bitch."

"Yes, Maya isn't it? I read about her briefly. And I saw all the pictures. You just had to screw things up for me, didn't you? I really wanted this. And more than anything I wanted this for you."

"Bullshit, Axel, you never do anything for anyone else. You wanted this for you," she shouted back at me.

"Sir?" Jennie tried getting my attention.

"Shut up. Don't interrupt me Jennie."

"You have always been a disappointment to me."

"Mr. Axeline?" Jennie said with more insistence.

I huffed and then poured myself a whiskey.

"Axel," Jennie yelled. "The markets are open."

"Why the hell didn't you tell me. What's happening?" I ran back over to my desk.

"Shares are being purchased from market houses around the world," Richard blurted.

I could feel my blood pressure spike.

"They know. Richard, dump everything!" I screamed. "Sell every last freaking share from that shit-hole of a vineyard. I never want to hear about Netuno again."

"Dad, what are you doing?" Jade shrieked over the phone.

"Jade, we're done. You are done." I yelled into the speakerphone.

"Jennie, hang up on her."

Jennie pressed the end button and I shook my head.

"It's done Axel, all the shares have been sold. We lost money, a lot of money," Richard stated.

"You mean I lost money. You're still getting paid today, but the question is, do you have a job tomorrow?"

Richard sighed, "You were right, Axel. Somehow they knew about the takeover. For a second, I thought we might have misinterpreted the situation, but as soon as you dumped your shares, there was a buying frenzy. I'm not sure who orchestrated the purchase, but they were very smart. They wanted control. Have another drink.

"Axel, I'll call you by the end of the day with another company you can destroy."

"Thank you, Richard, *you* always know how to make me feel better. You still have a job."

Jennie sat quietly in the office with me for several minutes, while I nursed my third whiskey of the morning.

"I'm sorry the deal fell through," Jennie attempted to console me, but I needed no consoling. I knew what I needed to do.

"Sometimes you lose. I haven't lost many deals over the years, but it just goes to show, you must hire the right people to get the job done. Jennie take a message for me and send it out by courier. On second thought, I don't want to waste any more money today, just text her. The message is: Jade, you're fired."

15

What Time is it Where?

Maya

7:57 AM (LISBON), 2:57 AM (MONTREAL)

8:57AM (AMSTERDAM), 11:57 AM (PEACHLAND)

SILENCE BLANKETED THE DINING ROOM as we watched the trade clock count down on the large screen TV. Euronext, the second largest stock exchange in Europe, opened in Amsterdam at 9:00 am. The plan was simple: Sachi's people were to buy as many shares as possible so that she would prevent the Axelines from become majority shareholders. If the plan failed, the Axelines would win. They could sell Netuno, or worse—Jade could become the boss …

We held a collective breath as the clock ticked down to zero and the trading opened. The only sound you could hear was Sachi on the computer. Her focus was unbreakable. Then it happened, the stock dipped.

"Wait!" Sachi yelled at her team as she typed furiously on the keyboard. "Stop buying. Someone is dumping their shares."

"Why is someone dumping shares?" Bento asked.

"It's them. They know we know," Sachi responded without taking her eyes off the screen.

Gervais inched closer to Sachi as she worked her magic. Then suddenly, she started barking orders into her headset.

I watched the stock price fluctuate and everyone held their breath. Then I saw it, the essence of a smile on Sachi's face followed by a laugh and the final barking order to "*kai, kai*, buy." Shortly after that, she closed her computer and thanked all the people on the collective lines.

Sachi removed her headset and took a deep breath.

"We did it."

"It's over?" Bento asked.

"Netuno is ours," she said with confidence.

"Yes, I guess that makes us partners now," Reinaldo whispered, with a deep sigh.

She walked towards the brothers and held out her hand to them, "Only temporarily, I promise. Sealing the deal with a firm handshake."

A little smirk formed on Mateus's lips. "Does this mean we are splitting all the expenses this year?"

Sachi laughed, "Sounds like a good discussion to have over a bottle of wine."

Gervais stepped in and kissed her. "You are amazing."

Sachi pulled back.

"What?" Gervais asked defiantly. "It's not like they didn't already know."

"What about my father?" Sachi asked.

"Let's not worry about that now."

Sachi smiled and kissed him back.

Carmo squeezed Puro's hand and the two of them breathed a sigh of relief.

"Well I think this deserves a celebration," Mateus cheered.

"Yes, let's celebrate! I'll get the champagne," Gervais yelled.

"Hey, I'm supposed to be in charge," Sachi teased.

"Not in my kitchen," he rallied back.

Sachi laughed and shook her head. "We'll see about that."

"Grab the case of champagne in the cooler," Gervais called out to a staff member.

"You had a case waiting in the cooler?" Sachi asked with a grin.

"*Oui*, I knew you could do it," he said, leaning in and kissing her again.

I stayed while the champagne was popped. Everyone began drinking and celebrating, but after half a glass my head began to pound and I had to leave.

I was relieved Netuno had been saved, but the truth was *my* situation had not changed. Cristiano was missing and I didn't know what to do next. I walked out of the party and into the lobby, where I heard Reinaldo on the phone.

"You failed, Branca. The Axelines didn't get Netuno. I'll give you the divorce. I'll give you half of everything I own, which is now exactly NOTHING! Except for my grandfather's old tractor in the back. Do you want it? It needs some work, but you can have it. If you have anything to say to me, call my lawyer. I don't want to talk to you anymore. You broke my heart, Branca. I gave you every part of me, but that wasn't enough for you was it? But that's irrelevant now because I don't need your kind of love. I have everything I need without you. *I* have a family. *I* have people who love me. By the way, Bento is marrying Carmo and you are not invited to the wedding. You are never to return to Netuno again. I'll have your things packed up and sent to your mother's in Spain. Goodbye."

I should have excused myself when I heard him on the phone with her, but I was drawn to the conviction in his words. He had loved his wife and she betrayed him. There was no going back for him. Sometimes love is just not enough.

After he hung up, I tried sneaking by without him seeing me.

"Maya? Why aren't you with everyone else?"

"Oh, I didn't feel much like celebrating," I said. Reinaldo raised his eyebrows in confusion, so I added, "Oh no, please understand, I am so happy about Netuno being safe, but as you know, I have a few of my own problems to work out."

"Yes, I am no stranger to problems. I take it you heard me on the phone?"

"I'm sorry. I can't imagine what you are going through. Did Branca have anything to say in her defense?"

"No, I left the message on her voicemail." He chuckled a bit. "I was pleased she didn't pick up. I am trying to be strong but standing up to her is new to me. I'll let the lawyers take care of the rest. Any news of Cristiano?"

Hearing someone else say his name landed heavy in my heart.

"No, nothing yet. The only thing I know for sure is that I'm not going home next week. I don't know what I am doing, but I'm *not* going home."

He smiled, "Well, if you need a job, there will always be one here for you at Netuno. Let me know if there is anything I can do to help."

My heart opened to the idea of even being asked. It was the sign I didn't know I was looking for.

People started emerging from the dining room, tipsy and relieved, and finding their way back to their regular lives. There were still grapes to tend to, wine to make, olives to pick, and an inn to run.

Puro walked towards us then shook Reinaldo's hand.

"So, how did the phone call go?" Puro asked with a little grimace.

Reinaldo laughed. "She didn't pick up, but that's okay. I told her she could have the tractor as part of the divorce settlement. I'm sure that will make her plenty mad. Besides, when she sold her shares, I am sure she was paid well. I literally have nothing else to give her."

"Are you alright, old friend?" Puro asked with concern.

"Yes, I think I just want to get back to growing grapes and leave all this love business to everyone else," Reinaldo sighed and walked away.

I looked over at Puro as he watched his friend step out of the room. "Thank you for sitting with me last night," I said. "You must be exhausted."

"Strangely, no. I feel good, reinvigorated. I'm going to call Maggie and tell her the great news. Did you know I'll be flying out to see her in exactly one week?" Puro said with excitement.

"I'm happy for you. I know how important you are to Maggie." Puro blushed unexpectedly.

I paused, thinking about the two of them. They had only known each other for a week before CJ's death but somehow that was all it took. They had established a deep connection, one that only they could really understand.

Seeing him, and his commitment to Maggie, I knew I needed to get started on finding Cristiano. But how? Where was I to start? Then it came to me: Mrs. Dutra. If there was anyone who knew something, it would be her.

"Puro, will you excuse me? I'm heading upstairs to change. Do you think you could call a car for me? I am going into Lisbon to see a friend."

"A friend? Why don't you wait until tomorrow Maya? It's been a long day and you've hardly slept. Not the best time to be making decisions."

I'm not sure if it was exhaustion, the last call with my father, or a growing feeling of desperation, but I snapped.

"I don't need a parent right now, Puro, I just need a car. I'll be down in thirty minutes." I turned and stomped off.

As I headed up the stairs, I felt horrible for the way I had spoken to Puro. He was just trying to help. When I landed on the top step, I closed my eyes, praying for some kind of reprieve from my erratic behavior.

Suddenly, I could see Cristiano there, standing in front of me with his hair falling over into one eye and sporting a mischievous smile.

"You don't get to smile at me, not even in my imagination," I yelled at him before opening my eyes and making him disappear.

⤮

My mind whirled as I stood in the shower. I tried to bring his face back, but I couldn't conjure it up no matter how hard I tried. I gave up and started thinking about seeing Mrs. Dutra. I knew it was a long shot, but maybe she had talked to him. Maybe she knew something that could help me find him.

When I was changing, a small note fluttered from my pocket to the ground. It was the blog password that Dalley had sent. I rolled the paper in my fingers and wondered if I could really do it. Could I take over her blog?

With Netuno safe, there was nothing stopping me from writing whatever I wanted.

I pulled out my phone and followed the simple instructions. When the site opened, I added my first blog post. When I finished writing, I pressed publish and threw the phone on to my bed.

My cell had barely bounced off the duvet when I saw the screen light up.

"Beth? Aren't you supposed to be sleeping? Don't you have class today?"

"How am I supposed to sleep? You are my best friend on the other side the world and you're in trouble. Maya, I just read the new post on the blog. Was that really you? What are you doing?"

"Am I in trouble? Maybe? I don't know anymore, but I know I am feeling very cranky. You didn't answer my question. What are you doing up? Are you monitoring the site?"

"Well, yes, someone needs to have your back."

"Always looking out for me. And to answer *your* first question: yes, it was me. I'm taking back my life."

"Are you sure this is the way to do it?"

"No, but at least I'm doing something. I've spent my whole life being afraid to do *something*. I kept thinking that by doing nothing, I would avoid more pain and sadness."

"I would hardly say you have done nothing in your life."

"Well I haven't done anything meaningful. And I've decided it's time to change. First, I'm quitting my job at the sprinkler company today."

"So, you're serious? You're not coming home."

"No, Beth, I'm not. I have to find Cristiano. I don't know how, but I'm going to find a way. And I can't do it while worrying about what's happening back in Peachland. When I was young, I imagined I could be an adventurer. Maybe it's time to start."

Beth sighed.

"What? Do you have something to say?" I asked pushing back at her sigh.

"Maya, what has gotten into you? Listen to yourself. I hate to say it, but you're sounding very bitchy and a little desperate."

I paused, taken aback by her reflection.

"Are you still there?" Beth asked with concern.

"Yeah, I am. It's just ... you're right, I'm not myself right now. I haven't slept properly for two days and I guess half a glass of champagne was still too much."

"Maya, I don't think you can blame your behavior on the champagne."

I knew in that moment I could snap at her or laugh at myself. "Why do you *always* have all the answers?" I asked half-jokingly.

She chuckled. "I don't, at least not for me. I only have the answer key for you and a class filled with six-year-olds."

"Are you saying that I'm acting like a six-year-old?" I let out a little laugh.

Beth skillfully sidestepped into a different conversation.

"If writing this blog is going to help you find him, then do it …"

I paused. "Beth? You said you read the blog, but did you like it?"

"Maya," she answered, sounding annoyed. "Get some rest, and then go do what you need to do. And yes—I really liked the blog."

16

Hazy Days Be Gone

Dalley

I woke Monday morning in a haze. I had no job, no friends, and I had just successfully blown up more people's lives than I could count on two hands.

When I left Netuno on Friday night, I had no idea where I was going. I just knew I had to get out of there. I drove straight to the airport and boarded the first flight I could, which landed in Hungary. When I arrived at my hotel I went straight to the bar, grabbed two bottles of whiskey, and went to my room. Saturday disappeared and by Sunday afternoon I woke with the most horrific hangover. Peeling myself off the floor, I peeked out the window to catch a glimpse of my host city, Budapest. It was beautiful.

Later that day I checked my blog, as torturing myself seemed quite appropriate, and there it was—there she was. Maya had posted a comment in her own name. Bold, but good for her.

A fleeting thought crossed my groggy brain as I wondered if she was wearing my boots. I rummaged through my purse and found the welcome note the brothers had given us on that first day when we arrived in Lisbon. Pulling out the phone I had bought at the airport, I texted Netuno. It was the safest way to get my message there and avoid talking to anyone. Cowardly yes, but effective.

After that I went back to the hotel bar and started drinking again. I didn't stop until the bartender cut me off and sent me back to my room. When I woke up on Monday morning, I was grateful that at least I was alone, as I remembered befriending a drinking partner at the bar.

The morning was painful. It felt worse than Friday, Saturday, and Sunday combined. Guilt, self-loathing, and Jägermeister didn't mix well, but I deserved to feel terrible. My only question was, for how long?

I checked the blog again—nothing new. I sat for some time, holding my throbbing head and walking through my life trying to figure out how I could have ended up alone and hungover in a hotel room in Budapest. And then it hit me. I had become my mother. I had become everything I never wanted to be: negative, bitter, and alone.

I rolled off the bed and crawled over to the shower, swearing off Jäger for the rest of my life. Then I started the painful process of sobering up. But when I moved, so did the last three shots of Jäger—and they decided to shoot back. I managed to get to the toilet in time, but the results were gut wrenching, to say the least. When I stepped into the shower, my recovery was hastened along because I had missed the window for hot water at my hotel. Being done with my pity party, I stood in the cold water, blasting myself with a full dose of real life, and did a point-for-point list in my head of all the mistakes I had made.

After my sobering shower, I went out into the city and found a quiet Internet café and a cup of Hungarian coffee that scrubbed any remnants of alcohol out of my system.

My laptop sat open and untouched for over an hour, and then it came to me. The answer was simple but true.

"I am supposed to be a journalist, but I haven't been for a long time. I need help."

My mind jumped to one face, one heart. I lied to Maya when I said I never thought about him. I lied to her about the airport. He didn't put me on the airplane and just let me walk away. He wanted me to stay with him. He wanted to teach me and to love me. I was young though, and I didn't trust my feelings. I didn't know that what I felt for him was love. I was so scared.

It didn't fully hit me that I had made the wrong choice until I was on my flight home. I kept hearing my mother's words in my head, acting as a silent tormenter.

"Don't you dare let a man change your plans," I could hear her bellowing. "They will tell you they love you and then they will use you up and throw you away. Be strong and whatever you do, don't get pregnant. No offense Dalley, but you were a mistake."

It was the longest flight of my life, and by the time I landed her voice had convinced me that she was right. I drove straight to her house and she was more than happy to assure me I had done the right thing.

Later that year she convinced me to have a hysterectomy. It was extreme, but she was extreme. Somehow her arguments made sense, or so I thought at the time.

She acted fast, sourcing out a private clinic, and before I knew what was happening, it was over. I woke up in the recovery room and she was gone. It was one of the worst days of my life. She had left me alone to face a new reality: I would never have a child of my own.

Soon after the surgery I discovered she hated me even more because I had the one thing she didn't: my whole life ahead of me without any responsibilities. I thought briefly about going back to him, but her words had twisted my thoughts around. Why would he want me? I was damaged goods.

So, I collected my things and moved as far away from my mother as I could. I found a small city newspaper and convinced them to hire me.

I'm not sure how long I sat in front of the screen, but when I returned from my trip down memory lane, I typed in Price's Portugal. And there it was: she had written her first post. I dove in, feeling both excited and a little resentful that she had taken me up on my offer.

Finding My Voice by Maya Wells

I'm not sure if writing this blog is the right choice, as my stomach is in knots, but when I stepped on the plane to Portugal three weeks ago I promised myself I was going to leave behind my old fears, my old life. So, here it goes.

I've spent most of my life always doing the right thing for everyone else. The problem with that is, when you finally decide to start doing the right thing for you, it can be confusing for those who love you and messy for yourself.

My world got even more complicated the day I decided not to get married. It was a painful process for everyone, but with a little time and luck I was able to take a step forward into this new life. I met Cristiano, fell in love, made some amazing friends, and found a magical place where I want to live. But life isn't a fairy tale, and with the good comes the bad. While in Portugal I also experienced betrayal, embarrassment, hate, and a new kind of fear. The kind of fear where you feel like your heart is being ripped out of your chest and torn in two, and you don't know how to put it back together. I'm not sure how much truth you want but I'll give you what I have.

The first truth I can offer is that Miss Price took my journal entries and used them for her blog without my permission. It didn't start that way, but somewhere early in her trip something happened. I'm not sure why she did it, but I know that it hurt me and a lot of others. The second truth is about me. I know most of you read the letter that I wrote and believe that I should have told Cristiano about his biological family the day I discovered it. You're right, I should have. I wish I could turn back the clock, but I can't, and I take responsibility for that.

Another truth is about deception. This section stars Miss Jade Axeline. Firstly, Cristiano did not have an affair with Jade. He was at her apartment to collect something Jade had stolen from me, and while he was there she manipulated the situation to make it look like he was doing something wrong, but he wasn't. Jade's next big lie was the image that she posted of my dear friend Maggie. Maggie is a dedicated mother and a true friend. The image Jade posted was a picture taken on the first day we all arrived at Netuno and not on the day Maggie's son died. Shame on you, Jade. And to top it all off, one of Jade's final schemes was that she and her father's company were trying to take over Netuno. (They failed, as of about an hour ago!!!)

I'm not proud of my part in this soap opera, and because of all this craziness, I fear I may have lost my Cristiano. He is a complicated soul who didn't deserve any of what was thrown at him, and so when he arrived in Portugal to set things right with me, the absurdity was in full swing and he ran.

Now, I have an opportunity to find him and set things right, but I'm afraid. I'm not sure I have the courage, but I must find it and find him, and maybe in the process I'll find a better me, too. Thank you.

Maya

When I finished reading her post, I was reminded how much I liked her and how much I wanted her to succeed. So, I decided to comment under a pen name, Kava Root.

Kava Root: *Keep writing. Never let anyone stop you from finding what you need in our big bad world, specially people like Dalley and Jade.*

Maya: *Jade and Dalley are nothing alike. Jade lives in hell, enjoying other people's misery, while Dalley is just lost in purgatory somewhere, waiting for the chance to do the right thing.*

Kava Root: *Hmm…Yes to Jade. Not sure about Dalley though!*

I closed my computer and sat still. "Purgatory?" I thought. "Maybe she's right, but how do I get out?"

I grabbed my wallet and unzipped a pocket I had been ignoring for a very long time. Inside was a little slip of paper I had kept for ten years. I dialed the number on it. It rang once, twice, and then I heard his voice.

"Hello?" he answered groggily.

"Who is calling you at this time in the morning?" A voice shrieked in the background. My heart sank. I was just about ready to hang up.

"Dalley? Is that you? It has to be."

I hesitated, "Yes." I took a sip of my now cold and bitter coffee. "I should have stayed," I said.

"I know," he answered flatly.

"I …"

"You miss me," he said with a tenderness I had not heard in a decade.

"I need you. I have been sitting on the edge of hell for weeks and my feet are blistered and burnt."

"Yes, I can imagine. I've been following you. Where are you?" he asked with a growing determination.

"Hungary."

"Yes, I am," he responded with one of his bad jokes.

"No, I meant the country."

He laughed, "Yes, I know. Where did you leave your sense of humor?"

"I think with you in Fiji all those years ago."

"Then I had better return it."

"Hey, who was that I heard in the background?"

"Just a distraction while waiting for you to call."

"Not sure if I am charmed or worried."

"Be charmed. Really, I've been waiting a long time. I'll book a flight. What city?

"Budapest."

"I'll be there in six hours."

"I'll be waiting." I hung up. My hands were shaking.

"What did I just do?" I blurted out to myself. "Holy crap!!" If I wasn't sober already, I sure as hell sobered up in that moment.

I paid my bill and started running towards the hotel. As I ran by a storefront, I caught site of my reflection and stopped short. Who was I looking at? I didn't recognize her anymore. I didn't want to be her. The fuchsia hair had to go.

"Time for a new look," I declared as I marched into the first hair salon I could find. "Something dark and sleek please."

17

You Can't Outrun Love

Cristiano

I'M NOT SURE HOW OR why I found myself in Paris, but there I was, standing on the steps of the Louvre. It was midnight and I was alone, or so I thought. I slumped down on the steps, holding my head in my hands, not sure what to do.

Then I felt a shift in the air around me and a hand landed gently on my shoulder.

"Cristiano, come with me," a voice said with a degree of fatherly sternness. It was Pierre la Nou, my parents' oldest friend and the last person to see them alive before they left for Egypt.

I followed him into the museum, where he gathered his things. He asked me no questions, except where I had parked my car. He took my keys and led me outside. He opened my car door and told me to get in.

When we arrived at his flat, I walked quietly with him up the old stairs of the four-story building. He unlocked the door and we stepped in.

"Please excuse my place. I don't have many visitors," Pierre said. "Your mother used to tease me that I would never find a woman if I did not get rid of some of this stuff. I tried and it was even almost tidy for a time, but history has always been my best friend —besides your parents of course. After they died, I just didn't feel like making any more friends."

"Yes, I know what you mean."

He smiled and motioned for me to sit down on the couch. I moved an ancient looking sculpture out of the way and collapsed onto the old sofa. For a moment, I imagined my mom sitting in the same spot, laughing and teasing Pierre about all his relics. She didn't like too much clutter and was always bugging my dad about the artifacts he brought back from their travels.

Pierre then opened the drapes and turned off the lights in the living room. The Eiffel Tower shone in the night like a beacon. My heart dropped as I remembered how Maya had yelled at a taxi driver to stop so we could get out to view the tower. She was as mesmerized with the tower as I was taken with her.

"I'll never get tired of seeing the tower at night," Pierre said in a whisper.

Suddenly the room was plunged into darkness. The tower lights had gone out.

"Ah, it must be 1:00 a.m.," Pierre said. "I think the city is trying to save electricity or something like that." He laughed and walked into the kitchen and turned on a small dim light which shone over the stove. "You hungry?"

I smiled. "Sure, I could eat."

Pierre offered a simple meal of bread, fruit, cheese, chocolate, and a café noir that should have kept me awake until the sun rose, but emotion and exhaustion incinerated the caffeine and it melted into my body like hot chocolate.

When I finished eating, he didn't ask any questions, just pointed me in the direction of his second room and told me to go to sleep. My mind and body were restless at first, but in the end, exhaustion won out.

When I woke, I was still wearing my clothes and shoes, and the scent of a good French espresso filled the air. Pierre was gone but had left a note.

I have your car for the day. Oh, I've missed driving this vehicle. Your father and I picked it out together. He loved this car. I'll see you for supper around 8:00 tonight. I'll meet you at the apartment. Lock up when you leave for the day. That is my subtle way of telling you to get out of the apartment today and wander. Just wander. Looking forward to hearing all about it tonight. Pierre

Although the space was quiet, I did not feel alone. Knowing that my parents had spent time there filled me with a comfort I needed. As I sipped my coffee, I began looking around the apartment. Pierre had so many amazing pieces. Where had they all come from?

While poking around, I found a shelf of old photos. There was even a picture of my dad and Pierre sitting in the car. My dad had the biggest smile on his face while he gripped the leather-bound steering wheel like he was a race car driver. It reminded me of how much he loved his car.

Next, I found several albums, each filled with images of them traveling together like the three musketeers.

I had no idea how close they were, as I had only met Pierre once when I was a boy and he brought me a shadow lamp.

After a round of photographic nostalgia, I locked up and headed out for the day. I was sad at first, being there without Maya, but I did as I was told. I wandered all over the city.

By noon, the sadness had lessened. Just being in Paris gave me a moment to breathe and think. I had heard about Paris being a life force of its own, but I'd never really understood until that day.

I walked for hours, my mind skipping from past to present to future. I didn't know if the flashes of my future could ever become my reality, but I had to try something because if I didn't, what were my options? Return to a Spanish nunnery? Wander the streets of Paris? Neither sounded like a good long-term solution. I had to figure things out and if I was going to do that, I needed answers. Answers to questions about my relationship with Maya and about my new family, but I had to start with my parents' death. I needed to close that chapter in my life; I needed to go to Egypt.

When I returned to the apartment Pierre was standing on the street.

"You almost had me worried," he shared half-teasing.

"No reason to worry, I just wandered a little farther than I had planned today. You were right, it was just what I needed to clear my head."

Pierre fussed with my keys in his hand, then finally blurted it out: "What's the matter Cristiano? What dropped you on my steps in the middle of the night?"

୶

As we sat down for supper, I took a breath and plunged into the tale, the whole thing from meeting Maya to discovering my adoption to running when I saw Maya in Steven's arms.

"I never knew you were adopted," he said, sounding a little hurt. "But that explains a lot. I knew they had been trying to have a child for many years, so when your father called to tell me they had a son, I always assumed you were theirs. When I saw you a couple of weeks ago, I did wonder how you got to be so much taller than your dad. As for your hair? Well I just figured it came from Rosa's side of the family."

Pierre paused, looking over at my mom's photograph.

"So, what are you going to do now? How are you going to get Maya back? You can't just let her go," he cried out. "She loves you! I know it. I saw it in her eyes!"

"Oh Pierre, I don't know what to do about Maya right now. You didn't see what I saw."

"Or what you thought you saw. You owe it to yourself to find out. Don't rely on your eyes alone to tell you the whole story."

"I know, I know you're right, but there are a few things I have to do before I can even think about going back. During my walk today, I realized I have some unfinished business to take care of. I need to go to Egypt, Pierre, to say goodbye to my parents."

Pierre's body shuddered. "No, you don't. You don't need to go there. Can't you just say goodbye from here?"

"No Pierre, I can't. I must go to the spot where the plane crashed. The authorities never sent their bodies back. They said there was nothing left. I've always felt incomplete since they died, like a piece of me was missing. There were always so many questions. They may have only been my adopted parents but …"

"But what?" He interrupted with agitation. "Cristiano, for god's sake boy, that made no difference to them. They spoke about you as if Rosa had given birth to you herself. I knew them better than anyone, and you were their child. I'm sure they never told anyone about the adoption because they never wanted you or anyone else to doubt who you were. You are Cristiano Lazaro."

"I don't doubt they did it for the right reasons, but I have another set of parents with an entire family out there. I always thought that the hole I felt in my heart was only because of their death, but when I saw her …"

"Maya?"

"No when I saw my mother, my birth mother, something shifted. I went to her home. I phoned her. Heard her voice. Something inside of me just made sense."

"What did she say to you?"

"I pretended to be someone else. She was so gentle and kind, so truthful."

"You got all that in one short conversation?"

"Yes." I responded defensively.

"Cristiano, I meant no harm. I just don't want you to lose sight of repairing things with Maya."

"I know Pierre, I'm sorry, but before I can go back to Maya, I must work this all out. It's very confusing right now. But I must go to Egypt and say goodbye to them, and then meet my biological parents. Please tell me you understand?"

Pierre walked in circles around his room, running his fingers over a series of Egyptian artifacts. Worry blanketed his face.

"Did you know your dad and I studied ancient Egypt relics together? He was the best researcher I have ever known. I could give him a task and he would not stop until he had the answer."

"Yes, he was very dedicated."

"You're right," he said simply.

"Right about what?" I asked not sure what he was talking about.

"You deserve some peace, and I might be able to help you with that. I'm sure everything has settled down in Cairo by now. Let me make some calls."

"Settled down?" Pierre was not making sense.

"It's nothing. The politics there are complicated. Nothing for you to worry about."

As he stepped away, I had a strange feeling that there was something he wasn't telling me.

18

The Group Project

Maya

AFTER SPEAKING WITH BETH, I felt a determination percolating within me. I dressed and then pulled out Dalley's boot box. When I opened it, the boots were patiently waiting for me. I paused as I ran my hand over the supple leather. A spark of anger shot through my body and I felt like throwing the boots off the balcony again. Ellen was right, before I could wear the boots, I needed to hear Dalley apologize. So, I left her boots in the box and grabbed my own, zipped them up, and ran out the door.

When I arrived downstairs, there was a quiet buzz in the air about how Sachi and her father had saved Netuno from the Axelines. I took a purposeful breath and looked around at my Netuno family and my mother. The scene in the lobby forced me to put my plan on hold as I felt a responsibility to stay with everyone for the day.

"Puro, can you cancel the car?" I asked. "I'm going to stay here today." He smiled and shrugged his shoulders, making no effort to pick up the phone. I stared at him. "You canceled the car already, didn't you?" I said.

He paused a minute. "Yes, when I saw everyone coming together, getting ready to work on the project, I thought it would be good for you to stay. I can't help the dad in me," he said sheepishly. "I'm pleased you changed your mind. I wasn't sure if you might be mad at me."

"No, Puro. There has been enough anger and confusion around here. I'm happy to be with everyone."

I joined the ladies who were sitting in the lobby bantering back and forth about wine and Netuno and what had just happened. I cringed when Josie started telling my mom about the encounter I had had with Jade after CJ got sick and Maggie had to fly home. I think there were some comments about toxic venom and being pathetic. It was not a story I would have ever shared with my mother.

"Good for you, Maya, that's my girl!" she shouted out, giving me a shove to the shoulder. I shook my head. She was so animated, listening to every word people were saying. I could hardly believe the woman sitting there was my mother.

The landscape of our group had changed but the intention was still there. We had one week left before the remnants of our little family found their paths back home and we were going to make the best of it.

Puro had ordered a bottle of port that now appeared to be the cause for so many stories coming to light.

"Do you want a glass, Maya?" Josie offered.

"No, thank you, Josie, no port for me. I need to keep a clear head today." I looked over to the desk. "Puro, can you get me a coffee? I'm going to check in with Avo before the actual planning starts."

"A coffee? Have we turned you from leaf to bean?" he asked teasingly.

"I'm not sure, the jury is still out on that one, but I am liking the flavor and the kick that it gives me. Cream, no sugar."

"I'm sure I can put something together," Puro nodded.

"Coffee over port? Maya, that's almost blasphemy," Josie teased.

I laughed and shook my head, then walked down the photo-graph-laden hall and turned a corner, which led me to Avo's room. When I knocked, there was no answer, so I entered carefully.

"Avo, it's Maya. Can I come in?"

I had spent so much time with Avo, but little of it had been spent talking. I knew she understood me, but always chose her words carefully.

She was standing on the balcony staring out into the vines. I walked over and helped her into the rocking chair that Puro must have brought in for her.

"Good morning, Avo."

"You haven't heard from him," she stated with little emotion.

"No, he's somewhere out there, on his own. I just wish I knew he was okay."

"He is. If he weren't, we would both know. Maya, you must let God take care of things right now. He will let you know when he needs your help."

"God or Cristiano?" I asked, half-serious.

She smiled a little. "In my experience, you will know when it's time to go and find him."

"God and I have had a bit of a rocky relationship over the years, I only recently started talking to Him again."

"You may not have been talking all these years, but He has been listening."

"How can you be so sure?"

"Well, He brought you and Cristiano into each other's lives, did He not?"

"I'm not sure anymore. If I'm going to give Him credit for that, then can't I blame Him for wrecking things for us too?"

"Hmm, yes, sometimes it does look that way, doesn't it? But I believe things don't happen in our lives without a purpose."

"If there is a purpose to this, I would love to hear His explanation."

She started to laugh. "Oh Maya, He has given you all the clues; you just aren't looking in the right places yet."

"So, you're saying God is sending me on a scavenger hunt?"

"No, not a scavenger hunt, but more like an archeological dig. He still needs you to do the work before you can find the answers. He sends us on these journeys to help us grow and be strong."

"How am I supposed to grow and get stronger from this?"

She sighed, "You already have."

"Are you not worried about him?"

"Yes, I am worried. My heart is aching, and my selfish side wants him back right now. But he is on his own journey—a much needed one. If all of this had not happened, meeting you, finding out about his past, even seeing you in Steven's arms …"

I gasped.

"Yes, Puro told me the whole story."

"I …"

"No, no." She held her finger up for me to stop talking. "If all of this had not happened, he would still be on the wrong path, moving farther and farther away from who he is supposed to become. By meeting you, he saw a glimpse of who he could be. Now he must search for how he can become his best self. I know he will find his way. He will return. We must give him time. You simply have to have faith."

"Faith." I crinkled up my nose and then gave her a kiss. She closed her eyes and started rocking in the chair. It was only a few moments before I heard her breathing shift. She had fallen into a light slumber. I stepped out of the room with the word *faith* dancing on my lips.

As I walked back to the lobby, my fingers touched my empty wrist and searched for my charm bracelet. I had promised myself not to wear it until I found him, but then I realized I'd made a mistake. I needed the charms close to my body, pressing into my skin, keeping me focused.

I ran back to my room and dumped the contents of my purse out onto the bed and found the box. I opened it and carefully placed the bracelet on my wrist.

I happily rejoined the group and found my coffee cup waiting for me on the table. As I picked it up, I heard the gentle sounds of the charms singing. I sipped the hot liquid, letting the memory of Paris and my love for Cristiano wash over me.

"That must be some fantastic coffee, Maya," Petra said, picking up on my lightened mood.

"Oh, you know, I'm just like you, coffee addicted."

"I don't believe that, but I'll let it go for now. So, does anyone have an idea what the group project should be?"

"I don't know," Josie responded, sounding a little woeful and looking over at Ellen.

"Why do you sound so sad, Josie?" Ellen asked.

"Oh, I'm not sad. I'm just not happy about you leaving early. I know you have to go, but I don't have to like it."

I looked around the table and the only fresh face I saw was my mother's. The celebratory buzz that had boosted everyone's morale was starting to fade, and the weekend's events had rendered the group silent.

Poking me hard in the ribs, my mom got my attention. "Maya, I think Puro needs you," she whispered. I turned around and Puro looked at me with exasperation, tilting his head in Carmo's direction.

"What?" I mouthed over to him. Then he leaned his head to Carmo again.

"Carmo, would you like to join us?" I asked, hoping that was what Puro needed.

"Yes, I'd really like that," she answered with a sparkle of excitement. Puro smiled and let out a sigh of relief.

As Carmo sat down, Petra poured her a drink. Carmo began to sip on the port politely, but it felt like she had something to say. Then my mom chimed in.

"Carmo, I want to thank you and Bento for all your kindness. Your father and Bento's family have gone out of their way to welcome me and I cannot begin to thank you for everything you have done for my Maya."

"Mom, really?" I said.

"Well, I think it is important to thank people who have done a great kindness," my mother answered. "It's just as simple as that."

"Oh Judith, I could not agree more," Carmo said, but she stumbled over her words. "Oh, I am so nervous."

"Carmo, what do you have to be nervous about?" I asked trying to help her settle down.

"You're right," she said taking my hand. "Okay, here it goes. This morning, after Netuno was saved, Bento and I started chatting. We decided we didn't want to wait until after the harvest to get married. We have been through so much together over these last few weeks and we want you all to be there. We talked with both our dads and we are wondering if everyone might be able to stay an extra week so you could … maybe plan my …"

"… wedding? For real?!" Josie exclaimed, jumping up and sending her glass of port sailing off the edge of the table.

Everyone laughed. It was beautiful and messy just like Josie. Puro grabbed a rag from under the desk.

"Well, it looks like we have a wedding to plan," he said. "I guess I'll volunteer to be the janitor." Smiling from ear to ear, Puro knelt to clean up the port. He paused for a moment. "Oh, I was supposed to leave for Vancouver to visit Maggie next Monday, but with this new development maybe I could go this week. Do you think you all can manage without me for a few days?"

"I think we can survive," Carmo said. She turned to me. "Maya, can you watch the desk if I have to help the group with wedding plans?"

"Yes, of course I can. Anything you need," I reassured her. My heart wavered a little, as I knew my journey to find Cristiano would have to be put on hold, at least until Puro got back. I remembered what Avo had said about faith. I had to believe this was my path for now, until the next road presented itself to me. I just had to keep my eyes open.

"Next step then, everyone needs to call home and see if it is possible to stay for an extra week," Carmo ordered.

"No need," I said. "I quit my job this morning. I'm not going home." My mother's eyes widened, and I thought I saw a crease in her forehead, but when I looked again, she was smiling.

Sachi chimed in. "I'm not going anywhere either, my rent is all paid for months," she said, letting out an unexpected giggle.

"My life is my own. I'm retired and I'm in," Josie stated.

I looked around at our ever-changing group: Carmo, Sachi, Petra, Ellen, Judith, Josie, and myself.

"Well I guess that just leaves Petra to confirm. What do you think Petra?" I asked.

"I think I can take a few extra days. I might even be able to convince my husband to come out for a visit."

Josie turned to Ellen, "Are you sure you can't stay?"

"No, I need to get back to my children. Francesco is coming to get me tomorrow."

Petra slipped out to make a call, and about fifteen minutes later returned with a look of anticipation on her face.

"I'm in too. I hope you don't mind an extra guest, Carmo. My husband has insisted he's coming to the wedding. He said he misses me. Imagine that," she said almost glowing.

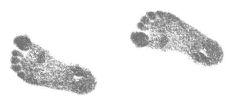

19

Fire-Breathing Butterflies

Dalley

I HADN'T BEEN NERVOUS ABOUT anything in my life since I was eight years old and auditioned for the role of a dancing flower in *Sleeping Beauty*. I told everyone I didn't want to do it, but secretly I hoped I would make it into the ballet. When my name didn't show up on the list, I blew it off, but inside the disappointment almost crushed me. I decided that hope was for the weak and I never wanted to feel weak again.

So, as I stood in the airport waiting for his flight to arrive, I was surprised by the feeling that crept into my body. Somehow, hanging out with Maya for three weeks had broken down my defenses. Hope was now showing up like an uninvited party guest.

I felt empty but still nauseous after three trips to the bathroom. I couldn't determine whether it was butterflies or a fire-breathing dragon that had found its way into my stomach. My eyes darted up to the arrival board. I had no idea where he was flying in from. He just told me to be at the airport in six hours. As much as I wanted to turn and run, a smarter self was telling me it was time to be still.

As another planeload of people filed out through customs, I waited … and then I waited some more.

Deep in my stomach I could feel the flutter and a deep burning sensation again. It was then that it occurred to me that somewhere between my anxiety and anticipation I had created a new species: a fire-breathing butterfly.

When I thought I could not wait a moment longer the doors slid open, and there he was. A little grayer and with lines a little deeper, but handsome—more handsome than I remembered. His skin was a golden brown, and from the ripples of chest muscles under his t-shirt, I could tell he had not abandoned his daily workout. He walked straight over to me, dropped his bag, and grabbed my face in his hands.

I spoke first, "I'm sorry."

"You should be," he said. "I've been waiting ten years for your call. I almost gave up."

"Why didn't you?"

He pulled me in closer and pressed his sun-chapped lips tight with mine. I resisted at first, but only for a moment. I had been fighting for too long. It was finally time to let something good happen in my life. I didn't deserve it, but I wanted to.

I kissed him back, diving headfirst into his world, our world, the world he had been taking care of for both of us since I walked away all those years ago.

"You asked me why?" he whispered. "You really don't know the answer?"

He studied my face with his eyes crinkled and filled with concern.

"Promise me you're not going to fight me or tell me you can't do this." He was serious. I had hurt him; I could hear it in his voice.

"Yes. Dagmar Ravn, I'm not going to fight you. I tried life without you and look where it got me."

He laughed, "Only my mother calls me Dagmar. But yes, you got yourself into quite a mess. I followed your work for years, but when you started the blog a few weeks ago, it didn't feel right. It wasn't you. I thought maybe that *editor* had finally broken you."

I half laughed, knowing it wasn't funny at all. "Yeah, something happened but it wasn't the editor. It was me. I lost my mind."

He touched my face gently, and then kissed me again and again. We stood in the same spot until several more planeloads of people filed past us. I had been in so many airports during my life and had seen couples standing right where I was, reunited in love, but I never imagined I could be one of them.

Then Fiji flashed in my mind. I should have stayed.

He pulled back. "Hey, where did you go just now?"

"Remembering," I said with some apprehension.

"About what?" he asked, stroking my cheek.

"About the day I left you and the scrap of paper you tucked into my pocket."

"I've been holding on to that phone for a decade you know."

"You kept the old phone?" I asked.

"Yes, I wanted to make sure I didn't miss your call."

"Why?"

"Because I wanted to be with you whenever you were ready."

"Am I? Even after everything I've done?"

"We all get lost. You just jumped off the path into a tiger-filled jungle and ran into a viper along the way. People got hurt. You got hurt. But you called me, asked for my help, and here I am."

No one had ever interrupted their life for me, waited for me. He was different, but then, I knew that from the start. He wanted to love me from the first time we met.

He looked at me and smiled again, "Do you have somewhere I can take a shower? I had a hectic time getting here."

"Yes, I imagine you did. Where were you traveling from?"

"It doesn't matter."

"I have a feeling I interrupted you when I called. Is there any unfinished business out there you need to take care of?" I asked coyly, trying to figure out if I just ruined someone else's life besides Maya's.

"No. I may have been stricken off someone's Christmas list, but I'm not worried about that. I told her from the beginning that there was someone else. She just never believed me."

"Do I need to send her a sorry note?"

"No, I don't think that would go over too well. What about that shower?" He touched my cheek again, causing yet another warm flutter to ignite.

"Yes, I can take care of that for you," I exhaled.

My heart raced uncontrollably and for the first time in my life I understood what it was like to be loved.

We ran out of the airport holding hands and acting like two kids. We giggled in the backseat of the taxi, with Ravn never breaking contact with me. The years melted away as we made our way to my hotel, and by the time I put the key in my room door, our first set of fresh memories were already being stored.

Then he stepped into my little sliver of chaos.

"It looks like I made it just in time," he said, nodding at the plethora of mini bar bottles strewn over the carpet along with potato chip bags and chocolate bar wrappers. "What did I tell you about drinking alone?"

"I don't remember," I said pushing him away.

"I think you do, but it's time to stop," he whispered into my ear. "Give me a few minutes while I take a shower, then we can clean this place up together."

"Or we could leave it for the maid," I half-joked.

"No, we need to take care of this ourselves. Don't you agree?"

"Do I have a choice?"

"No," he said simply. Then he walked into the bathroom and closed the door.

I was grateful for the moment alone. Looking around, I was mortified by the state of my room, so I tucked my hair behind my ear and went to work. He was still in the shower when I finished.

I walked over to the large open window and gazed out. Budapest was the perfect place to start over.

It wasn't until I felt his hand on my waist that I knew he was there. I didn't turn around at first, as those dastardly fire-breathing butterflies ignited when he touched me. I just pushed my body back into his, hoping that the flames would be doused by the water droplets that soaked my shirt, but no such luck.

"Looks like we have a few extra minutes," he whispered, pulling me in closer, then spinning me around like a top. "I told you I would help clean up."

"That wasn't the mess I needed help with."

"I know," he answered sincerely. "So, what do you think we should do with our new-found time?"

His towel was slung loosely around his body, resting precariously on his hips.

He didn't wait for my answer, "There's a wet spot on my back I can't reach. Can you help me?"

"I need a towel."

"Here, take mine," he said, offering his without hesitation.

I knew in that instant he was my last and only. But I still felt that I didn't deserve to have Ravn come back into my life so easily.

"Look at me," he said in a commanding voice. "We will fix it. We will find a way—together."

I believed him. I had to.

I took the towel he offered and wiped the remaining water from his back, then dropped it to the ground and ran my fingers over his warming skin. His body shivered under my touch. Without missing a beat, he stepped forward and launched himself across the bed I had just meticulously remade.

～

Wrapped in cotton bed sheets, we finished eating and lay silently together. But the silence did not last for long, as my guilt at what I had done to Maya and my friends was starting to eat away at me. I wasn't sure when it had happened, but somewhere along the way I had developed a conscience.

"Ravn, what am I going to do? This whole situation is such a mess."

He pulled me close. "Well, the first thing I am going to do is get some new clothes. The circumstances of my departure did not allow me to pack any of my things before I left for the airport."

"Circumstances?" I grimaced.

"Like I said, don't worry about a thing except maybe buying me a new pair of pants."

I made a quick call to the front desk to have some new clothes delivered for Ravn. While we were waiting I checked to see if Maya had posted another blog.

"You are going to drive yourself crazy, Dalley. Could you at least wait until we get dressed to start righting your wrongs?"

"Oh, I can save the world wearing a sheet, but if you want to opt for a towel be my guest; you know how that turned out last time," I chuckled.

"The sheet it is then if we are going to get even a stitch of work done before my new clothes arrive."

As I read Maya's newest entry, I felt a pang of jealousy, but tried to push it away as I did not want to be that kind of person. "Well, good news. Maya is embracing this whole blog thing," I said not doing a great job a hiding my feelings.

"Don't sound so excited, Dalley. You were the one who offered her the opportunity."

"Yes, I know," I said. "I just didn't think she would actually use it."

Ravn looked at me with a little annoyance. "Well, what did she say?"

"She added a short post hinting there is going to be a wedding at Netuno very soon. She didn't say who was getting married, but I'm guessing Carmo and Bento."

Ravn looked confused. "And they would be … ?"

"Oh yeah, sorry. They're the son of one of the owners and the estate manager's daughter. They have been friends since they were children."

"By the look on your face, I'm thinking we're heading to Portugal for a wedding?" Ravn said, trying to read my mind.

"Yes, that's the plan I'm hatching. Mind you we may have to forge an invitation to get in, but …"

"Oh, I don't think even a forged invitation will get you through the doors after the stunt you pulled. You are going to have to arrive with a spectacular gift and an apology of a lifetime."

Ravn's words stung, but I knew he was right. I was going to have to do something more than spectacular.

20

Being Still

Maya

TUESDAY MORNING CAME WITH AN uncomfortable stillness. There was no breeze or bird song, just a blanket of grey and the need for me to shelve my worries about Cristiano. At least I knew it was going to be a busy day, starting with dropping Ellen at the airport followed by some wedding shopping in Lisbon.

I decided to take advantage of the trip into town to pick up a tablet. My work on the blog had become important to me and typing it out on the phone was ridiculous.

Writing the second blog post proved to be quite interesting for me. While the content was somewhat benign, readers were reacting swiftly. What surprised me most was the flash of anticipation I felt as I checked to see how many had read the post and who liked it.

I packed up my bag for the day, making sure Christopher was placed securely inside. Then I slipped on my fleece pants and an old t-shirt. As I walked past the mirror, I was shocked to see someone I thought I had left behind in Peachland. I didn't like the look of her, so I quickly stripped down to my underwear and threw on one of my new summer dresses and fixed my hair and makeup. Before walking out of the room, I looked again in the mirror and smiled.

"I may not know what to do next in my life but at least I'll do it with a little style." I leaned in and kissed the mirror, leaving my mark.

When I arrived in the lobby, Josie was buzzing around, handing out to-do lists for the day. I took my list and scurried out to the waiting SUV to take ownership of a window seat.

As much as I wanted to join in the banter that erupted once we were on our way, my heart wasn't in it. Instead, I slipped Christopher out of my bag and started to write.

> *Tuesday Morning,*
>
> *I'm on my way to Lisbon, trying to block out all the chatter, but right now all I can hear is my mom and Josie laughing. Imagine that: my mom laughing. Not just smiling or chuckling but laughing and holding her stomach. I didn't know it was possible.*
>
> *I feel sad. How can I be sad when she is so happy? I'm putting my sunglasses on to hide my watering eyes. I don't want her to worry. I don't want her to stop laughing. I refuse to let even one tear sneak out— oh shit! There's one. And another.*
>
> *Petra just took my hand and squeezed it gently. I guess sunglasses don't hide everything.*
>
> *The laughter has settled, and it looks like everyone is taking a break to enjoy the beautiful drive to the airport.*
>
> *With the quiet, I have some time to indulge in my writing, maybe write a story—yes, that will make me smile.*
>
> *A story within the truth.*

The cottage was still when I woke, so still in fact that my heart stopped briefly as I strained to hear both their breaths. But instead of hearing them breathing, I heard the faint sound of his guitar dancing through the open window and landing on my pillow. I smiled as I pulled the pieces of my sleepy brain together and then snuck out to see them. This was one of my favorite parts of the day. Every morning, Cristiano scoops up our little one on her first waking and takes her out to the garden. He sings and bakes and shows her the beauty of all the things he loves to do. He says he does it to give me a little uninterrupted sleep, but the truth is, he loves their quiet time. He has her strapped to his chest and she watches his every move. I'm not sure how he plays the guitar at the same time, but they are magical together. I can never stay unnoticed for too long, for both sense my presence. She is only three months old but there is something special about our little one. She sighs when he sings, like she knows how much he loves her, like she understands the magic of where she is. I stroll into the garden and her eyes meet mine. I take our precious bit of magic and rock her in my arms until she is asleep. Cristiano has a hot pot of tea steeping for me and a fresh loaf of bread cooling on the table.

In the distance I can see Avo walking on the path towards the cottage. Her steps are slow, but her heart is peaceful. It has been a year since the wedding, and our lives have become the fairy-tale I always dreamed of, minus the evil queen. There is always an evil queen, but not in my story!!!! The cottage has become our home where Cristiano, Avo, Senda, and I live. Cristiano

quits his job at the airlines and takes over managing the
vineyard at Netuno...

What a lovely dream. Gotta go. We just arrived at
the airport.

Maya

We leapt out of the vehicle and hugged Ellen as Francesco grabbed her luggage. I could see how hard it was for Petra and Josie: they had become especially close to Ellen during our time at Netuno. They worried about her, but truthfully she didn't look worried.

"Hey Maya, remember, forgiveness before the boots," Ellen reminded me before she walked away.

I laughed, "I'm working on it."

"Sachi, keep cooking, that is what you are meant to do—and don't let anyone keep you and Gervais apart."

Sachi smiled and nodded her head with an understanding. Everyone else gave their final goodbyes and waved to Ellen as she passed through the gates and headed back to her life. I wondered what she was going to do when she got home. We had all changed so much in those three weeks; it was inconceivable that any of us could just go back to our old lives without bringing a piece of Netuno with us.

The remainder of us piled back into the SUV. While everyone else prepared for our day of wedding shopping, I slipped on my headphones and fell back into my writing.

⌘

Once we arrived in town I told everyone I wanted to head out on my own, but Petra would have none of it. She was coming with me, whether I liked it or not. I finally relented, giving in to the concern I read on her face and not wanting to make a scene of any kind.

As we gathered our things, I felt a twinge in my heart: the last time I had been in Lisbon, I was shopping with Dalley. While Petra led me away from the group, my mom waved. She looked happy.

"May I have the list Josie gave you?"

"Why?"

"During the car ride it was decided that when we arrived, I was to take you on whatever mission you needed, and everyone else would do the wedding shopping," Petra answered.

"What are you talking about?"

"The list please," Petra responded with little room for discussion.

"But …" I started to object.

"But nothing. Maya, while we were in the SUV, we tried talking to you, but you were so deep into what you were writing, you didn't hear us. Your mom thought it best if we left you alone. By the way, I really like her. She is so nice and smart and such a great storyteller."

"Smart? Storyteller? My mother?" I asked in disbelief.

"Yes, Maya. As we were driving she told us this intense story about Isabella of Portugal. It's crazy to imagine what mothers had to go through 500 years ago, and in some ways not much has changed," she sighed while shaking her head.

I was curious to hear the story, but at the same time, a little hesitant. Petra must have sensed it as she paused briefly.

"Relationships with parents are complicated."

"Yes, they can be," I smiled back at her.

She gave me a little nudge and suggested we stop for a coffee. While at the café, Petra launched into the story that my mom had told while we were driving into town.

"Your mom shared that after suffering for so many years with her depression, it was important for her to understand it better. During her research, she stumbled upon the story of Isabella of Portugal. Your mom appears to have put together a theory that Isabella could have suffered from severe postpartum depression. It was clear she felt a kinship with Isabella in some small way and thought it important to tell us both their stories."

"Both?" I sighed. "Truthfully, I know little about her except the most obvious. She's a bit of a mystery to me."

"Well, maybe when you're ready, the two of you can start unravelling the mystery together."

"That is an interesting idea. I'll have to think about it."

"So, what is our plan for the day?" Petra asked changing the subject.

"I'm not really sure," I answered, holding back.

"You're not telling me the truth. We only have one agenda today and that is to help you find what you are looking for. What do you need?" she asked me again.

I knew she would not let me do this alone, so I relented and filled her in. "I need to buy a tablet."

Petra never asked why, just pulled out her phone and called someone.

"Who was on the phone?" I asked with a little curiosity.

"Oh, that was my assistant back home. I had her find information on several local computer shops and send it so we don't lose any time."

"Are we on a timeline?"

"That depends on you."

"I really do want some sort of device."

"Yes, I am sure you do, but it feels like there is something else. No need to argue with me."

Of course, she was right. There was a visit I wanted to make, but I didn't have an address or any idea of how to find the place. My lip quivered when I said her name.

"Mrs. Dutra," I sputtered. "I need to go see a woman named Mrs. Dutra."

"Well, now we're getting somewhere. Where does she live?"

"Here in Lisbon. I've only been to her apartment once, with Cristiano. I don't know how to find it. The building was constructed in the 40s. It's art deco style, no elevator, four stories, no rentals."

"Is that where Cristiano lives too?"

"Yes," I whispered.

"No need to be shy about this. My father was a private detective. I helped him hunt down people when I was in high school for extra money. I know who to call, just leave it to me."

While Petra dialed the phone again, she looked more determined than ever but by the end of the call her determination appeared to be blotted out by exasperation.

"The first search revealed a lot more Dutras than I would have thought. What is Cristiano's last name? We can use it to cross reference."

"Lazaro. Cristiano Lazaro."

"Cristiano Lazaro, his name just rolls off your tongue doesn't it?" She made another call and within two minutes, her frown turned into a grin. "We should have an address very shortly. Let's go get that tablet."

We were in and out of the store in less than thirty minutes.

"Have you heard anything yet from your people?" I asked nervously.

"Maya, you need to calm down. Let's go get a drink."

"Drinking would be a bad idea for me right now. My head is already spinning."

She sighed, "Okay, let's go get some food and maybe you can tell me why you needed to buy a tablet so badly?"

I took a breath, "Maybe."

As we sipped our coffee and waited for our food, Petra looked over the ridge of her cup, with the question hanging on her lips again.

I stared down into my hot milky drink, not sure how to explain it without sounding crazy.

"I've taken over Dalley's blog."

A look of understanding flashed across her face. "Oh, so that's what he was talking about. Interesting."

"Who? What?" I asked feeling confused.

"My husband. He received a message from your father, asking him to put a hold on the legal work for a few days. Maya, what's really going on?"

I squirmed in my seat. "At first, I thought it was all about Cristiano, that maybe he might read the blog and choose to come home, back to me."

"And then?" she asked leaning in with curiosity.

"The truth is, as more people started to read what I wrote, it felt good to be heard. Almost exciting in a weird way."

"Oh, so you are channeling your inner Dalley now?" Petra said with a slight hint of disapproval. I sighed wondering if I had made a mistake. Seeing my reaction, she quickly changed her position.

"Maya, I think there is some merit to the idea, but you need to get a little more proactive than just a blog. You need a plan."

"I have one," I said defensively.

"Well let's hear it, because every day someone's missing, it makes them harder to find."

"He's not missing. He ran away, and I don't know if he wants to come back," I pouted.

"Do you believe he loves you?"

"Yes, I think he does. He told me he loved me."

"Do you believe you are meant to have a life together?"

"Yes, I do," I responded with surprising resolution.

"Then you need to stop *worrying* about finding him and just go out and do it."

"That's my plan.," I responded with frustration. "I was going to stay at Netuno for the week, and then leave on Friday night."

She burst out into laughter.

"Do you think it's stupid?"

"No." She placed her hand on my shoulder, sensing that one more challenging comment would send me into tears. "I just think you're not going to be any use to us during the week while your heart and soul are somewhere else. We have Carmo and your Mom and they are awesome. We can get everything done for the wedding without you. Can you make me a promise though?"

"It depends," I said breathing deeply now.

"Depends on what?"

"It depends on what kind of promise you want me to make," I chuckled a little.

"Oh, Maya. All I want you to promise is that if we get one solid clue from Mrs. Dutra, you are not going to come back with me today. You are going to take off in a different direction and find Cristiano." Petra paused, "and maybe have an adventure or two along the way."

"Petra, that is crazy. I can't just take off. My mom came all this way to be with me and I promised Carmo I would help at the inn."

"Yes, I know. Carmo will understand. As for your mom, she and I had a chat in the car and all she wants is for you to find happiness. Maya, she is stronger than you think and so are you." Petra took a moment to gather her thoughts. "She's worried about you, Maya."

"Worried about what?"

"About you falling into another depression."

"Another? I don't know what she's talking about," I said, with more than a hint of prickliness.

"Mm, maybe the three months you spent sitting in the garden, drinking tea, wrapped in a quilt?"

"Oh, it wasn't that bad, was it? I went to work."

"Look, Maya, I wasn't there, so I don't know. But she basically said you scared the crap out of her."

"I don't think I was really depressed, just frozen by my fears."

"Sounds a little depressing to me. Either way, the idea of you taking off was hers. While we were driving in, she was watching you write in your journal and asked if I could bring it up with you."

My heart felt confused.

"She also told me to tell you that she'll be there when you get back and is looking forward to meeting Cristiano."

"So, it's all settled? Is everyone else in on it too?" I asked sarcastically.

"No, but Josie is going to be irritated that she didn't think of it first."

Petra reached over and handed me a credit card. "Your mom asked me to give this to you."

"I can't take this." I pushed it back at her.

"Yes, you can, because if you leave today and do not take it with you, your mom is going to be upset. She wants to help you, Maya. Please let her. Besides, you need to be back at Netuno next week for the wedding. That's not nearly enough time to do any permanent damage to her credit," Petra laughed.

"Love isn't just an adjective, it's a verb," Petra stated.

"Seriously, Petra?"

"Yah, I heard it somewhere, but it's a good one, isn't it?"

"Yes, you're right, but how could I just leave? I don't have any of my things."

"Ah, let's see. You have your Paris purse. How about your passport?" I nodded. "You also have your journal and a credit card. That's pretty much all a girl needs to travel these days."

I laughed nervously and said, "What if I get into trouble?"

"You'll figure it out. By the way, your mom said you need to buy some clothes—she wants you looking your best when you meet Cristiano. She also said Aunt Olive would tell you to buy a new lipstick, not sure what that is about."

"The Lipstick Theory."

"The Lipstick Theory?"

"Yes, you have to meet my Aunt Olive one day." I paused. "So, you and my mom took care of everything?"

"Almost."

Petra took one last sip of her coffee and looked down at her phone.

"We're in business. You ready?"

21

A Mother Knows

Judith

My stomach flipped as I held my phone tightly and waited for a text from Petra. I wasn't sure if I had done the right thing. I knew Maya had changed since she'd arrived in Portugal, but had she changed that much? Then I heard the familiar ding that let me know I had a message.

Hi Judith, well you were right. She had a plan in mind and did need help. We are in a taxi right now on our way to Cristiano's apartment to meet someone. I told her about your plan. She was a little nervous at first, but I think I sold it. What good is twenty years in advertising if I can't use my skills for good too.

Thank you Petra. I can't wait to hear what happens next. I had better go. Josie is poking me. She needs help picking out ribbons and fairy lights. Can I tell her?

Yes, better you than me. Oh, and can you call Carmo and let her know that Maya won't be back until the wedding? I think Carmo was expecting her to help at the front desk with Puro away.

Oh dear, I might have made a mess for everyone.

Don't worry, Carmo will figure something out.
Petra

"Who were you texting with Petra?" Maya asked suspiciously.

"Your mom," I answered matter-of-factly.

"Oh, is she okay? Worried?"

I fibbed a little. "Yes okay, no not worried at all. She just wanted to know if I had shared her plan with you yet. I told her we are moving into Phase Two and I would let her know when we have something. Change of subject: Maya, what are you going to ask Mrs. Dutra when we arrive?"

"I don't know," she answered, looking lost.

"Well you better think of something. We've just pulled up to the address."

When Maya looked at the building, she became flushed and started taking micro breaths. I thought she was going to hyperventilate if she didn't settle down.

"Well, I can see this is the right place. Let's go in."

"No, Petra, I have to do this by myself," she said, calming her ragged breaths. "You have done so much already, but if I am really going to make some steps forward in my life, I need to know that I can do some of them on my own."

I was uncomfortable with her going in by herself, but I admired her for taking hold of the situation. Although her first steps were unsteady, she became more confident as she got closer to the door. She pulled her shoulders back, straightened out her body, and readied herself to face whatever was behind door number one.

Maya

I could feel Petra watching me intently from the taxi. I knew she wanted to come in with me, but I had to do it alone. I wasn't sure what I wanted to say to Mrs. Dutra, but somewhere in the conversation I had to convince her to let me into his apartment.

One knock on her door was all it took before she answered. She stared at me for several seconds, then smiled and leaned in for a hug.

"Maya, Cristiano's not here. He's away," she offered in broken English.

"Where? Did you see him? Was he here?" I asked with a note of desperation.

She patted me on the arm. "No, he is not here but he did call me about another matter," she said, wrinkling up her nose, "he also told me he was on his way to Porto," she commented, clearly not knowing the impact of sharing that knowledge.

My heart jumped. "Porto?" My next question sat on my lips until she took my hand and squeezed it.

"What is it, child?" she asked, now with concern.

I could feel the tears forming and did everything I could to hold them back.

"Did you know?" I asked, reluctantly.

"Know what?" she smiled.

"Did you know he was adopted?"

"Yes," she responded with an unexpected release of breath. "Does he know now?"

"Yes, he found out a few weeks ago. His Avo sent him a letter."

"Yes, the letter. I remember."

"Mrs. Dutra, can you please let me into his apartment?"

She hesitated.

"Please …" I cried out in frustration. She looked at me with pity. "I need to find him as soon as possible."

She sighed with resignation, then handed me the key and started rambling in Portuguese. She held up her hands like she was trying to tell me something but struggled to find the English words. Then she turned around, walked back into her apartment, and slammed the door.

As I walked up the stairs, I worried that I had upset Mrs. Dutra and wondered what I could do to make things right with her. As I stepped closer to Cristiano's apartment, my worry turned to confusion as a southern twang rang out into the hallway.

"Jack!!" I barked.

I had the key in the door and was ready to charge in, but the chances of him possibly being naked were higher than I could take. That was an image I did not want to have seared into my brain.

I knocked quietly at first but that was ineffective. I tried again with more force. When my second attempt failed, I made a fist and started to pound.

Jack whipped the door open. "Maya? What are you doing here? And why are you pounding on my door?"

"*Your* door?" I said, gritting my teeth.

"You know what I mean. Why are you here?" he asked, like somehow I was the last person he thought he would ever see.

"The question is, why are you?"

"Cristiano told me I could stay here for a few weeks or so."

"So, you talked to him?"

"Oh, Maya. Come in out of the hallway. If you don't, Mrs. Dutra is going to get mad at me again. She is a mean old lady."

"She is not!!" I yelled.

"Well, she hasn't been very nice to me."

"Why? What did you do to her?"

"Oh, it doesn't matter. Cristiano told her I was coming by, but I guess I caught her when she was napping. Ever since then, she looks at me with an evil eye. I think she thinks I have done something to Cristiano. But I know my southern hospitality will eventually win her over. Anyway, what can I do for you?"

I was still taken aback about seeing Jack, but pulled myself together. Thankfully, he had pants on, so that was one less trauma I had to endure.

"Jack, why didn't you text me back?" I paused, knowing being mean was not going to get me anywhere with him. "I thought maybe, just maybe, he would stop here first."

"No, when he left Setubal he headed North."

"I know he's on his way to Porto to meet his parents. I just don't know how to find them. Please Jack, can you help me? It's the least you can do."

"No, that is not the least I can do." He stood with his arms folded. "I cannot believe how much grief the two of you have caused me in the last two weeks."

I leaned down and picked up a pillow off the couch. I could smell him.

"Grief? I caused you grief?" I could feel my blood starting to boil. "For someone who claims to care about him, you sure have a funny way of showing it," I snapped back without regret.

Jack sighed then uncrossed his arms and moved in to give me a little nudge. Stepping back to avoid him I tripped over the edge of the coffee table and tumbled back onto the couch.

"You okay?" he asked with genuine concern. Now it was me who had my arms crossed. I held myself tightly trying to push the tears back once again. "Maya, you need to relax," Jack's voice softened, "Give me a minute, I have his parents' number and address in the other room."

He walked away, leaving me alone in the living room. My eyes began scanning over the coffee table and the magazines that lay untouched from my last visit to Cristiano's place.

Then *it* caught my eye: the envelope with the letter, Avo's letter. I slid it out from under the magazines. Just then, Jack came out of the room. I panicked and shoved it into my bag. My heart started to pound. I felt stupid and wanted to leave. My phone pinged and a cold sweat formed all over my body.

"It's just me," Jack said flatly, seeing my emotional reaction to the sound of the text. "Maya, he's not going to call you—at least not yet," he added when he saw the panic in my eyes.

"Shut up, Jack," I bit back.

"Well that's not very nice," he said, laughing loudly.

"Jack, I think I had better go." I walked over to the bookshelf that held Cristiano's jar collection.

"I don't think that's a good decision Maya," he said. Defiantly I stuck my tongue out at him and slipped one of the jars into my bag.

"Mature, Maya, real mature."

"This coming from a middle-aged man who lives in a hut?" I rebutted. "What do you know anyway?"

"Apparently not as much as you," he said sticking his tongue back out at me.

I left without saying another word, my anger taking center stage as I huffed out of the apartment. I wasn't sure who I was madder at: Jack or myself. When I stepped off the last stair, Mrs. Dutra was standing by her door. I handed her the key.

"I don't like that man," she said, wrinkling up her nose again.

My anger subsided long enough for me to answer, "Yes, he can be difficult, but he has always been good to Cristiano."

"Well, okay. Maybe I will give him a second chance but only because you said so."

❧

The taxi was waiting for me, but Petra was nowhere to be found.

The driver looked at me and shook his head. "She told me to tell you, you have everything you need," he said. "And that she would see you back at Netuno. She also said Judith would be fine and that I was to take you wherever you wanted to go—where to, Miss?"

"Porto. I need to get to Porto.

22

Reflection

Maya

THE TAXI DRIVER DROPPED ME at the Gare do Oriente train station. The next train to Porto was not departing for three long hours, leaving me with just enough time to sit and have a panic attack or take the credit card my mother had given to me and go shopping.

Luck was on my side, as the train station was connected to one of the most beautiful shopping centers I had ever seen, the Vasco da Gamma. Walking into the center, I was taken by the modern architecture and the amazing lighting. I didn't feel like I belonged there at all, but I was not going to let that stop me.

I walked around trying to find clothes I liked but it was much more difficult without Dalley. Then I saw it, a store called Cortefiel. The clothes on the mannequins in the window were perfect. They were a mixture of both the old and the new me. Light and flowy, yet comfortable and fitted. I walked through the doors and was immediately greeted by a staff member.

"*Bom Dia, Como posso ajudá-lo hoje?*"

"English?" I asked.

"Yes, a little," she responded. "Help? Can I help you?"

"Yes, please. I need everything." I waved my hands over my body, indicating that I needed a whole outfit, maybe even a whole wardrobe. "I leave for Porto on the next train," I said, showing her my ticket.

She looked at her watch. "Oh … Gaspar? Gaspar? I need help."

Within a few minutes, I had a treasure trove of salespeople huddled around me. Tereza, the first young woman I met, shared my story with the others. She had Gaspar take me to a dressing room. It was not long before Tereza and Gaspar were handing me more clothes than I knew what to do with. I trusted them and only said no to one outfit before remembering I was the new and improved Maya: new hair, new heart, new clothes, and hopefully a new future.

While I was paying for the clothes, Gaspar disappeared briefly then came running back into the store with a beautiful travel bag. He placed all my new clothes into the bag and pushed it towards me.

"I, I … *obrigado* Gaspar and Tereza." I hugged them both.

"Good luck, Maya Wells, we are rooting for you and Cristiano," Gaspar said. Noticing my surprise, he added, "One of the girls recognized your face and name."

I covered my face, feeling embarrassed.

"No, no, no, that Jade," he said shaking his head in disgust.

"Yes, I have to agree with you," I smiled.

Then Tereza handed me an envelope. "We thought you might need this." I opened it and inside there was a gift certificate for a massage.

She smiled, answering the quizzical look on my face. "They have a new service on the train where they offer massages. We thought you might like it."

I hugged them again before leaving, then ran to catch my train. I'd never had that much fun shopping before, not even with Dalley.

I had booked a premiere seat on the train because I knew I would need some quiet time. I only had two and a half hours to try to figure out what I was going to say to Cristiano's biological mother when I rang her doorbell. After realizing that there was no manual for meeting his family, and that I was just going to have to trust my instincts, I handed it over to the universe.

With nerves bristling I called the porter over and showed him the beautiful envelope that Tereza had given me.

We walked through several cars, my heart racing as I was not sure even a massage could calm me down. But it was paid for, and if I got any more nervous about my trip to Porto, I really was at risk of having a panic attack.

The massage car was beautiful. Music played in the background, setting me at ease, and lightly scented oils filled the air. A woman took my envelope and handed me a robe in exchange, then motioned for me to undress behind a screen.

When I came out, she looked the other way as I hung up the robe and crawled under the pristine cotton sheet draped elegantly over the massage table.

She held several bottles of oil under my nose, letting me choose the scent I preferred, then carefully dripped the warm oil on my back. Slowly, she began moving the oil over my skin and speaking calmly to me in Portuguese with her safe and soothing voice.

My body slowly let go as she worked the oil into my muscles. As I relaxed, my heart and mind wandered, taking me to the night I heard Cristiano play his guitar at the nightclub, then transported me to the costume shop when he kissed the small of my back. My body shivered in delight at the memory. Then, without notice, my mind took an abrupt turn to a different scene: all I could hear was Puro in the hotel lobby calling his name, yelling for him to come back.

My sadness rose to the surface and my body gave way to quiet sobs. I covered my face, but the woman touched me on the shoulder, letting me know it was okay to cry. To finish, she took a warm cloth, gently wiped me down, then left me alone. I sat up slowly, wiping the tears that were still rolling from my eyes. They wouldn't stop. Why wouldn't they stop? Then I felt it. It was like someone was squeezing my heart and I could hardly breathe. I just wanted to hear his voice, to see his face.

Once I returned to my seat, I found myself staring out the window while holding my breath. It was not until I caught my reflection in the glass that I let out a sigh.

Raising my hand, I touched the window's cool surface while imagining Cristiano stroking my cheek. I closed my eyes and pictured his fingers traveling down my neck. I could feel my body flush as I focused on memories of our date at the festival: his arms around me, his lips on mine. I needed to find him. I had to trust that our love would take me where I needed to go.

⁓

When we arrived in Porto, my first steps off the train were a little shaky. I hailed a taxi and gave the driver the address for Cristiano's parents' house.

I had no idea how far we had to go, but when the driver turned up a steep road and stopped at the top, I saw a house. It was simply spectacular. Stepping out of the vehicle, my heart was pounding so hard I thought it might break through my rib cage. There I was, standing alone on a dirt road in a foreign country, not sure what to do next. There was no going back for me though, so I walked to the front door and knocked.

23

A Long Story

Maya

EUPHEMIA WAS THE MOST HANDSOME woman I had ever seen. Her skin, her hair: she was him somehow, or he was her. It was so startling I could hardly speak.

"*Ola*," she said, her voice magical and soft.

"Hello," was all I could say for a moment. As she looked at me with no recognition, I realized she had no idea who I was. If Cristiano had been there, he hadn't mentioned me. Her beautiful face showed no fear or anxiety, only a simple curiosity about why an English-speaking stranger had just been dropped off at her doorstep.

"Um, my name is Maya Wells."

"Hello, my name is Euphemia. How may I help you?"

What happened next surprised us both. I had hoped to do this without tears, but I was a mess.

"Are you injured? Do you need help? What is the matter, Miss Wells? Please come in."

I could feel kindness emanating from her as she watched me carefully, waiting for me to speak again. My eyes met hers and I wondered:

What was her life like? Was she happy? Did she ever think about Cristiano? Was his story really mine to tell?

But there I was standing in this woman's entrance way, crying. She deserved an explanation; she deserved the truth.

So, taking a deep breath, I began. "I'm not sure where to start," I said.

"Oh, dear, maybe from the beginning would be a good place. Would you like something to drink or eat?"

"Tea, please, if you have it."

She nodded and smiled so warmly, then invited me into her living room and asked me to sit. While I waited, I admired all the beautiful furniture and décor. It was apparent every piece was unique, handcrafted, and chosen specifically for the space. Everything had a purpose, a reason to be there. Then I saw it, leaning up against the wall. I walked over and ran my hands over the board. I closed my eyes, and for a moment, I could imagine him on the water, smiling as he broke through the waves. I missed him so much.

"Do you surf?" I jumped about a foot off the ground. "Oh dear, I am so sorry. I didn't mean to startle you," Euphemia said.

"No, that's okay. Yes, well no. I don't surf. I tried once but it didn't go so well," I laughed, sort of.

"My husband surfed when we were young and used to make his own boards. That is one of his."

"It's beautiful," I said in a whisper as I ran my hand along the finished wood.

"Oh, thank you. He wanted to get rid of it, but I told him we needed to keep it, even if it doesn't quite go with the décor."

She placed a tray on the table that held the tea, a bottle of wine, and a lovely selection of food.

"I thought a glass of wine might pair better with the cheese and olives. I hope that is okay?"

"Oh, thank you, it's perfect," I said.

Euphemia poured me half a glass of wine and handed it to me. I stared at her and then took a sip, wanting to speak but unable.

"Please, tell me, what brings you to my home? Do you know my husband or my children?"

I smiled. "You could say that."

She looked curiously at me.

"Could you please explain? I am feeling confused. Maybe it is my English."

"No, it's not your English. I'm sorry. This all must be so odd, and you are being so gracious. But like I said, I don't know where to start."

Then I thought about the letter in my bag. Avo had told the story so beautifully. I could not imagine trying to tell it in my own words so, hands shaking, I pulled the envelope out of my bag and offered it to her. The truth was, it was her story too.

At first, she looked confused, then I saw it, the recognition of the name. She gasped, lost her footing, and fell back into the chair.

"Euphemia, are you okay?"

"I don't know. What is this?"

"It's the reason I'm here."

Her hands began to shake, and her face became flushed. She tried to speak again but no words came out.

"Can I?" she asked in a whisper.

I nodded my head, not sure I could find the right words either.

With some hesitation, she pulled the letter out of the envelope. "Can you read it to me?"

"If you wish." My heart was beating so hard again, I thought it might explode. I wasn't sure I had done the right thing, but there was no walking away from it.

Before I began, his name fell off her lips like it had been sitting there her whole life.

"You know my Cristiano?" Tears formed in her eyes. "You know my son?" her voice hitched as she said the word.

"Yes."

I laughed again and then we both started to cry.

"Read," she said, pushing the letter back at me.

And so I began. Page after page of truth and heartache, of love and death, of broken and healing hearts, and then I stopped, knowing Cristiano had not read the last few pages and wanting to leave that just for him.

She sat, breathing slowly, her face stained with ancient tears she had been holding onto for twenty-eight years. Then something shifted. I could see the wheels of her mind turning. A thousand questions were dancing on the tip of her tongue.

"Why did no one ever call us? Tell us? I thought he was happy. That he was with people who loved him," she said.

"Oh, he was. Avo loved him—loves him—more than life itself. She had wanted to tell him about the adoption after his parents died, but she just never found the right time. Cristiano was a complicated soul from the beginning."

I paused, thinking about the extra layer of truth not found in Avo's letter—the truth about her husband finding Cristiano at fifteen. "There is something else you need to know," I said, but before I had a chance to tell her, I heard a key in the door and then a tumult of laughter.

"Hello Euphemia, what's for supper? We're starved."

Marcos walked into the room followed by his two children. I gasped, trying to hold back my surprise. It was like looking at my Cristiano only twenty years from now. I wasn't sure if I could speak, but Euphemia did that for me."

"Marcos, this is Maya Wells. Children, please go upstairs."

Marcos studied his wife's face and knew something was very wrong.

"Children, go upstairs right now," he said. "Mom and I need to talk."

The teenagers looked at me. They wanted answers, but clearly were not going to challenge their father. After they left, Euphemia ran to him.

"Marcos it's a miracle. Miss Wells brings us news of our Cristiano." She held the letter tightly to her heart, like she was holding on to him. Then she turned to me. "I didn't even ask how you know him?"

I watched the interaction between Cristiano's parents carefully. "I guess the only way to explain myself is this: Your son is the man I love."

She stepped closer to me, studying my eyes. Then she placed the letter on the table and gently took my hands in hers.

"What's the matter? Where is he? Why isn't he here with you?" she asked.

"It's very complicated," I explained. "He only found out about the adoption three weeks ago, and about you and Marcos and the family this past week."

Marcos stepped towards us, clearly wanting me away from his wife. "Miss Wells, I think you should go. You are upsetting my wife. Please stop with your stories."

My anger flared. "They're not stories. It's true, it's all true. Jack knows how to keep a secret, but he is not a liar."

"Jack?" Euphemia said, looking at me and then turning to Marcos. "Your old friend Jack? In Setubal?" She swiveled back to me and pulled me closer, holding my wrists tightly. "How do you know Jack? And what does this have to do with Cristiano?" she yelled pushing me away and grabbing the letter, frantically looking for answers.

"Marcos," she said sharply, while holding up one page. "Almost fifteen years ago you went to see Jack. He called you about a young surfer he had been teaching. When you came back that day, you wouldn't talk about the visit and you brought back one of your old boards, but not your first."

I watched her carefully as the pieces came together.

"You told me the boy could surf but that you didn't meet him." She breathed in deeply, then let out a low, slow sigh. "Did you know it was him? Did you know it was our son?"

Marcos covered his face with his hands and collapsed in the nearest chair. I didn't want to be there. I didn't want to hear the next part of the story. I started to move toward the door, but Marcos jumped up and stopped me.

"Why did you come? Why are you doing this to us? He has a family. What do you want?" he screamed at me.

"I don't want anything. I just want to find him," I cried.

Euphemia broke in, yelling at Marcos. "No, he doesn't have a family. His parents are dead. They died in a plane crash when he was seven," she yelled, throwing the letter at him.

Marcos looked stunned as the pages fluttered to the floor. "No that can't be. I left him there because he was happy."

"Who? Cristiano told you he was happy?" she screamed.

"No, Jack. Jack told me that Cristiano was loved. That he was fine. I had no idea about the plane crash."

"But you knew it was him," Euphemia continued. "You saw our son and you didn't tell me. How many times? Two, five, ten? How many times did you watch him surf? And you never talked to him? Even to say hello?"

She turned to me. "Does he know?" she held her breath. "Does he know that Marcos was there? That he saw him?"

"Yes, but he only found out that information a few days ago."

"Euphemia, I'm sorry," Marcos uttered. "I would have told you if I had known about his parents. I would have talked to him. I would have done things differently."

"But you didn't. For almost fifteen years you've known about him and you didn't tell me." There was a long pause.

Euphemia turned to me. "Maya, I need a few minutes with my husband and the children." She moved to an arched doorway and waited for Marcos to join her. They went upstairs, leaving me sitting in the living room alone.

Ten minutes later, I saw Cristiano's brother storm down the stairs and run out the front door. His sister followed, but she didn't leave. She walked into the living room.

"So," she said with some curiosity. "I have another brother. I did not see that coming. I always wondered why my father was so strict about my dating rules. Now I know. Hi, I am Jacinta. And you are?"

She was so joyful, but she also had a little edge about her. "I'm Maya Wells."

"How did you meet my brother Cristiano?" she asked.

"The short story: he saved me from a scalding cup of tea at the airport. He is a flight attendant. Then he wrote me a letter and asked me out on a date. He changed my life."

"Wow, that is very romantic. Do you have a picture of him?"

"Yes, I have a few on my phone."

"Where are you from?" she asked as I dug through my purse for my phone.

"I'm from Canada—a place called Peachland."

"That sounds beautiful. Oh, I wonder if I can find pictures of him online." She grabbed her tablet.

"No!! Wait," I screeched.

"Why? Is he a criminal or something? Are you?" she laughed.

"No neither of us are criminals," I said. "But I have to warn you and your parents about something. If you Google me or Cristiano, we will show up on a blog that was written by a journalist from the States. Most of what is said is not true. Some of it is, but it's a long and complicated story."

She started to laugh. "Oh my god, I think I know what you are talking about. I haven't read it, but a few of my friends were telling me about it. This whole thing is so weird, kind of crazy." She paused. "I can't believe my parents kept a secret that big for so long, and that my new brother is Internet famous. Where is he?" she asked with an innocence that could only make me smile.

"I like you," I chuckled sidestepping her question for the moment. "And he is going to like you too."

"Really, what is he like?"

"He is honest and loyal. Hardworking, kind, insightful, and musical. He can play the guitar and sing. He can dance and surf and make bread."

"Bread? He sounds like a carbon copy of my dad—our dad—except for the bread-making part. My mom won't let *him* into the kitchen. That is so cool. I hope he will want to teach me."

"His Avo taught him. She is amazing, almost …"

"Magical?" Euphemia said, poking her head into the room. "I see the two of you are getting to know one another."

"Mom, did you hear all the cool things that Cristiano can do. I can hardly wait to meet him." She paused, then faced her mother. "Why did you never tell us? He's my brother."

Euphemia's eyes teared up again, but then she smiled, "I should have known from the time you were little that you would have been able to handle the truth about him and me and your father. I was worried though. I wasn't sure how your brother would manage. He has always been a little moody."

"A *little* moody?" joked Jacinta.

"I wanted to believe that Cristiano had a perfect life and I didn't want to ruin that for him," Euphemia said. "I had always hoped that when he was told about the adoption, he would come and find me, but that day never came."

"This is so messed up," Jacinta remarked. She turned to me. "How did he find out about the adoption?" she asked earnestly.

"His Avo wrote him a letter about three weeks ago. I have it here if you want to read it. If it is okay with your mom." I bent down to pick up the pages from the floor tucking the last two in my purse.

"He had an Avo? We never had any grandparents. We weren't allowed to see them." She looked sadly over at her mother.

"Yes Jacinta, I'll tell you the whole truth, but can you give me a couple of days?"

"Can I read the letter?" she asked, looking at her mother but already reaching for the pages I held in my hand.

"Yes, of course you can. Avo has done a much better job telling the story than I could ever do."

Jacinta settled into a chair and started. After reading the first few pages, she looked up. "Mom? I can't believe this. You were sixteen? How could your parents make you give him away?" Then Jacinta looked at me. "Was Cristiano angry when he found out about the adoption?"

"No, he wasn't mad or even sad. He said he felt relieved, and that certain parts of his life made more sense."

Euphemia was ringing her hands and clearly needed to ask me something.

"Euphemia, what is it?" I asked, feeling horrible for causing her so much distress.

"Maya, I asked you earlier where he was, but you never answered me."

She needed to know the whole story. They all did. I took a breath and handed over the last bits of truth that I had been hanging on to.

"Last week, both of our worlds took a turn. All his truths came out as well as a bucket of secrets and lies. It was messy and too much for him to manage. So, he got into his car and drove away."

"What kind of car does he drive?" Jacinta asked innocently.

"Jacinta, what does that matter?" her mom barked at her.

"It's okay, Euphemia," I said before turning to Jacinta. "It was his dad's, his other dad's." I stopped. "A beautiful silver sports car from the '60s. It means the world to him."

Euphemia staggered backwards before steadying herself with the table.

"Mom, are you okay?" Jacinta said, running over to her.

"Oh, Lord." The color drained from her face. It looked like she was replaying a scene in her mind but did not like the ending.

"Euphemia?" I asked, worried that she was going to faint.

"He was here," she stammered.

"He was here?" I felt panicked, excited. I was close. "When?"

"What do you mean he was here?" Jacinta interrupted us.

"I mean, I saw him. A few days ago, I saw a young man on the road to the house. He was in a silver sports car. I was on the balcony. I waved to him but he didn't wave back; he just drove away. I stood for a long time, watching the dust settle on the road. Something … I knew something was different about him, of course I knew. He is my son." She started to cry again, and Jacinta held her as she wept.

"Mom, it's going to be okay. We'll find him. Right, Maya?"

"Yes Jacinta, I'm going to find him. I have to."

The front door slammed. "Zef! Zeferino, stop. Stop running away from me," his dad yelled at him.

Zef stood on the stairs and yelled back, "You guys are the biggest hypocrites I have ever met. Everything you have ever told me is a lie. I always knew that there was something wrong. It always felt like I was second best. Now I know the reason why. I was your replacement for him." He ran up the stairs and I heard another door slam.

The house became very silent. Euphemia's tears stopped and she raised her head. She looked over at a broken Marcos and smiled. "Don't worry dear. Zef will find his way and so will Cristiano. I have faith that our family will be together very soon," she said.

She looked over at me. "Maya, it's getting late. You need to stay with us tonight."

She didn't give me a chance to respond but continued speaking.

"I mean, I would like you to stay with us. I want to find out more about … everything," she said gently. "But I have to take care of a few things this evening. Jacinta, please take Maya out to the guest house and bring her something else to eat. I will see you in the morning, Maya. Everything will be much calmer, I promise."

"I'm sorry I turned your world upside-down," I said.

"No, Maya," Marcos spoke softly. "You turned it right-side-up." He walked slowly out of the room and headed up the stairs.

24

Unearthed

Cristiano

PIERRE AND I STAYED UP late into the night, with him researching information on the crash and me trying to get the voices out of my head.

I had no doubt Pierre would accomplish his task, but I wasn't so sure about mine. The voice I had heard in the garden and then in the car disappeared before I could even understand where it came from. But there was another voice too, one that had been with me since I was child. It was like a lyrical whisper or a song being cast around me like a cloak. It had been with me for many years like a quiet comfort blending into the background and only showing itself when I was still enough. As I lay on the bed evaluating my sanity in that moment, I strained to connect the voice with someone. At first, I thought it had to be my mother's, but as I closed my eyes and searched my memories, I recalled one of our secret beach days. I was standing with my mom, listening to the ocean roar while grabbing hold of the warm sand in my toes. That was the first time I remember hearing the voice. I asked my mom what she was singing, and she laughed. She told me she had not been singing anything, and then said something about it being the song of the waves.

I was confused as a child; a part of me wanted it to stop but the other part didn't. I never asked her about it again, even when I heard it and I was not near the ocean. It was never scary. It was just a part of me.

I opened my eyes, realizing that the subtle song had been playing in the background my whole life. Only over the last two days it had gotten louder—so loud, in fact, I could no longer ignore it. It was as if the voice was trying to get my attention. Then, just as the tower's lights went out on my second night in Paris, it came to me. I recognized the voice. I realized who it was: Euphemia, my birth mother. Hearing her on the phone, seeing her on the balcony, it all made sense.

Somehow, it was always her. She was inside my heart from the beginning. She never left me. I closed my eyes and slept soundly that night.

On waking in the morning, Pierre appeared not to have moved from where I left him the night before. He was disheveled but ecstatic.

"I found it. I may owe a few people favors for the rest of my life, but I found it. The Egyptian government are very tight lipped about everything, but I was able to put pressure on a few people. With a little *extra* encouragement, we got the coordinates for where the plane went down, plus a little bit more."

"What do you mean?" I asked with anticipation.

"Well, the small carrier that flew your parents went bankrupt after the crash. No one would fly with them. After that, all their assets were crated up and stored. Egypt's latest set of politicians have decided to auction off the contents of several storage facilities and the airline's crates are among some of the assets. More interesting than that, I was able to get a copy of the manifest of the crates."

"How the hell did you pull that off?"

"Oh, don't ask." He shook his hand waving off that part of the conversation. "I know you were young, but do you ever remember getting their luggage back after the crash?"

"No, we received nothing. The only thing the airline did was let us know they were dead."

"You never received a settlement from the airline?" Pierre was offended by the information.

"No. I don't think Avo would have taken it even if they had offered. My parents had a very sound life insurance policy from the university. What is in the crate?"

Pierre paused. "Office stuff and … luggage, two pieces of foreign luggage."

"Pierre, whose luggage was it?" I stepped closer to him my anticipation turning to anxiety.

"It didn't say, just that the bags had French airline tags." He looked at me. "Cristiano, they flew out of Paris before heading to Egypt. Their luggage should have been on the plane, but …"

He handed me a folder and I read through it quickly. It popped out at me as if highlighted.

"The plane was overweight. They left the luggage behind," I breathed out slowly. "Pierre?" I asked.

"Yes, I know you have to go. I knew there would be no sense in trying to talk you out of it so … grab your things. There is a taxi waiting for you outside. I took the liberty of booking you a flight to Cairo."

25

Digging

Dalley

"Ravn, have you found anything?"

"Well, looks like she posted last night. She's in Porto right now."

"Porto? Why is she in Porto? Let me read that."

Hi everyone, it's me again. I'm in Porto right now. Took the train up from Lisbon yesterday. Beautiful trip. Did you know they give massages on the trains here? What a treat. But that's a story for another day.

Left the girls in charge of the wedding plans. Even my mom is getting in on it. Last text I got from her was that she was redesigning a dress for the big event. Now for the emotional plea …

Cristiano, if you read this, know that they love you and want you and … so do I. Maya

Sending you all good thoughts and wishes from Porto, and remember, never let fear stop you from doing what is in your heart. Still not giving up.

From Porto, Maya

"Oh Maya, your declaration of love was perfect, but it would have been nice if you could have told me why you are in Porto, '*know that they love you',* what is that supposed to mean?" I threw the laptop across the bed hitting Ravn in the leg.

"Hey, watch where you're throwing the technology," Ravn said, sliding it under his arm and pretending to protect it from my frustration.

"I need to know what's going on. I have to talk to someone down at Netuno," I said with exasperation.

"Do you really think that's the best idea? Let's see if we can do a little more research first. You're really not anyone's favorite person right now, except mine of course."

"Thanks Ravn, that's very helpful."

"I'm just being realistic."

"Well, favorite or not, I may have someone who is willing to talk to me."

"Who would that be?"

"I'll let you know if she picks up." I did a little digging and found Jade's number in some of my notes I had put together before coming on the trip. I pushed send and turned on the speakerphone. Ravn shook his head and started to laugh. The phone rang twice and then I heard her familiar acidic tone.

"What!! What the hell do you want?"

I heard Ravn chuckle; she really was everything that I had described. Uncharacteristically, I panicked and wasn't able to say a word, but Ravn moved in seamlessly.

"Dagmar Ravn here."

"What? Who is this?" she spat out.

"Sorry, I'm calling from overseas, bad connection. Hello? I'm a free-lance reporter looking for Jade Axeline. I was just following up on some …"

"Rumors? Well they're all true. My father recently fired me without due cause from his firm and I plan on suing him for breach of contract."

"Can we set an interview time for tomorrow?" Ravn looked at me, grinning and making it up as he went along.

"No, but I can give one to you right now," she responded sourly.

I stood in the hotel room, waving my arms around, searching for a piece of paper where I could write down a series of questions for him to ask her. He held his hand up, letting me know he had things under control.

As he settled into the interview, he was magnificent. He led her down the exact path I wanted. She answered every question he asked plus ten more. It was like she was under his spell.

"So, are you going to ask me the question everyone is dying to know?" she spat at him through the receiver.

"Only if you want to share," he offered invitingly.

"I feel like I can trust you to tell my side of the story."

"Absolutely, I will be fair, more than fair. Please, Jade, tell me what this is all about?"

"This was all about some crappy little winery in Portugal that my father wanted. He thinks I messed things up for him, that I tipped our hand about the takeover. But it wasn't my fault. I blame that bitch, Maya. If she had just stepped out of my way at the airport in Montreal and let me have the stupidly gorgeous flight attendant, none of this would have happened. He should have been mine!"

"Really?"

"Yes, really. What man in his right mind would choose her over me? And in addition to that she was very mean. Can you imagine, she called me toxic waste!"

"Toxic waste? Yes, that is very bitchy." Ravn looked over at me for confirmation.

I nodded my head and laughed to myself, remembering when Maya told me about her encounter with Jade on the veranda.

Jade continued to prattle on. "I know. Have you seen her blog where she names me as a thief? It's not true. I've lost everything because of her, and I left a comment letting her know what I think of her."

"You did, did you? Are you referring to the blog Price's Portugal?"

"Of course I am, you idiot."

"No need for you to be rude, Miss Axeline."

"Oh, that's not rude, I haven't even gotten started."

"With me or the bitchy blog writer?"

"Oh, I think I like you."

"Thank you, that is very kind."

Ravn pointed at me to go on the computer and see what Jade had written.

As I checked the comment, I couldn't help but start typing a reply.

Ravn was quite impressive—he continued his conversation with Jade while at the same time trying to wrestle the computer away from me before I added anything to the blog. It was too late. I smiled, pressed return, and off the reply went into cyber space, not as Dalley but under my pseudonym.

"Dalley Price, she was the journalist who set up the blog? What did you think of her?" he laughed as he fished for more fun facts about me.

"Yes, she's the one. I liked her at first …"

Ravn looked over at me and smiled while she blathered on.

"… she was deceitful, worse than me. She stole Maya's journal writings and posted them as her own, but like I said, I liked her …"

He interrupted her. "So, you went to Portugal to gather information for your father, and then your father's company tried to buy up enough shares to take over the winery? But somehow the people at Netuno found out about the takeover and disrupted your father's plans. He blames you for blowing up the deal, so he fired you and canceled your credit cards. You blame Maya for everything. Is there anything I'm missing?"

"Only that I am the victim in all of this. Maya ruined my life and when I find her I'll be happy to return the favor, actually a little excited about it. Don't tell my dad but I kept his expense card."

"I won't say a word."

It was right about then I couldn't listen to one more word of her crap. I launched myself across the bed and tried to grab the phone. Ravn scooped it up before I could get it and ran into the bathroom.

I was left to lie on the bed, waiting for him to finish. When he came out, he looked stern at first, then broke into great laughter.

"That was so much fun. You are going to have to cancel your number when she puts the pieces together. She's not going to like you anymore."

"Oh, I couldn't care less if she likes me. And the phone is a throw away. What else did you learn?"

"She said she was flying back to Europe soon and offered to *meet* me."

"She propositioned you. Slut!"

"Yeah, do you have a picture of her?" he smiled.

My nostrils flared.

"Don't give it a second thought. I've had enough candy while waiting for you all those years. I've lost my sweet tooth."

"I'm not sure what to say to that. Some people may think that's a little crass?"

"It may be crass, but it's true. You want me to be truthful with you, right?"

"Yes, but only when I ask. You don't need to add extra commentary."

He shrugged his shoulder. "Whatever you want, Dalley. I am here to serve."

"Good. Now if you could summarize the call for me that would be extremely helpful."

"Axel's plan failed. Netuno is safe. She hates Maya. Her father fired her, and she has limited funds. She's carefully following Maya on the blog. She's flying back to Europe, no reason offered except that she had a vendetta against Maya. Dalley, she's dangerous."

"What do you mean, 'dangerous'? She is a spoiled brat who just lost her only means of paying for her next Prada bag," I countered.

"No, I think there is more to her than that. I've met a lot of people and only a few who are truly vindictive. If she really thinks that Maya ruined her life, then we better find Maya and Cristiano before she does."

A cool chill ran over my skin. I didn't quite know how to respond.

"Maya's trip to Porto—I remember reading something about that town in one of your blogs. Somewhere in Maya's letter that you published she mentioned the city. I think it had something to do with Cristiano's birth parents."

"Oh, you are impressive." I went to make a call, but he grabbed the phone from my hand. "Stop being so grabby."

"You owe me for the interview with the shrew. I'm hungry, take me out to eat."

"I don't remember you being bossy when we first met."

"Well then, I guess we need to spend more time together. You think I'm bossy? I think I've learned to get what I want."

"And what exactly is that?"

"You."

26

Maya the Conqueror

Maya

HOLDING MY JOURNAL TIGHTLY TO my chest, I stepped onto the small balcony and embraced the view. As I watched the sunrise, I thought about the last few months of my life, and how not getting married had led me on a journey of new love and self-discovery.

Wednesday Morning, Cristiano's Parents' Home, Porto

Something changed for me this morning as I breathed in the crisp air of this beautiful place. I allowed an awareness to touch my heart. As many times as I have said that I don't want to be afraid anymore, up until now I was still allowing the secret seeds of fear to germinate in the tiniest of spaces. It's almost like I wanted to fail. Well not fail, but not succeed. I was afraid to learn something new, afraid I wouldn't be good enough at whatever I tried. Funny thing is the last few weeks have made me realize that I've always been good enough, right from those days when I used to sneak out of the house and climb my peach tree before sunrise. I finally get it.

What I now know is that better and different were right in front of me the whole time. They were always in my grasp, as they are now. I guess it just took ... well it just took time.

Worry stones have been the impediment I cast again and again on my path, setting myself up to trip and fall.

As I make the decision to move forward and find Cristiano, I know I cannot erase all my worries, but I can at least cast my anxieties off. And if I ... when I stumble again, I know it won't be because of the stones I have placed in my own way.

I feel a fresh confidence developing within. My past is just that, my past. I cannot erase it, but I can learn from it. I'm on a mission and nothing can stop me.

Until next time,

Maya the Conqueror

Events of the past three weeks flashed before me like a digital picture frame on double speed. My mind stopped on Bento and Carmo, two of the kindest people I had ever met and whose love was proving to be the binding agent that would keep our new Netuno family together for one more week.

❧

"Netuno Winery and Inn, how can I help you?" Carmo's voice was like coming home. I smiled.

"Carmo, it's Maya."

"Maya! Petra said you took off on some secret mission to Porto. What are you doing there?"

"Honestly, Carmo, I wasn't sure at first. It was scary. Then I met her."

"Met who?"

"Cristiano's birth mother, Euphemia."

"You went to Porto to meet his birth mother? Really? Are you sure that was such a good idea?"

"No, not a first, but then she started asking questions and I started answering. She is amazing. Then I met his father and his siblings. Things got messy last night. Lots of tears and a few slammed doors. His little sister surprised me though. Her name is Jacinta. She cannot wait to meet Cristiano. His brother on the other hand, well that may take more time. But that's not the reason why I'm calling. I wanted to apologize, as I'm not going to be back until the wedding."

"Maya, I know. And don't worry, we have everything under control. Your mom is the best. She is taking an old dress of mine and redesigning the whole thing for the wedding. It is going to be beautiful."

"Yes, she sent me a text about the dress. She is very excited."

"Maya … you *are* going to find him." Carmo jumped in, changing the subject. "I cannot believe how brave you are. I don't think I could have just taken off without knowing what I was going to do next."

"Oh, I don't know about that." My words lingered a little. "I think you would do anything for Bento if you thought he was in trouble, and he would do the same for you. I know Cristiano, and …"

"You love him, and he loves you," Carmo said, finishing my sentence.

"Well, I know I love him, but I guess I'll just have to see how he feels about me when I find him."

"Maya. He loves you. Don't doubt that … you can't ever doubt that."

"Thank you, Carmo. Hey, has Puro left for Vancouver yet?"

"His flight leaves today. Francesco is coming by very shortly to get him."

"Can I talk to him for a moment?"

"Let me see if he's free."

I waited for a few seconds, listening to the morning hustle and bustle of the inn through the open line. Then I heard his voice.

"Maya, I only have a minute. Carmo said you are in Porto. I trust you to do the right thing. Just find him and bring him home."

"Thank you, Puro. Have a safe trip and send Maggie my love. Tell her I miss her."

"I will. I have to go. Be careful Maya."

He hung up before I had a chance to speak to Carmo again. Then there was a knock on my door.

"Good morning, Miss Wells," Marcos said through the door.

When I heard his voice, my heart jumped. He sounded just like Cristiano, an older version but eerily similar. I opened the door with a little apprehension, not sure what to expect after the evening's events.

"Good morning, Marcos. Please, call me Maya."

"Maya, I wanted to come and apologize for my and Zef's behavior yesterday. My reaction to you and the news you brought was inexcusable. I hope you can accept my apology. And my son's as well. It came as a shock to him, as you can imagine."

He stood awkwardly in the doorway. "Marcos, would you like to come in?"

"If it's not too inconvenient."

"No, not at all. I would love the company."

"I have asked Jacinta to bring us some coffee. Is that okay?"

"Yes. I am getting used to all the coffee that people drink here. Puro was the first to make me drink some when we were out on a walk one day."

"Puro? Who is that?"

"Oh, I'm sorry. Puro is the manager at Netuno. It's a vineyard close to where Cristiano was born.

"Oh, yes, I have heard of the family who owns it."

"Puro has been with the vineyard for many years and runs the daily operations of both the vineyard and the inn. He was old friends with Cristiano's fathe … Oh, I'm sorry."

"No need to be sorry. He is his father. I'm the one who should be sorry." He sat down. I couldn't help but be caught off guard when he tilted his head and his hair fell into his eyes. When he looked up, he saw me staring. "What is it Maya? Did I say something wrong?"

"No, it's just that you and Cristiano look so much alike. It is a little unnerving for me. Your hair, your mannerisms."

"Really? We look alike? When I saw him as an adolescent on the water, I couldn't tell. I could only see that he surfed better than me. Does he still surf? What does he like to do? What does he do for a living? How did you meet? Where are you from?"

I started to laugh. It was clear no one had talked to him from the night before, but that was okay. I was happy to tell him all about Cristiano. "Yes, he still surfs when he can. He keeps a series of boards in his apartment in Lisbon, and a couple with Jack, but they're not talking right now. Cristiano is mad at him. He punched him when he found out Jack had been keeping secrets from him."

"Yes, I have to say I'm a little mad too. I can't believe he didn't tell me about Cristiano's parents that first time he called me."

"Truthfully, Jack didn't know for sure if Cristiano was yours until you arrived that day. He had suspected, but thought it was too coincidental. Then when you saw him and you put the pieces together, his suspicions proved true. He would have introduced him if you had asked. But you didn't."

"I know. I have thought about that day for years. It still haunts me that I walked away from him."

"Jack said you came back to watch him several more times. You knew who he was, but you never said anything to him or Euphemia."

"I know, I was a coward. Each time I went down after that first, my intention was to stay, to tell him, but I didn't have all the facts. The only thing I knew for sure was that that he didn't know he was adopted. It was a messy situation, but Jack should have told me that Cristiano's parents had died."

"I know, I was mad at him too, but Jack didn't mean any harm. He thought he was doing the best thing for Cristiano by not telling you."

"Yes, well … I guess we all keep secrets for different reasons."

"Keeping secrets, I know all about that."

He paused, thoughtfully. "Tell me more about him, please."

My heart felt lighter just thinking about him. "Where do I start? He sings and plays the guitar beautifully. He's part of a band when he is not working. He looks a lot like you, and he is really good at his job."

"What does he do for a living?"

"He is a flight attendant for Portugal Air. He flies most of the overseas routes but picks up some of the European flights when needed. He is kind and generous, loyal, loving, and right now … a little lost."

He looked concerned but held off on asking the series of questions I knew were inevitable.

"Maya, where did you meet?" he asked, trying to keep the conversation as light as possible.

"We met at the airport in Vancouver while I was on my way to Portugal. I spilt a cup of tea all over myself and he came to my rescue with a handful of towels," I laughed feeling a little embarrassed.

"A charmer and a hero."

I smiled. "Yes, a bit of both. He saved me in more ways than one that day."

Marcos stood up, walked over to the window, and stared out pensively. "Maya, what's going on? Why are you here?"

I took a breath. "Maybe we should have this chat with you and the family together. I started to explain it to Jacinta last night, but I figure it best if we did this one together. Have you read the letter yet?"

"Yes, some of it. I got as far as the morning I had to say goodbye to him."

"I suggest you read the rest of it. It will help you better understand Cristiano and all he went through before he even met me."

Marcos nodded in agreement. When the two of us turned, Jacinta was standing at the door with our coffees. I wasn't sure how much she had heard, but I had to assume everything.

"Dad, mom told me to tell you she is ready to talk."

"Well, Maya, I guess this is my chance to set things right with my lovely wife. Jacinta, can you stay and keep Maya company?"

She smiled, and her eyes sparkled. "Oh, I have so many questions, especially about the blog. I stayed up all night reading it."

"The blog?" Marcos inquired.

"Oh, I wouldn't worry about it Dad. I'll fill you in later with a condensed version." She looked over at me and winked.

I shook my head and was thankful she had brought the whole pot of coffee, as it looked like we were going to need it.

"So, Maya, I thought it was time you meet my moody brother. He won't talk to my dad right now, but I convinced him he should be here for the conversation about the blog."

My face went red and I could hardly believe that the blog was going to be my introduction to his brother and sister. "Sure Jacinta, where is he?"

"Oh, he's hiding in his room, I just have to text him." She sent a note and within a few seconds her phone pinged. "Zeferino is on his way," she said.

"Zeferino?"

"God of the west wind, or something like that. My dad chose it. Mom couldn't decide what to call him when he was born. I think I understand now why it was so hard for her, with having to give Cristiano away and all."

I nodded, not saying a word, just trying to listen.

"You know, we never met any of our grandparents. I always thought it was so weird, but that was one conversation that was not allowed in our house. After a while, I stopped asking questions about them, but Zef pushed our parents. He always wanted to know why we couldn't see them, and like clockwork, when he pushed, mom would start crying and walk out on to the deck. Then Dad would yell at Zef and the door slamming would start. I guess they never felt like they could tell us the truth."

"I don't think anyone knew how to talk about that truth."

"Yes, truth seems to be a high commodity around here, very expensive," Zef said, standing in the open doorway.

"Please come in," I waved to him.

"Miss Wells, my apologies for making a scene last night." Zef was far more composed than the night before. It appeared he had been doing some thinking, trying to assimilate the new information.

"Please, call me Maya. No apology needed. There was nothing easy about any of the conversations that happened last night."

"Yes, that is very true."

There was a pause and a collective deep breath in the room.

"Zef and I spent the evening talking. I told him all about the letter. Then he and I read through the blog together," Jacinta said, nudging her brother.

I covered my face, feeling extremely exposed.

Zef walked over and sat down beside me. "Maya, with what's happened to both you and Cristiano, I can only imagine how you must feel. Having your lives offered up to the world in such a way is a terrible violation. I do have one question though. You have continued to write the blog in your own hand. Why?"

"Truth?" They both nodded. "It sounds silly when I say it out loud, but I am hoping that at some point Cristiano will read the blog and realize that I am trying to find him. That I love him, and that whatever he is going through, he does not have to do it alone. I just want us to leave behind all the horrible parts and pick up where we left off."

"Paris?" Jacinta interjected.

"Yes, Paris." I smiled.

"Do you think he is following at all?" Jacinta asked innocently.

"I am not sure about him, but I did see someone called Kava Root show up and tell Jade off in not so many words. So, I know I have a least one reader on my side.

"No … you have three for sure," she said pointing at herself and her brother.

"Where do you think he is?" Zef asked with genuine concern.

"I don't know," I contemplated aloud and then took a sip of the strong coffee.

Zef wrung his hands, stood up, and started to pace. "Jack should have told my dad about the accident, my dad should have told my mom about seeing Cristiano, and you should have told him right away about us. Maya, where is our brother? My mom cried most of the night; she couldn't even talk to dad. I'm not sure what they are talking about right now, but … it sounds like he had a difficult life."

"Your mom and dad made a good choice, gifting him to his adoptive parents. They loved him more than anything and when they died, his heart shattered. Avo and a few others stitched him back together and it stuck for a while. But over the last few days, everything came undone. What you didn't read on the blog was what happened the night he left."

Zef and Jacinta leaned in waiting for the next part of the story.

"Cristiano flew back early to explain to me that the pictures you saw were not real, that he did not cheat on me. Many people back in my other life were worried about me, including my ex-fiancé, Steven. *He* flew out attempting to save me from something that wasn't even real. Long story short, Cristiano walked in and saw him holding me just after I had had a panic attack and kind of fainted. With everything else that had happened and all he had found out, seeing me with Steven was his breaking point. He jumped to conclusions about what he thought he saw and drove off. I literally ran after him as he drove away that night and eventually followed him here."

"He was here the other day. Why didn't he come to meet us?" Jacinta asked.

"That's a good question. I don't know, but more than likely he didn't want to upset your lives. He was probably worried about you and your brother, and not sure what to say to your mom and dad. I'm guessing he was simply scared. I know I was when the taxi dropped me off at your house yesterday."

"But you came in," Zef said, sounding slightly annoyed.

"Yes, but if I had my own car, I might have driven away."

"I don't think so," Jacinta said giving me a hug.

"Oh Jacinta, thank you."

"You are family now," she said openly.

My shoulders relaxed.

Zef took one last sip of his coffee. "Hey, are you guys hungry? I'm starving. I didn't eat supper last night—too busy slamming doors." We all laughed. "Let's go make some breakfast," he offered as his stomach growled.

I walked back into the main house listening to Jacinta and Zef tease each other and try to figure out what we should eat for breakfast. As I looked around, Marcos and Euphemia were nowhere to be found.

"Mom and Dad must have gone out on one of their *walks*," Zef said sarcastically, looking over at Jacinta.

"Their walks?" I asked curiously.

"Oh, yes," said Jacinta. "Whenever we were little and they didn't want us to hear their arguments or discussions, they would head out into the hills on one of their 'walks', but they always came back holding hands."

"This is going to be a long walk before she holds *his* hand." Zef smirked. "Waffles, I'm in the mood for waffles."

I smiled, remembering Cristiano's story about eating waffles with his parents.

"Waffles would be perfect, but I have to warn you. The only thing I really know how to make is bread and peach pie," I explained apologetically.

"You bake bread *too*?" Jacinta asked.

"Too?" Zef questioned.

"Yes, Cristiano's Avo taught him how to bake bread," she said, looking at her brother. Jacinta then stared at me and opened her eyes with hope. "Does that make her our Avo too?"

I smiled, "Yes, she is everyone's Avo, and I can guarantee you, she will love you very much."

"Oh Zef, did you hear that, we are going to have an Avo."

He laughed, watching his sister dance around the kitchen with a spatula in her hand singing into it like a microphone.

"Cristiano would love this. He will love this," I shared with Zef as he heated up the waffle iron.

He smiled thoughtfully. "So many things make sense now."

"What do you mean?" I asked.

"When we were growing up, sometimes it felt like mom couldn't love me, not completely anyways. She was so open with Jacinta but when it came to me, she always held back. It was like her heart was preoccupied—and it was." He smiled as he poured the batter into the machine.

"I'm so sorry, Zef. This whole thing is such a mess."

"No, not really a mess. Well maybe, but at least we—they—have a chance to set things right. I have an idea of what they are going to say to me this morning, but I can't imagine the conversation they are going to have with Cristiano when they finally meet."

"We just have to focus on finding him first, and then we can figure out the rest," Jacinta said, holding both our hands tightly.

The scent of melted butter and toasted waffles filled me up for the moment as I sat with Cristiano's brother and sister, imagining the day we would all be in the kitchen together.

"Hey, you two, waffles are ready!"

27

Close Encounters

Cristiano

As we stood at the front door of his apartment, Pierre hugged me tightly.

"You don't have to do this," he entreated.

"Yes, I do. Don't worry, it will all be fine," I said, trying to calm his newly-awakened nervous behavior.

"Your parents wouldn't have wanted you to take the risk. I shouldn't have started poking around."

"I asked you to. I can take care of myself. I've been doing it for a long time. I'm just going to say goodbye to them, collect their things, and be back in a few days."

He reluctantly released me from his embrace.

I squeezed his hand tightly. "Pierre, I have to go."

"Be careful. I had to do a lot of digging and pull in some old favors to get the exact coordinates for where the plane went down. And with their luggage resurfacing after all these years … just please watch yourself. We don't know what really happened."

My body jerked. "'What really happened?' What is that supposed to mean?"

Pierre grimaced. "Nothing. Just do what you have to do and come back—Maya loves you and that is not the kind of love you can just walk away from."

Shaking my head, I handed my car keys to Pierre and stepped into the taxi.

The drive to the airport was quiet; so quiet, in fact, that my nerves began to bristle. All I could focus on were Pierre's last words. What did he mean, 'What *really* happened?'

☙

When I passed Portugal Air, memories of saying goodbye to Maya after our magical weekend flooded back. My heart ached, I was torn. I thought about flying to Lisbon instead, fighting for her, becoming the man she believed that I could be, but I wasn't. Not yet anyway. I had to go to Egypt and find a way to let go of the pain, to let go of the past. I had to take back my life and stop waiting for the next wave to crash down and split me in two. If there was even the slightest chance for Maya and me to have a future together, this had to be the first step.

When I arrived at my gate, the flight had been delayed by four hours due to a sandstorm. There wasn't enough time to leave the airport and too much time to just sit and think, so I went in search of something to read and a good cup of coffee.

Maya

While we were finishing breakfast, Euphemia and Marcos came strolling through the door holding hands. They looked around at the dirty kitchen but only smiled.

"Would you like some breakfast? Zef stopped slamming doors long enough to meet Maya and make some waffles," Jacinta laughed.

"Thanks, Jacinta," Zef said, shaking his head. "Yes, we worked everything out and thank goodness, as now I have an alternate sibling to choose from when Jacinta is being annoying."

"That is quite enough, Zef," his father said half-jokingly.

"Oh, don't worry about me Dad, I have lots of ammunition this morning. Look at his hair, and the waffles, well …" Jacinta volleyed back at her brother.

"What's the matter with my waffles?" Zef picked up a waffle, ready to start a morning food fight.

"Enough you two. I am glad to see that things are almost back to normal," Euphemia said, jumping in. "Maya, Marcos and I have talked things through and we both agreed." They looked lovingly at each other, and then she continued, "What can we do to help you find him?"

"That is so kind but that's one of the problems. He's not really lost and I'm not sure he wants to be found."

"Who would he turn to?"

"I don't know." I could feel myself flushing and my breath starting to quicken.

"Yes you do, Maya, think," she said, pushing me.

I sighed, "The most important people in his life have no idea where he is: Jack, Puro, Avo …"

"I'm guessing he is searching for answers. Who would he go to for more information about his parents? His other parents." Marcos smiled with difficulty.

I started pacing around the kitchen, searching through my brain, then it came to me, "The only other person I know would be Pierre La Nou, an old friend of Rosa and Michel's who lives in Paris and works at the Louvre. We saw him just over a week ago," I paused briefly. "Can I take a train from Porto to Paris?"

Jacinta laughed, "You could, but why would you? It would take you forever." She turned to her parents. "Mom? Dad?"

"Of course, Jacinta. Marcos, could you please book the next flight to Paris for Maya?" Euphemia asked, leaving no room for discussion.

"Oh, I couldn't," I objected.

"Yes, you can," Zef said. "Once my mother offers something, there is no going back. Besides, you need help finding my brother, right?"

"Yes, I do."

Euphemia touched her heart. "Maya you came all this way to find him, knocking on a stranger's door and taking a chance that few people would ever do. You unearthed a family secret that should never have been buried and offered us a chance to be whole. I know you love him."

"Mom, you need to relax a little bit," Zef suggested as politely as he could.

"Yes, I know," she said, acknowledging Zef's advice. Then she turned back to me, "Maya, you need to go and bring him home."

"Paris it is then," I exhaled, trying to keep my nerves at bay.

"Can I come?' Jacinta jumped in.

"NO!" both her parents shouted with firm resolution. Zef laughed out loud and shook his head.

"Nice try, Jacinta. You start back at school next week."

"Why do I need school when I could travel and have a life adventure?"

"Next time, Jacinta. I promise," I said, seeing her disappointment. "Anyways, I'm not sure what kind of adventure your brother is taking me on and when I do find him, we will have a few things to work out before he will be able to come and meet you. But I promise, I will tell him all about you."

"I want to see him before I start back at school next week." Tears started to glisten in her eyes. Her heart was so open and true. "Please," she pleaded.

"Jacinta," her mom walked over and wiped her tears.

I took a breath, "I will do my best to find him."

"I know you will," Euphemia responded.

"Maya, your flight leaves in just over two hours. We had better go," Marcos said while grabbing his keys, and a waffle off Zef's plate.

I ran back to the guest house to get my bag, but before I left I added a short blog entry.

Hi Everyone, this entry is for Cristiano, wherever he is.

I never thought I could be this bold but here I go: Life has gifted me with the next step in finding you. I am heading to Paris. I have to believe that the place which brought us closer together in so many ways will offer me the clues I'm looking for, and remember what I wrote to you:

… I promise to love you like no one has ever loved you before; to walk with you into the darkness knowing we will always find the light. To bring you joy and laughter when you least expect it, and to humble myself when I have hurt you and ask for your forgiveness. I'm not perfect, but with you in my life I strive to be a better me and for that reason alone I could love only you … I love only you Cristiano.

Maya

Dalley

"Dalley, Maya is online and just posted a short blog—more of a declaration, mind you."

I threw myself across the bed and rolled on top of him so I could see what she wrote.

"That was very impressive," Ravn laughed. "I didn't know you could dive and roll with such precision."

"I have many talents you don't know about yet, but for now let me read the blog." My insides cringed when I thought about what I had done to her.

"She really loves Cristiano. Does he love her too?" Ravn asked while re-reading the blog over my shoulder.

I chuckled, "Yes, it is quite nauseating and sweet at the same time. Those two should be together. Their love story is the real thing."

"Not like ours you mean?" Ravn raised an eyebrow.

"Let's leave our sordid tale out of this."

"If you say so, but I like our story. And Dalley—I'm happy that we have our own love story to tell."

I looked over and smiled then turned back to the screen.

"Dalley what are you typing?"

"Oh, I just need to add a comment to support her. Even if she doesn't know it's me."

Kava Root: *Paris is beautiful this time of year. Good luck! When he reads this, he would be a fool not to come running back to you.*

Within minutes several other people commented on her blog including Jade.

Jade: *You're right Kava Root. She's going to need all the luck she can get. And I can confirm that he is a fool because he rejected me.*

"Jade is such a wench. When you spoke with her, did she mention where she was flying into?"

"No, but I am sure she'll let us know soon enough. She's not particularly good at keeping secrets."

"Ravn, we need to go to Paris. We need to help Maya find Cristiano."

"That is very noble of you. Are you sure?"

"Yes, I have to make things right with her."

"I'm not going to argue. Paris it is then."

"Thank you, Ravn. I love you," I added before I knew what had popped out from my lips.

He looked over at me standing with my hand over my open mouth. "Of course you do. And I've loved you since the day I saw you wearing sparkly flip-flops before they were even fashionable."

"You remember my footwear?" I blushed unavoidably.

"I remember everything about you."

"Okay, you win." I shrugged, knowing we were venturing into more serious territory.

There was a brief pause as he tapped away on the computer.

"Just booked the flights. We leave very shortly."

"Ravn, can you check the flights that are coming into Paris from Porto? There can't be too many."

"Dalley, you're not going to try and meet up with her at the airport, are you?"

"I am. How else am I going to get her to forgive me? I'll chase her down if I have to."

"For the record, I'm not sure the chasing her down part is a good idea," Ravn warned.

"Well, I am. I know Maya. She'll forgive me if I can just get her to look at me." I wasn't sure if it was true, but I had to try.

28

From Here to There

Maya

I STEPPED ON TO THE plane with no spilled tea, fanfare, or questions. Marcos had booked me into first class and for that, I was very thankful.

As I settled into my seat, I went into my purse to pull out my headphones but realized I had forgotten them back in the limo. I pushed the call button and stared out the window while waiting for a flight attendant.

"Hello, Maya, what are you doing up here in Porto?"

I recognized her but could not place her name.

"Silva," she said, pointing to herself. "I work with Cristiano? We met on the flight to Portugal three weeks ago and again last week when you flew out of Paris," she responded with a little hesitation.

"Yes, I'm sorry Silva." I let out a sigh. "It is good to see a familiar face. I honestly don't remember much from the Paris flight. Not a great night." I wanted to ask her if she had heard from Cristiano, but I held back. "I had a few personal things to take care of up north."

Silva paused, watching me carefully. "Can you imagine, two Wells women in one week on my airplane."

"Two?" I asked with confusion.

"Yes, I had the pleasure of flying with your mom out of Vancouver on the weekend. She is wonderful. What a lovely woman. How was her stay in London? I set her up in one of my favorite hotels."

"I'm not sure, she didn't talk about her trip very much."

"Oh, I'm surprised. She didn't tell you about the young women at the airport who discovered she was your mom?"

"No, she didn't tell me, but I did see the pictures. I am beginning to realize I am not as anonymous as I once was."

"That is one way to put it. In Portugal, you are a little famous right now, Maya, you and Cristiano."

"I don't think so Silva. I wouldn't call it famous, maybe infamous."

"Oh, no, I think we would leave that title to be shared between Jade and Dalley. They're the ones who created this mess."

"I don't know any more how much it matters whose fault it really is."

Silva looked thoughtfully at me and changed the subject. "Well, you can be assured no one will bother you up here. What can I get for you today?"

"Nothing too dramatic, just a set of headphones please."

"Of course. Anything else?"

"A cup of tea would be great if you have it. I tried the coffee at the airport, but it wasn't quite what I was looking for."

She smiled. "I'm sure I can find something that will work." When she returned with my headphones and tea, she knelt beside me and whispered in my ear.

"He loves you. He would never cheat on you. He just wouldn't." She then gave me a little side hug and I couldn't help but well up and let a few tears go.

"I know, Silva, but things are more complicated than you know."

"Everything is more complicated than we would like it to be, Maya."

That's when I took a little leap. "Silva, I don't know if he has contacted you but last Friday night, everything fell apart. It was a perfect storm of unfortunate circumstances and when things got really messy, he ran. He literally ran away."

"Oh, Cristiano, you are better than that," she whispered quietly to herself. "Please be patient with him, Maya. He is very quick to blame himself when something goes wrong."

My heart broke for him and what he had gone through in his life, and I felt desperately guilty that somehow I had made things worse.

"Maya, this isn't your fault, you are the best thing that ever happened to him. Meeting you unlocked a part of his heart he only imagined."

"I know, I felt it too. I never believed I could *want* to feel so connected with anyone. It scared me, but I couldn't say no to him, his voice, his heart, his hair."

We both burst into laughter. It felt good to laugh.

"Maya, never underestimate the power of the people who are put in our path. I don't believe we have only one soul connection in the world, but I do believe that when we meet one, it is our responsibility to take hold of it and nurture it for however long it lasts in your life."

"Do you think ours is over?" I asked with fear rising in my tone.

"No, far from it, I think that right now though, *you* need to be fighting hard for *both* of you. It appears this situation has thrown him out into the wilderness, and he may need some help finding his way back."

"You sound like you know a thing or two about fighting for love."

"Yes, my husband had some similar traits to Cristiano, but at the end, he died with peace in his heart, knowing he was worthy of being loved and had learned to love himself.

My heart ached for the love she lost and for the love I had to find. "Have you heard from Cristiano?"

"No not directly, but I did hear that he submitted a leave of absence request. At present, he's been pulled off all the rosters. I switched my shifts this week, as I don't like to fly overseas without him." She grabbed my hand. "And look where I turned up—on your flight, on this day, working first class. We are always where we are supposed to be."

She paused, then added, "I'm worried about him, too. Any ideas about where he might be?"

"Well I started in Lisbon at his apartment, then up to Porto where I met his birth parents. No luck though. He had been there, but I missed him by a few days. I'm on my way to Paris to see if he is staying with a friend."

"Well, it sounds like a good place to start. Maya, as much as he thinks he doesn't need anyone right now, he does."

c⁊ɔ

The two-hour flight passed quickly as I threw myself into a world of musical distraction. When the announcement was made that we would soon be landing, I removed the headphones and felt the charms on my bracelet tumble into one another. I missed him so much my stomach ached.

As the wheels touched down, Silva skipped over and gave me a hug. "When you find him, make sure to tell him he's worth it. And when he shakes his head and tries to disagree, because he will, tell him I said it is not up for discussion."

To avoid the whirlwind of excited passengers, I waited until the plane was empty, then held my bags closely to my chest and walked off.

As I made my way through the busy airport, the stress and fatigue of the day began to take its toll. All I wanted to do was find the exit and take a taxi into the city. I stopped to catch my breath and studied one of the internal maps posted on a wall, but my life hit an unexpected bump.

Turning around I literally smacked into another traveler who was passing by. The two of us and all our belongings went flying. Both of us ended up on the airport floor. 'Sorry' spilled from my lips before I even saw her face.

"You must be Canadian," the traveler said. "No need for sorry, it was just an accident."

Over the next few seconds, my world shifted into slow motion. The voice was so familiar. Then it happened. I turned my head and our eyes met. A flash of anger surged inside of me like I had never experienced before.

She must have seen it on my face, as the second thing that came out of her mouth was: "Please don't hit me! I just started eating solid food again."

My jaw clenched shut and as much as I wanted to yell and scream, nothing came out. For a moment, I thought I had lost my voice again.

"Funny meeting you here," she laughed nervously.

"Is it really? Is this funny? A chance meeting. You don't do anything by chance. You are calculating and manipulative and I wish I had never met you. You ruined my life."

"Calculating and maybe a little manipulative, but ruined your life? Really? That's a little over the top don't you think, Maya?"

Again I stopped myself from punching her, as I didn't want to get arrested in France, but I did think about it for just a second.

"Maya, listen to me," she yelled while holding her arms up to protect her face. "I made a mistake, a whole series of them. I started the stupid blog because I was too weak to say no to my editor and I kept writing because my ego was liking all the attention. I convinced myself by consuming many glasses of wine and all your chocolate that no one would get hurt. I highjacked your life through your writings and our friendships and embellished the stories for my own benefit."

At that point I stopped gathering my things briefly and just sat there. People walked around us like we were a hazard spill.

Dalley continued: "My editor loved it and the readers were eating it up. I negotiated with myself that I needed your stories more than you needed your privacy. I was wrong. I was jealous."

"Jealous? Jealous of what?" I saw the look on her face. She was desperate, sorry. Looking for forgiveness and a second chance. She kept going, but I was already starting to soften.

"My priorities got all turned around. I lost sight of what was important to us, you and me."

"You? Who are you? I don't know," I said feeling confused by Dalley's flip in personality.

"Yes, you do. I am your friend. I haven't been a good one, well actually a bad one, but I am here now."

"Friends? Really?" I wanted her to work a little harder. I turned away.

"Maya, I'm sorry." Genuine tears began to fall. "I screwed up. For the first time in my life I had a group of real friends and I ruined everything. The truth is, if you walk away, you still have a life with people who care about you."

She was right, I had people who cared, but did she? She waited for me to talk again as I contemplated how much longer I wanted to be mad at her.

"Okay, so answer me this. Where does Jade fit in?" I asked.

"An evil villain," Dalley joked half-seriously.

"Don't make me laugh. Remember I'm still mad at you. Evil villain?"

"Yes, she really is. She is crazy," Dalley said with a smirk.

"Being mad at you is taking too much energy and my Grandma Stella always told me anger causes the worst kind of wrinkles." I paused then added, "Nice hair."

"Thanks, but why aren't you wearing my boots?"

"Oh, Ellen made me promise I wouldn't wear them if I was still mad at you. They are back at Netuno."

"I bet you regret that now—Maya, I am really sorry," she welled up for a moment again, this time holding on to the tears.

I wasn't sure what had changed in her life, but something else had happened besides me.

"I know, I believe you. I don't forgive you a hundred percent yet, but I believe you."

At that point, we were both silent, sitting on the floor in a French airport not knowing what to do or say. Dalley started collecting her things and I stood awkwardly having no idea what to do next. Then, from behind a pillar came a very striking and tall older man who spoke directly to me.

"Maya, thank you for giving her a chance. All she wants to do now is make things right."

"I guess the question is, what is right anymore? And who exactly are you?" I asked, trying to understand how the stranger fit in.

"Feeling a little chippy, Maya?" Dalley added while putting her arm around my shoulder.

"Well, if Dalley Price can cry when she apologizes, then I guess Maya Wells can create an edge."

We both broke into a chuckle and took a breath at the same time.

"This is Dagmar Ravn, the old *friend* of mine from Fiji," she offered, answering my question.

When she said the word 'friend' she threw such a twist on it, I knew she was trying to remind me of something. I thought back to our conversation on the flight over to Portugal when she told me a little about herself.

"Fiji … Fiji?" I smiled, putting the pieces together and remembering the story she told me about the man she met when she was there.

Dalley raised her eyebrows. "Yes, Fiji."

Ravn started to laugh. "Well now that we have established that Dalley and I met in Fiji, can I buy you ladies a drink? I think the two of you have a few things to talk about, and the flight in from Budapest was a little too turbulent for my nerves."

He seemed funny, kind, direct. "I'll take you up on that drink, Dagmar Ravn is it? But I'm not sitting beside her yet," I huffed in her direction.

"Let me know when you're done being mad at me and want to tell me what the plan is to find Cristiano," Dalley volleyed back.

"Find him? You want to help?"

"Yes, that's why you're here, right? At least that is what you wrote in your last post."

"Yes." I said simply, realizing that in some strange way I had led her right to me. "The truth is, I'm not sure what I am doing here, and I don't have a plan." I paused for what felt like forever then jumped back in. "I could use some help if you have any ideas."

We went to an airport pub, and during our time together Dalley talked and talked. She was different. I wasn't sure if it was because of him, but she looked brighter, happier than I had ever seen her. While we ate, she came clean about everything from taking pictures of my journal to eating all my chocolate bars. She apologized for tearing our room apart in Netuno and for leaving everyone to pick up all the pieces.

After she had emptied her pile of guilt on the table, I needed to know more about our own personal villain.

"So, tell me more about Jade? How crazy is she?"

"Certifiable," Dalley replied. "And now more than ever since the Netuno deal fell apart. Her dad fired her, kicked her out of the company, and cut her off. By the way, nice work on saving Netuno. I need to hear more about that later."

A rush of pleasure washed over me as I heard about Jade's misfortune and then a trickle of guilt followed because I felt so happy.

"Maya, don't start going soft on me. She got what she deserved."

"I know, but did her dad really kick her out of the business?"

"Yes, Ravn did an 'interview' with her yesterday. She is furious—at you. She kind of blames you for everything."

"He?" I turned to Ravn. "You did an interview with her?"

"Yes, Dalley wanted to find out what was happening, and so I gladly obliged—being a journalist and all that."

"I get the feeling more happened in Fiji between the two of you than you shared with me before."

"You told her about me?" Ravn's eyes brightened. "That is so cute."

"I am not cute, but yes," she said, feigning annoyance.

"I knew it. You never forgot me either." He leaned over and kissed her with such familiarity, it was like the two of them had never been apart. The relationship already had grooves of understanding and acceptance.

My face betrayed me. I was the one jealous now, and sad.

Ravn released Dalley and she studied me carefully before saying another word.

"Maya, after I left Netuno and ended up in Budapest, I didn't know what to do. I was a mess and hit rock bottom. While floundering around down there, I realized that the first real mistake I made was the day I left Dagmar in the airport."

"I told you, only my mother calls me Dagmar."

Dalley smiled.

"When I called Ravn, he dropped everything to be with me to help me find my way through this mess. I know I played a part in this situation with Cristiano leaving and I will do whatever I can to help you find him," she stated earnestly.

Dalley's heart was sincere and it helped to dull the pain about Cristiano's whereabouts.

"Thank you, but I can't let you wear all the blame. Cristiano is a complicated man. My only goal now is to find him, introduce him to his family, and bring him home."

Ravn coughed to get our attention. "Let's see if we can hasten things along for you, Maya. No one should ever have to wait as long as I had to to set things right with the person they love," he added with a serious tone.

Dalley squeezed his hand then gave me a nudge. "So, where do we start? The guy's not a master spy. We should be able to track him quite easily."

I adjusted myself on the bar stool and momentarily got lost watching the crowds as they rushed down the large corridors trying to catch their planes.

"Did you see that, Dalley?" I shouted.

"See what?"

"I don't know." I stood up and craned my head into the path of oncoming foot traffic.

"Maya!!!" Dalley yelled while pulling me back.

"I thought I saw …," I said while continuing to scan the ever-changing crowds.

"Who?"

"Just my mind playing tricks on me." I peered into the sea of people, looking, just looking.

"Well you almost got yourself decapitated in the process. I was asking you before—where do we start?"

I shook off the moment, then went into my wallet and pulled out his card. "We start at the Louvre with a lovely man named Pierre La Nou."

29

Not Moving

Maya

Driving in the taxi with Dalley and Ravn was quite surreal. I could hardly believe I was in Paris, *with* Dalley, after everything she had done, but I had to give her a chance. Besides, if I was going to find Cristiano, I needed her help. My sleuthing abilities were nonexistent, and it felt like my memories of being in Paris with Cristiano were nipping at my heels and not allowing me to think clearly.

As the city skyline came into view, I touched my tear of bravery which hung quietly around my neck. A surge of emotion began searching for an exit plan, but I didn't want to cry. Not there, not in front of them. So, I pressed the pendant into the nape of my neck, causing a reactive cough that snuffed the tears' plans for escape.

I opened the window and let the afternoon air carry me to our next destination. When we arrived at the Louvre, my heart began to beat faster, and a wave of doubt hit me hard.

"This is crazy, Dalley. I need to leave."

"Maya, this is our only lead. We need to talk to this La Nou fellow. Trust your instincts. This was the first thought you had."

Ravn interjected, "The truth is, Maya, many times when I was out in the field, researching a story, the only thing I could trust was my instinct. It kept me alive more than once."

"But I'm not a journalist or a detective. I don't have instincts like that," I said, feeling deflated.

"That's where I think you are wrong," Dalley said. "I think your instincts about me were spot on when we met. You were open but had an air of caution. With Cristiano, your instincts told you to just go for it. What about the first day when we were in Lisbon? And we went to the market. You trusted the taxi driver, knowing he was going to come back."

"Well I hoped he would."

"Hey, I am on a roll here. Oh, and just a couple of hours ago, you trusted me when you had no reason to. That has to be instinct."

"… or insanity, but let's go with instinct."

Before Dalley and I could continue Ravn interrupted, offering up some journalistic advice. "Before I go into any new situation I like to know about the people I am dealing with. Maya, tell me about your first impression of Pierre La Nou."

I thought back to the first time I saw him. "He was refined with a little edge around him, and clearly had a strong attachment to Cristiano and his parents. He loved them like family. He admired them. But a part of him looked lonely, and when he gave me his card and told me to call him about anything, I believe he meant it."

"That's good. Let's go with that then," Ravn said as the taxi dropped us off. While walking across the parking lot towards the museum, my heart was pounding in my chest. I tried to push away the memories of that day Cristiano and I spent at the Louvre, but I was losing the battle and coming undone. I stepped over a curb and started to fall, barely catching myself. It was then that I saw it: A familiar vehicle parked near a loading bay. By the time Dalley and Ravn saw that I was gone, I had dropped my bag and broken into a full sprint.

Dalley yelled, "Maya, where the hell are you going?"

"It's him, he's here," I screeched.

By that point, I had garnered some attention from a few guests and security. But they didn't see a desperate woman trying to find the love of her life followed by her two friends. All they saw were three people running at top speed towards an open cargo bay behind the museum. Not suspicious at all.

When I arrived at his car, I jumped into the driver's seat and frantically started searching through his glove box, throwing papers around and looking for something, anything. I found receipts for gas in Portugal, Spain and France and the passenger seat was covered in breadcrumbs.

"Spain? He went to Spain without me?" I was furious. I wanted to see Spain with him. "He must be inside."

"Maya, what are you doing?" Dalley yelled, highly aware of the approaching security. "Have you lost your mind? Get out of that car right now!"

"I can't. It's his. You were right, Dalley. He's here. I'm not going anywhere until he comes out."

"Maya, whether he's here or not, it is best if you get out of the car right now," Ravn insisted. "We are no longer dealing with just security, but the police are on their way too."

I was crazed though. It didn't matter what anyone said. I was not getting out of the car until he came back. I put my hands on the wheel, closed my eyes, and refused to let go.

"Maya, this is not the time. We have to find Pierre and he will help us find Cristiano." Dalley tried to convince me but I was immovable.

"I told you I am not going anywhere," I screamed.

By that time both security and the police were yelling at all of us. I didn't realize but Ravn and Dalley were on the ground and the officers were trying to uncurl my fingers from the steering wheel. Ravn was trying to explain in his broken French what was going on, but the situation was quickly getting out of hand. Everyone was yelling at me in French and English, but I didn't care. I wasn't moving. I tightened my fingers on the leather-bound steering wheel and closed my eyes tighter. I could feel him through the warmth of the leather, and I wasn't letting go. I couldn't, I literally couldn't. That's when it got silent.

I'm not sure how long I sat in the car, but it was not until I heard a familiar voice coming from the passenger seat that I was willing to open my eyes.

"Well, you do know how to make an entrance, Miss Wells. First the purple velvet couch and now Le Louvre security and the police as you take my car hostage."

"Your car?" I answered with a puzzled look.

"Temporarily, until he returns."

"Returns?" I was crushed. "He's not here?" I asked, the crack in my heart widening.

It was then that he waved everyone away, and Ravn explained as best as he could what was going on. The security looked annoyed, but the two police officers smiled and said something about *l'amour*. Soon the crowd dispersed, and we were the only ones left, Pierre with his hand on my shoulder and me still grasping onto the steering wheel.

"He's not here," I repeated, but that time as a statement. The words that fell next from my lips started as a gentle ooze, then became frenetic. "Well isn't that perfect. Of course he's not here. That would be too easy, and why would he want to make it easy on me? He comes into my life. Makes me fall in love with him. Feeds me magic bread. Makes me think I might have more to offer to the world than sitting at a desk. Then he just runs off when things get complicated. What's wrong with me? Why wouldn't he fight for me—for us?" I stopped and sighed. "Pierre, where is he?"

Pierre broke into a smile. "The two of you are quite a pair, do you know that?" he chuckled.

"How can you laugh?" I asked, starting to find my quieter self. "What do you mean?"

"Oh, both of you love each other and yet you cannot trust yourselves enough to accept that you are worthy of being loved by someone else."

Pierre's words stopped me short.

"He loves you Maya, but he is confused. He didn't fight for you not because he didn't love you enough. He ran because he thought he didn't deserve to win."

I was dumbfounded. "I don't understand."

"When you came into his life, he was offered a flicker of what it was like to hold love in his hands and in his heart. Then your lives were shaken by a series of facts and fiction and he was flooded with self-doubt and anger, but it soon turned into something else: a need to find the truth—his truth.

"After he left Netuno that night, he realized he had unfinished business with both sets of parents. And when he found himself on my doorstep, he soon discovered that before he could take any steps towards his birth parents or back to you, he had to deal with Rosa and Michel's death first. He needed to collect their belongings and say goodbye.

"His parents' bodies have never been found as most of the plane was incinerated on impact. It had been assumed that their luggage went down with the plane, but we recently discovered that their bags didn't make it on to the flight. The luggage has been in storage this whole time. The contents of the storage unit are being auctioned within the next day or so. I booked a flight for him and he left today for Cairo."

"Cairo? The airport? Today?"

"Yes, Maya, today," Pierre assured me.

I felt numb. "It was him. He walked right past me." I stopped talking and could feel every part of me shutting down, shutting out all the voices and the sounds and turning inside myself.

"Maya? Maya! What's the matter? What is it?" Pierre called my name, then shook my shoulder gently, but I ignored him. I liked the place I was going. I didn't want to come back. It was quiet. It felt almost peaceful. It was the opposite of everything I had been feeling for days.

"What are you doing?" I heard Dalley ask angrily. Her voice sounded far away.

Pierre stuttered, looking for the words, but clearly my state of mind had caught him off guard.

"What did you say to her? Something is very wrong. What did you say to her? The very last thing," Dalley yelled at Pierre.

Pierre was flustered and I was frozen.

"I told her I put Cristiano on a flight to Cairo, just a few hours ago."

"Ohhh crap," Dalley uttered. "Ravn, remember when I pulled her back while sitting on the bar stools? She thought she saw something. It was him." I felt a hand on my shoulder. "Maya, snap out of it. This is no time to disappear!" Then I felt a sharp sting on my cheek.

"What the hell, Dalley? You slapped me," I cried, almost jumping out of the seat.

"Yes, and I would do it again. There is no time for indulgence or feeling sorry for yourself. Get out of his car right now."

"This must be Miss Dalley Price," Pierre interjected. "I have been reading all about you in the last couple hours."

"So, you've read the blog?" she said curtly.

Pierre chuckled. "Yes, most of it. Quite the situation. Looks like you have some fans who think your methods are quite inspiring."

"Well, I am trying to change my ways. Just ask Maya," Dalley said, pulling her shoulders back trying to defend herself against Pierre's cynicism.

I rubbed my cheek while Dalley informed Pierre of her new-found noble pursuit of friendship.

Then Ravn stepped in. "I don't know about anyone else, but I think we should find a place to stay for the night and then go for a drink," he said.

"No, take me to the airport, I'm leaving for Cairo right now," I insisted.

"No, Maya, you're not," Ravn said simply.

"Yes, I am," I barked defiantly.

He smiled and said, "We need to know more about what is happening before any of us jumps on a plane to find Cristiano. Besides, like I said, I need a drink, some food, and a good night's sleep. We need to make a plan and do things the right way."

I stepped out of Cristiano's car, but not before I ran my hand one last time around the steering wheel, following the indentations his fingers had made in the leather.

"Ravn, I think you're right." My stomach grumbled and I realized that although I'd ordered something at the airport, I didn't remember even taking a bite. "Maybe it is best if I have something to eat and avoid fainting again. Twice in one week is too much."

"Yes, let's try and avoid any more drama this afternoon, shall we?" Dalley teased.

Pierre stepped in.

"I think that is a good idea, Maya." He looked from me to Dalley and then to Ravn. "I finish here at 7:30. I'll make reservations for 8:00 at one of my favorite restaurants. Please text me the name of your hotel and I'll swing by and pick the three of you up."

As we walked away, I rubbed my cheek. "Hey, Dalley, are we even now? Can we agree no more punching or slapping?"

She threaded her newly darkened hair around her ear and looped her arm in mine. "I agree, but only if you come shopping with me and help me find a new pair of boots. I gave my favorite pair away to a friend of mine just the other day."

I smirked. "You must like her, or you felt *really* guilty about something."

"Maybe a little bit of both," she said, smiling.

In the end, I sent Dalley shopping without me, asking her to come by later and show me her new boots. My hotel room was small, but it had a tub and that was all I needed. After hearing about Cristiano being in Egypt, my insides had started to churn, and my anxiety began to prickle under my skin. I knew something was not right but I wasn't able to do anything to help him, at least until the morning.

After soaking in the tub, I ordered a café au lait, wrapped myself in a towel, and slipped Christopher out of my purse. I needed something to do and Christopher was the perfect distraction.

Dear Friend,

Just months ago I was planning a wedding to a man I didn't love and sitting at a desk answering phones and selling sprinkler systems back in Peachland, and today I almost got arrested in the parking lot at the Louvre.

Truth is, it got a little crazy. I don't remember much except that the police had their hands on their guns. The things a girl will do for love, hey. How embarrassing, all because I refused to get out of Cristiano's car. Not really refused—I just couldn't. My fingers embedded themselves into the leather. It was like I could almost feel him holding my hand.

Not sure what I'm feeling right now. I think a mixture of determination, fear, and a dose of anger that keeps rearing its ugly head every time I think of the whole situation. I'm worried about him and I'm mad at him. I wonder if my parents ever got mad at each other. They went through a lot, but I never heard them fight. I don't know … All I do know is that I have to find a way to shift the anger, but it may take me seeing his face, understanding what's really going on in his head.

Be positive, Maya. You know you will find him. You have no choice.

He loves me, I know he does.

Maya

I could feel a chill settling over me and thought it best to stop feeling sorry for myself and get dressed for our evening out. I was sure Pierre had more to tell us and I needed to look and feel the best I could.

I went into my bag and pulled out one of the lovely outfits that my shopping friends at the train station in Lisbon helped me pick out, as well as the diamond earrings Cristiano had purchased for me in Paris. I dressed slowly, thinking about him and briefly letting go of my worries. Instead, I allowed my love to take the lead at least for a little while.

The earrings sparkled and his bracelet sang. If he was listening, I had to believe he could hear me.

I closed my eyes. "Cristiano, I love you."

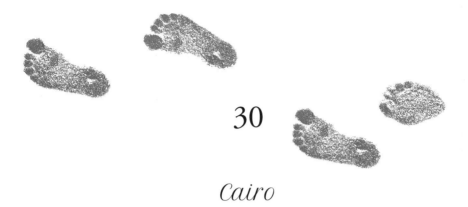

30

Cairo

Cristiano

"I love you too," fell from my lips as the lights in the cabin dimmed.

I wasn't sure why I had said it, but the elderly woman sitting beside me smiled and nodded her head like it was completely natural.

"Love travels beyond time and space if you are open to receiving it." Her words floated in my direction.

She closed her eyes and drifted off, leaving me wondering. The flight seemed long and I started to feel restless. I tried to distract myself with random thoughts, but my mind kept drifting back to the last few conversations I had with Pierre before getting into the taxi.

He talked about Maya loving me, and then made some cryptic comment about what really happened with my parents. Pierre's words were like splinters in my fingers. I needed to deal with both.

I shifted in my seat, wishing I had more space but finally allowing myself to close my eyes and settle into a restless slumber. A sudden drop in air pressure jolted me out of my rest and caused a collective gasp to ring out through the cabin.

"I don't want to run away from anything anymore," I whispered, as Pierre's words rolled around in my thoughts.

My seat mate opened her eyes and touched my hand. "Well, I guess it is time to turn around and face what's been chasing you," she said.

Before I had a chance to respond, we began a rather dramatic descent into Cairo. Extreme turbulence left passengers tightening their seatbelts and hanging on to the arm rests with pressured grips. Everyone, that was, except my new elder friend who was having the time of her life.

"I feel so alive when the plane drops like that; sometimes the flights are so boring, no bumps at all," she smiled broadly.

I chuckled. As a flight attendant, I'd never had anyone ask me for more turbulence.

As the plane rolled to a stop I realized I did not know the name of the adventurer who sat beside me.

"I'm sorry, how rude of me, what is your name?"

"My friends call me A.D."

"A.D.?"

"Yes, just A.D."

"Well, it has been a long time since I laughed that hard, A.D."

"*Merci*, my new friend, and you are?"

"Cristiano."

"And what is her name? The one you love."

I paused, almost afraid to say it, "Maya, Maya Wells."

"Now, doesn't that feel better?" she said, patting my leg.

We walked off the plane together. Her last words to me were, 'Stop running and start walking. You will learn more along the way and may even have some fun. And, when you are ready, you will turn around, and face what's been chasing you, but you don't have to do that part alone.'

I smiled as she melted into the crowd.

⁓

The dry desert air hit me as I stepped out of the airport. It was a different world. I had never been to Egypt, never set foot in the country where my parents died, but there I was, standing alone, trying to find my ride to the hotel. It was early evening and the sun had already set. The energy on the sidewalk was frenetic with tourists looking for transportation and drivers doing whatever they could to convince people to come with them. Pierre had said to look for an older gentleman; his taxi light would be off. I was to offer him 50 LE to get to the hotel but settle on 100 so he'd know it was me.

While searching for Pierre's driver, I locked eyes with a man trying to hide behind a pillar. It felt like he was staring right at me but when I looked again, he was gone.

The hair on my arms stood up and I walked to the other side of the platform. I had been all over the world, but something was different about that place. I walked a few steps away from all the voices and saw an older man standing by a taxi singing to himself.

His taxi light was off. "Are you driving tonight?" I didn't want to mention Pierre's name quite yet.

"It depends on who you are." He pulled out his phone, looked at the screen, then smiled back at me with recognition. "Yes, what is your price?"

"50 LE?"

"Is that all he can afford?" he shook his head, smiling.

I started to laugh. "No, but he told me to start there and settle on 100."

"Sounds fair."

"Where to, Cristiano?" he asked casually as we got into the taxi, but not before I caught him doing a visual sweep of the area as if he was looking for something or someone.

"Thank you for coming to pick me up," I said with gratitude.

"Where are we going?" he asked again.

I went into my bag and found the paper where Pierre had written his notes—Pyramid Lofts Homestay."

"Interesting choice. You here to look at the pyramids?"

"No. Pierre didn't tell you why I was coming?"

"No details, just that you had to take care of some family business. Sounds interesting. I hope it all goes smoothly."

The rest of the drive was uncomfortably silent.

When we arrived at the hotel, he pulled my bag from the trunk then touched my arm, startling me.

"Please be careful Cristiano. Twenty years is a long time, but Egypt has a longer memory."

"Thank you for your concern." I paused for a moment. *What was he talking about? Twenty years?*

He continued, "If anyone asks why you are here, just tell them you are a tourist."

I was not one to buy into cloak and dagger stories, but the driver started to worry me. I had a feeling he knew more about my situation than he was saying.

"Can I hire you privately to drive me for the next few days?"

He took a breath, rolling the offer around in his head. "I'll have to think about it," he said with a nervous tone flooding his voice. "I'll come back in the morning and let you know."

I had obviously upset him, so I waved goodbye and stepped towards a little café attached to the hotel. As I turned to watch him drive away, I saw the man from the airport again. On any other day, I would have thought it a coincidence. It might have been reckless, but I decided to confront him. As I walked towards him, he turned away, then started to run.

"What the hell? Why are you running?" I yelled. I thought about going after him, and even took a few steps, but decided against it.

I was exhausted and not in Egypt to get involved in other people's problems; I was just there to solve a couple of my own. But when I turned back to the hotel, my driver friend had returned. He waved me over.

"Please get in. I do not think it is safe for you to stay here."

"Thank you, but I will be fine," I said with some annoyance. I was getting frustrated with other people worrying about me so much.

"No, this is my country. I do not think so. Pierre would kill me if anything happened to you. Please get in and I will take you somewhere safe."

"I don't know you."

"You know me enough and I know you better than you think. I am a friend."

I was right. He had been holding out on me. Hoping it was the right choice I crawled back into the taxi.

Egyptian music now played quietly in the background as we drove away. His driving was fast and evasive. I tried to convince myself it was just a typical ride through the streets of Cairo, but I knew better. He soon turned down a darkened street and shut off the engine.

Breathing out heavily he sighed, "I think we lost them."

"Lost them? Someone was chasing us?" I asked with growing concern.

"Did he not tell you anything about the time before?" The man looked genuinely concerned.

"Who? Pierre? The time before what?" I could feel an edge forming in my tone and my anger was not far behind.

The man looked surprised at my response. "Pierre asked me to keep an eye on you, to make sure nothing happened to you while you were here."

I'm not sure if it had been all the travel or just the stress of the previous few days, but I bit hard into my response. "Okay, if you don't start explaining what you are talking about right now, I'm getting out of this car and both you and Pierre can go to hell. Start from the beginning. How long have you known Pierre La Nou?"

There was a long silence, and for a moment, I held on to the door handle preparing to leave.

"We've been friends for over twenty years," he sighed. "We met here in Egypt while he was doing some research for a specific item. My name is Ammon."

With a deep breath, I let go of the handle, knowing I was too tired and confused to be angry anymore. I just needed to know what was happening, "It's nice to meet you Ammon, but you have to tell me what is going on."

He started the car and as we drove slowly down the darkened street, several more questions began emerging.

"Come on Ammon. If you were sent to help me, please explain. You must know more."

"Truthfully, I am not sure what I am supposed to be explaining. I'm confused why Pierre didn't tell you everything before you got here," he sighed loudly again.

I could see the man was distressed. "Okay, Ammon, let's start with this. I am going to ask you some simple questions. Please just do your best to answer them."

"I will," Ammon answered with a nod.

"You know Pierre La Nou, but did you also know my parents?"

"Yes," he stated. "Pierre set us up much like he did with you and me. I was hired as their guide when they were here in Cairo all those years ago."

"Oh …" was all I could utter. I thought I was prepared to hear the next part of their story, but as Ammon began, thoughts of them in Cairo flooded my mind and my anxiety began to rise.

"I will get to their story, but first I just have to say I could hardly believe it when I saw you because you look nothing like your parents."

"Yah, well, I was adopted."

"That explains that, doesn't it," was all he could say. Clearly, he too was just finding out about my complicated past. "Hmm, interesting. Did Pierre know?"

"No, actually, neither did I until just a few weeks ago. This is all pretty new to me."

"Well, you just never know what secrets people are keeping, do you?" He shook his head.

I looked at him and half-smiled. We both paused, took a breath, and he launched into their story. "My wife and I spent a lot of time with your parents while they were here. Actually, every day. And every day they talked about you. By the time they were getting ready to leave, it felt like we knew you."

I smiled, imagining my mom talking to his wife. "She always liked to talk about me."

"Your mom and dad loved you very much. While they were here, we showed Michel and Rosa around Cairo and took them to every relic and coffee shop for miles around. There were so many laughs. Your dad was very funny."

"My dad was funny? I don't remember that." I searched my memory for something to grab on to but could only see the burnt waffles and gentle smiles he gave my mother. My heart felt happy and sad as Ammon continued to tell me stories about their trip to Cairo and all that they did during the last week of their life.

"Ammon, I don't understand something though. Although I was young, they always explained to me what kind of artifact they were picking up before they left on their trips. When I think back though I can't remember anything about that trip."

I searched my memories for that last day. They weren't themselves; something was different. "Do you know what they were looking for?"

He let out an exasperated breath. "Yes and no. I suspected it was the same relic Pierre tried to acquire several years before I ever met them, but I never asked, and they never offered to tell me."

"Why? They weren't doing anything illegal … were they?"

"No, no, they were good people, but they were not the only people searching for the artifact. I think they just wanted to keep my family safe."

"Safe? Ammon, none of this makes sense. My parents collected antiquities. They always described what they did as very boring."

Ammon shot out a quick breath. "There was nothing boring about what your parents did for a living." He paused. "Many years ago, when Pierre was in Egypt, before your parents came, he was looking for a specific relic. While following some leads, he discovered that he was not the only one searching for this item. Due to a confrontation with a certain group of people, he had to abandon his search and make a quick exit from the country. A few years later, your parents returned on his behalf. They never told me exactly why they were here, but I assumed they were looking for the same piece Pierre had been searching for."

Anger shot through me. "So, Pierre sent my parents to Egypt to find what he could not?" My stomach soured. "What were they all looking for?"

Ammon paused.

"Just tell me already." My irritation rose. "What difference does it make at this point!"

He swallowed hard, almost afraid to say it out loud. "Pierre said it was like a ghost relic. A piece of history that had taken on a life force of its own. It has appeared and disappeared over time. There are no photographs, only sketches and stories."

The hairs on the back of my neck bristled.

"Pierre was quite obsessed with it. After he left Egypt, he phoned me regularly over the years, asking if I had heard any news."

Exasperated and exhausted, I rudely interrupted, "What was it then? Jewels? A sculpture?"

Ammon paused again, as if he was not sure if he should say it aloud.

"A hair fork," he whispered.

"A hair fork?" I laughed. "Like a woman's hairpin? A stupid hairpin?" I threw the words at him.

"Oh, no, Cristiano, not just any hair pin, but supposedly the hair pin that Cleopatra VII used to kill herself."

"You have got to be joking. Cleopatra? This is all about some dead queen's hair piece?"

But Ammon was not joking. He was serious, and I had obviously insulted him horribly.

"I'm sorry Ammon, that was rude. My parents did teach me better than that. Please continue."

"This is no joke, Cristiano. Cleopatra is woven into the fabric of Egyptian history. There are many versions of her demise, but Pierre believes she died at her own hands after dipping the tips of her hair fork into the venom of an asp. Then, at the perfect time, she pricked herself to avoid the humiliation of capture by her enemies."

My body collapsed into the taxi seat. "What am I doing here? What does this have to do with me and my parents?"

My anger began to fade and was replaced with resignation. "This whole thing is ridiculous, Ammon. Please just take me to my hotel."

"There is nothing ridiculous about this story, Cristiano. It has been over two thousand years, and the tales of Cleopatra whirl around our country as if she were still alive. I can assure you there are people who take the topic of our 'old queen' very seriously."

"Like I said, I have nothing to do with this. I just came here to say goodbye to my parents, collect their luggage, and go home."

"Their luggage?" A look of surprise crossed Ammon's face.

"Well, now it looks like I know something you don't. Pierre is quite the secret keeper."

"Yes, it appears he is. But I am sure he has his reasons."

"Oh yes, I am sure he has an explanation for everything," I snapped back. "So, simply, he sent my parents down to Egypt to collect his relic and they died."

"Your parents and Pierre were best friends. When they died, a part of Pierre died too. You must know that."

"I don't know anything except that they died because of him."

"No, they died in a tragic plane crash."

"Whatever. It doesn't matter now," I barked back.

Ammon was quiet, then changed the subject.

He smiled. "My wife and I had them for supper the last night they were in Egypt. They talked about you as the light of their lives; they were so proud of you. I didn't understand all the English back then, but my wife explained it to me. She laughed at the stories they told about you and cried when your mother talked of how much she loved you. We hoped that one day we would get a chance to meet you."

"Can I meet your wife?" A dose of adrenaline shot through me with the anticipation of speaking to one of the last people who talked to my mom.

Ammon's face softened and saddened. "I'm sorry Cristiano, she passed away six years ago."

"Oh." My body went flat. "I am sorry for your loss Ammon. Can you tell me more about the night before they left?"

"Of course."

"That night at supper, your mother and father had a disagreement. She wanted to go home a few days early. I remember her saying they had found everything they needed, and she felt like they were being followed. Your father disagreed with her, saying she was just missing you. He desperately wanted to see the pyramids, but finally relented about going home early, as she became quite upset. So, he called Pierre that night and let him know they needed to come home. Pierre then booked a flight for the next day."

"That day at the airfield, your mom was so excited." Ammon continued. "All she could talk about was how much she missed you. We stayed to watch the plane take off." He paused.

"You could see the explosion from miles away." His eyes filled with tears. "My wife cried for days wishing your dad had convinced your mom to stay. When I called Pierre, he fell apart; he felt responsible. He loved them very much.

"It was quiet for a few days, then about a week after the crash, people started knocking on our door asking questions about where I had driven your parents. We concluded that they must have found the hair fork while they were treasure hunting, and that the men following them were the same people who had driven Pierre out of Cairo several years before."

I sat frozen in the seat. This all seemed so far-fetched. Impossible. My parents weren't treasure hunters, they were simple university professors, teaching classes and collecting items for museums and private collections.

"Well, what happened to the hair fork then?"

Ammon shrugged his shoulders. "We don't know. My wife and I assumed the relic went down with them in the plane but when I got a call from Pierre that you were coming to Cairo, I wondered if he had found it. I wondered if he was sending you to retrieve it for him. I didn't ask him any questions and all he told me was that you needed my help."

"Do you think the relic could be in their luggage?" I asked.

"I don't know, but I think someone else thinks it's possible."

"Why? Why would you say that?"

"Cristiano, maybe it is best if I just take you back to the airport. I will call Pierre and let him know it is too dangerous."

"No!" I yelled. "I have to be here. I have to say goodbye to them. I need to see where their plane went down. I need to collect the last of their things. I don't care about some stupid conspiracy theory."

"Okay then, we need to get smart. I need to know exactly what happened since you got off the plane."

I thought back, "When I stepped outside of the airport, I was looking for you, your taxi. There was a man behind a pillar. I thought he was staring at me and then he disappeared. I saw him again outside of the hotel. I went to chase after him, but he ran away. Then you came and here we are. Do you think this man knows who I am? Who my parents were? Is he the one looking for the relic?"

"Oh, Cristiano it is not just one person who is looking. It is the Ptolemites."

"The Ptolemites?" I smirked slightly. "Who are they?"

"This is no joke; they are the descendants of Cleopatra. They believe their royal position was stolen from them two thousand years ago and are on a mission to restore their place in history. They believe Cleopatra was murdered and did not in fact die by her own hand. They think that somehow the hair fork could be proof of how she died. With that proof, their family would be restored to some kind of power."

"Okay, so somehow the Ptolemite zealots are tracking me now? Is that what you are saying?"

"I know this sounds impossible, Cristiano."

"No, not impossible, but ridiculous. And if it is true, how could Pierre not have told me the whole story? If you knew what I've been through in the last three weeks …" I smiled a little bit and rubbed my forehead, trying to make my newly formed headache go away.

"Either the Ptolemites think you have the fork, or that you know how to get it."

I laughed. "I simply came to say goodbye to my parents. To visit where the plane went down. When Pierre told me about the luggage, I thought it would be good to collect their things and maybe find my dad's watch. He hated to fly with it and always had my mom pack it away for safe keeping," I said, looking longingly out the window.

"Okay, okay, do not worry. Tonight, we will lay low. We'll go back to my place. No communication with anyone until tomorrow, not even with Pierre."

"Oh, that's not a problem. I have a feeling if I talked to him right now, I might say something I regret."

31

Sambuca Returns

Maya

A KNOCK CAME ON THE DOOR.

"Maya, I'm back from shopping." Dalley paused. "I'm going to take a little nap. Can you text Pierre the name of the hotel?"

I waited for a moment, smoothed my hair down, then got up and opened the door.

"What took you so long?" she asked, sounding slightly annoyed.

"I was deciding if I wanted to talk to you."

"Really?" she asked, showing some uncharacteristic vulnerability.

"No. I'm just teasing, Dalley."

"Oh, I knew that. You're not funny though."

I sighed and looked down at her feet. "Where did you find *those* boots?"

Dalley shifted gears completely in response to my question. "Hilarious, aren't they? I couldn't resist. Not quite the leather I was looking for, but they are very sparkly. A statement on their own, wouldn't you agree? Talking about statements, where did you find that outfit? That's not one of ours. Have you been cheating on me? Letting someone else pick out your clothes for you?" She fell back to the wall, feigning righteous indignation.

I blushed, then cracked a smile. "You're right, you caught me red handed. After I ran away and started searching for Cristiano with just the clothes on my back, I was left to my own devices to clothe myself properly. Then, as luck would have it, I was saved at the train station by some retail shopping gods who helped me out of my clothing predicament."

"You look good," she added earnestly. Then she turned on her sparkly heals and headed to her room. "Off for my nap. Can you wake me when Pierre is on his way? I only need a few minutes to get ready."

❧

I went back into my room to text Pierre.

Hi Pierre, I hope you had a good afternoon. We are staying at the Citadines Saint Germain des Pres Paris.

Oui, I know it well. I will be there around 7:50.

Have you heard from him? Has he landed? Does he know I am here?

His flight landed a couple of hours ago. A contact of mine will let me know when he is settled at the hotel. We should hear something soon.

Oh okay.

Maya don't worry. Cairo is a very busy place.

I don't know what that means 'a busy place'.

It means there are no timelines there. All we can do is wait and pray.

Pray? Why would we need to pray?

No reason. It's just a good thing.

I'm not so sure about that. God and I are still trying to work out a few things.

❧

I left the hotel with just a walk in mind, but as I turned right, I started running and didn't stop until I looked up and found myself at the one place I was *not* trying to find. It was like God was having a little fun with me. I walked up the steps of the old church. It was not grand like Notre Dame, but had a humility and beauty of its own. When I walked through the doors, I felt like I was suspended in time, surrounded by something I could not describe. So, I did what any good wayward Catholic would do: I bent down and started to talk. Not pray, just talk.

"Dear God, it's me Maya. Not sure how I ended up here tonight, but I'm starting to get the idea that there might be more going on out there in the universe than I wanted to admit. I guess a thank you is in order. Since I left home, I have experienced so many different emotions in such a short time. I didn't know I could feel all those things, or maybe I did but I was too afraid to allow it. I've been scared, sad, mad, happy, euphoric, confused, but not lonely. Is that because of you? This is the third time in less than three weeks I have taken off running and ended up with you. That cannot be a coincidence. So here I am. I need some clarity and strength to make the right decision. I know I am responsible for my own life, but …"

"No buts …"

My heart leapt out of my chest as the voice boomed all around me.

"Hello?" I looked up into the intricate stained glass ceiling, waiting for a response, willing for the first time in my life to truly accept 'anything' that was going to happen.

When the tap came on my shoulder I almost fainted, not expecting Him to touch me.

"Maya? Are you okay? I'm so sorry to have startled you."

I turned around and saw Ravn standing over me. "Ravn? What are you doing here?"

"Well, let's start with this: I am not God. I saw the way you looked up when I interrupted you. Just a little bit funny. Dalley is going to love this story."

"Oh, I am sure she will."

We both laughed then took a seat on the pew.

"How *did* you find me?"

"I was downstairs in the lobby when you were leaving, and I saw you turn right and start to run. It was a little odd, so I followed you, just to make sure you were all right."

I laughed out loud again, as I held my hand to my chest, waiting for my heart rate to return to normal.

"Did you really think I was God?" he asked with a lingering chuckle.

"I wasn't sure what to think, but for a moment, maybe? Then you scared the absolute crap out of me."

"Sorry about that." He smiled. "I can see why Dalley likes you so much."

"Ravn, this whole thing with Dalley is a little confusing and overwhelming. I'm still not sure how to feel about what she did. Before I found out about the blog, she and I spent a lot of time together. We were friends and she hurt me. I have never trusted people easily, and when I met Dalley I was a little hesitant, but I took a leap. I just need to know, is she for real? Does she really want to make things …"?

"Right again? Yes. Dalley is terribly sorry for what she did. One day she will tell you her whole story. Maybe it will help you understand her. It isn't an excuse, but it may explain a few things and the choices she has made. But right now, her only mission is to help you find Cristiano. And the truth is, her mission is my mission." He glanced at his watch and before I could even comment he skillfully changed the subject. "What time are we supposed to meet Pierre?"

"7:50 or so."

"Do you feel like another run? We're late."

"Dalley wanted me to wake her up."

"No worries, I took care of it. When I left her, she was completely awake." He smiled and gave me a little wink.

I chuckled. He was so sweet. "You seem to be taking care of a lot of things for her lately."

"I've been waiting for a long time to even have the chance. What's surprising is that she's letting me."

❧

When we arrived back at the hotel, Dalley and Pierre were in the lounge having a drink, laughing like old friends.

Mid-laugh, Dalley looked up and waved us over.

"Maya! Ravn! Where were you two?"

"Oh, we were just making a deal with heaven," Ravn said, leaning down to kiss her on the top of her head.

"You don't say?" she looked up. Their eyes locked for a moment, just long enough to show me the connection between the two of them.

Pierre called the waitress over and asked for two more glasses so we could all share the bottle of wine.

"No, thank you. I'm good, I don't feel like drinking," I said.

Ravn cleared his throat. "Well, I am not going to refuse a drink, but wine is not on my list tonight. I feel like a … scotch. I've done too much cardio today."

Pierre ordered a scotch for Ravn and when they brought the drink, there was also a shot of something that he had the waitress place in front of me.

"Maya, we must share one drink together before we start talking about Cristiano again," Pierre insisted.

He was right, I did need something, as I had been less than sane earlier in the day when we met. So, I threw back the shot and cringed as the liquid slid down my throat. Vague memories of second-year university wafted up into my nostrils.

"Oh my God, Sambuca." I coughed and sputtered.

I had hated Sambuca ever since Beth took me to that cast party. I don't remember much except being outside and flames dancing from my lips. I shook my head again, trying to shake the taste out of my brain.

"You wait until you taste the coffee in Egypt. You'll have to do more than shake your head," Pierre said smiling.

"I will be sticking with tea, then," I said, trying to imagine sitting somewhere in Cairo, sharing a cup of tea with Cristiano and laughing our way through the mess of the past week.

"Their tea is pretty intense too, just be prepared."

"I'm trying to prepare myself for anything."

During the teasing, I started to relax. I wasn't sure if it was the shot of liquor or the company, but I was feeling a little bit better until Pierre received a text that had him walking away from the table.

When he returned, the look on his face scrubbed the Sambuca from my system and all that remained was a bucket full of nerves.

"What is it, Pierre?" I asked, standing at some form of attention.

"Maya, please sit down." He then looked at Ravn and Dalley. His eyes widened, and I could see that something was wrong, very wrong.

"I'm sure everything is fine," Dalley tried to convince me. "Who was the text from, Pierre?"

Pierre took a deep breath. At first it looked as if he was trying to think up a story, then his shoulders collapsed, and he began talking.

"I was nervous about Cristiano going to Cairo, but he insisted on it." He turned around and looked to see if anyone was watching.

"Pierre, I appreciate a good mystery, but I don't think Maya does right about now," Dalley quipped. "Please tell us what's going on."

"Let's go somewhere more private."

Ravn paid the bill and Pierre ordered a taxi. We made our way to the front door, no one uttering a word. My legs felt like jelly and I could feel a dull buzz vibrating through my body. Something was wrong, I could feel it.

Pierre guided me into the back seat of the waiting vehicle.

"What's going on, Pierre?" I asked, attempting to stay calm. But I could feel my heart start to quicken.

"Pierre is just being cautious, Maya," Dalley spoke up. "At this point we know nothing."

No one said a word as we headed towards the restaurant, not even Dalley, which scared me even more. While I sat in the back seat, I wrung my hands until they hurt. I could feel the acid churning in my stomach. As I looked up, I saw Pierre watching me in the rearview mirror. His eyes were filled with worry. The silence was finally broken by Ravn.

"Pierre, it might be time to let us know what was in that mystery text of yours."

"Maya, I don't want you to worry." He paused thoughtfully. "The text was from the hotel." He paused again, clearly struggling. "They asked if my guest was still staying with them as he had not checked in yet."

When I first heard the cry, it sounded far away. I couldn't imagine what would make someone scream like that, but the answer was quickly revealed when Dalley started shaking me and I realized the sound was coming from me. Two more shakes and the screaming stopped but the Sambuca rebelled, deciding to do a full reversal and show itself.

"Stop the car. Maya's going to be sick," Dalley commanded.

Pierre began yelling in French at the driver.

He was able to stop in time, but it only took a few minutes to cause a formidable traffic snarl as I leaned out the taxi door, vomiting up the remnants of Sambuca and a few airport fries.

Pierre had the driver take us back to the hotel as quickly as possible. While the driver was cursing, Pierre was muttering. The closest translation I could come up with was a repeated phrase of 'he's safe, he's safe, he's safe.'

Dalley held my hand as I hung my head out the open window, hoping the rushing wind would rid me of my worry, but it only numbed me long enough to get me back to the hotel lobby. She sat me down on a couch, and the moment Pierre walked through the doors behind us, she jumped on him.

"You said you did not feel good about Cristiano going to Cairo? Why? What else is going on? Did this have anything to do with his parents' death? Why were they in Egypt in the first place? What is the real reason?" Dalley barked question after question as if she had him in an interrogation room.

Pierre held his head up with some effort and tried to answer her questions. "Please let's do this somewhere else.

"Oh, I'm not going anywhere with you until I get some answers, and I am not letting you near Maya until we know more."

So, Pierre began. "His parents were doing me a favor," he tried to explain.

"Some favor," Dalley bit at him.

"I did not put them in harm's way on purpose if that is what you are saying Miss Price. We had worked together for years, picking up artifacts from all over the world. I just couldn't go back to Egypt to do that job myself." He paused, "I needed their help."

Ravn interrupted. "But why couldn't you go back, what happened when you were there before? Look Pierre, if we are going to find a way to help Cristiano, we need to know everything."

Pierre looked uncomfortable, like he wanted the conversation to stop.

"I'm getting there, please give me a minute." I watched him carefully as he shifted in his seat. "Let's just say, my last visit there didn't go well. There were some people who did not want me in the country; I had to leave without what I was looking for. Several years later, when I heard that the piece had resurfaced, I asked Cristiano's parents to go for me. I knew it was selfish, but I didn't think they would be in any danger. We had it all planned out. I had tracked it down to a certain destination, but just before they left I found out it had been sold again to an antique shop. I didn't know the exact name of the shop, but I had an idea where it might be. The plan was for them to quietly find the relic and if they couldn't, to stay a few days in the country as tourists. Michel had always wanted to visit Egypt. When they found the piece, Michel called and let me know. I didn't expect to hear from them again, but he called back a day later and said Rosa wanted to come home. She said she felt like someone had been following them. I booked a flight for them to leave the next day.

"When I got the call from Ammon about the crash, my life fell apart. I wasn't sure if the crash had been an accident or if it was sabotage. They were my best friends …" He covered his face to hide the tears. "And they were dead because of me."

"And the relic?" Dalley asked with agitation, not letting his tears get in her way.

"I never thought twice about it again. I assumed it went down in the plane with them."

Dalley barked at him, "Sabotage? Cristiano's mom thought they were being followed. Were they?"

Pierre looked at me then straightened up.

"More than likely, yes."

That's when I exploded. "So, who was following them? Did you know about these people before you sent them? Did you tell his parents? Wait … did you tell Cristiano about these people?" I felt like I was going to be sick again. "You didn't, did you? You sent him down there not knowing about the relic or the people who had been following his parents. Shame on you. You are disgraceful."

Pierre looked like he had been hit hard by my words, but I didn't care.

"So why did he go down there?" I pleaded with Pierre for answers.

"Closure, Maya. He needed to see where his parents died so he could finally say goodbye and move forward with his life, with his new family, with you. But there is one other thing you need to know."

"Just one?"

"You need to know that I've read your blog entries. I knew you were looking for him, but he didn't. You need to understand that once he decided to go, I couldn't stop him … you can't imagine what it was like at the funeral. No bodies, just empty caskets. So, when he asked me, I could not say no. I felt responsible. I made some calls and that's when I found out about the luggage being left off the plane and stored for all these years."

"So, you knew I was searching for him and you didn't tell him?"

"Not in so many words. I told him you loved him."

I swallowed back another surge of bile. "Pierre, where is Cristiano right now?" My anger and fear growing wider and deeper by the second.

"I know he landed, but he never registered at the hotel. I asked my friend Ammon to pick him up, but he is not answering his phone. Maya, I don't know where he is." Pierre slung his head into his hands.

Ravn interrupted my escalating anger with a practical question. "Pierre, who are the people who ran you out of the country all those years ago? And why do they want this relic so badly?"

Pierre slumped back into the couch. "They are called Ptolemites. They're descendants of Cleopatra the VII. They have been trying to restore their royal position in Egypt for generations and believe the relic will prove they have a right to governmental power and wealth."

"You have got to be joking," Dalley said. "Egypt has been running a republican government since the revolution in 2011."

Ravn jumped in. "You're right, Dalley, but the Ptolemites are no joke. I heard about them in my travels. Nobody took them seriously until the last few years. A reporter friend was looking into them last year and had to make his own quick exit out of Egypt when they didn't like the questions he was asking."

"The Ptolemites you say?" Dalley responded, pulling out her computer and starting some research of her own.

"I'm sorry, Maya, there's nothing more I can do," Pierre said touching my shoulder. "I'm sure we'll hear something in the morning."

"What does that mean?" The dam burst.

"It means it is going to be a long night," said Ravn as he knelt in front of me.

I smiled, stood up, side-stepped Ravn, and started walking to the exit.

"Maya, where are you going?" They all began to shout.

"Well, you all can go to sleep and wait around, but I am flying out to Egypt. Right now," I announced firmly. "Pierre, take me to the airport."

Ravn caught me before I got to the front door. "Maya, I respect your new-found fearless attitude towards danger, but we need to find out more information before we head down there. It's not a place you want to be without a plan and an exit strategy, especially if you're not there *just to see the pyramids*. And if the Ptolemites are involved in any way, we need to be extra cautious. Let's sit down for a bite to eat and we'll figure something out. I promise."

I knew Ravn was right, but I didn't want him to be. I couldn't eat, but I did agree to sit with them. As they began planning, I nursed a cup of tea and forced myself to imagine something positive that could come from all the chaos that was whirling around us.

❧

If only I could have convinced my imagination to stop thinking the worst, I might have been able to sleep for more than thirty minutes at a time. Instead, around 3:30 a.m. I gave up and wandered down to the hotel café.

I sat down on one of the lounge chairs and curled up in a ball with my journal in hand.

It was then I started to cry. They weren't the ugly tears I expected, just a relentless flow that appeared to have an endless source. Then, from the corner of my eye, I saw a waiter approaching. He handed me a latte and a handkerchief. I dabbed my eyes and took a sip without even asking who or why.

As I began to write, I felt someone sit down next to me. She didn't say a word but pulled out a brand-new set of knitting needles and two balls of yarn. I smiled, unexpectedly comforted by the fact that Dalley had told me the truth about her knitting when we met that first day.

"I heard the nights in Egypt can be rather cool," Dalley said simply. As she knitted, Dalley talked about random things, trying to distract me.

"Knitting? Really?" I asked, mesmerized by the speed of her hands and the clicking of the needles.

"Yes, I wasn't joking when I said it relaxed me. Mind you, that wasn't the reason I started. When I was a teen, my mom made it perfectly clear I was not allowed to learn to cook or clean or do anything that someone might misinterpret as being 'old fashioned.' So, I decided to learn to knit, as I knew it would make her madder than hell. She used to say awful things about the other mothers at school, especially all of the stay-at-home moms. There was a time she cut up the sweater I was working on, broke the needles, and wrapped everything up in a box with a ribbon on it. I just threw it away and started over."

Dalley went on to describe a life with a mother who hated being a mother. I could not imagine hating your own child. I felt desperately sad for her. At one point though my head began to bob, and her words blended. The last thing I remember was feeling lucky that Judith was my mom. It may have been a hard life with her depression, but I never doubted her love for me, even if she couldn't always show it.

It wasn't until I heard Dalley's voice again and opened my eyes that I realized I had fallen asleep. She had sat with me in the café until the sun came up.

"Maya, it's time to go. Our flight to Cairo leaves shortly," she whispered.

"Have you heard from Pierre?" I asked, snapping awake.

"No, but on another topic I really think we should let someone at Netuno know you are going to Cairo. If anything happens to you they will never let me attend the wedding."

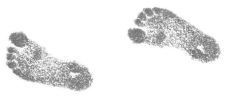

32

What is Safe?

Maya

As we sat at the gate, waiting to board the flight to Cairo, I called my mom. Though calm on the surface, I could feel slivers of anxiety creep into her goodbye and before she hung up, she let me know that Avo had insisted on going back to the cottage and asked if she could speak to Dalley.

I reluctantly handed her the phone, worried about what my mom might say to her. The conversation though appeared to be quite uneventful until I saw Dalley wince.

"She is? She does?" Dalley responded to something my mom said to her. "If she would like. I would be happy to." Dalley waited quietly on the phone then stood up and stepped away. I saw her pacing back and forth as she said little and listened hard to the other person on the line.

"I will, Maggie, I promise," Dalley said quickly, wiping a tear away before handing the phone back to me.

"Maggie is in Portugal? I thought Puro was going to Vancouver," I asked with confusion.

"He did, and then Maggie asked if she and Tim could come back. She thought a change of scenery would do them both good."

"Sounds complicated."

"When is life not? Your mom was very gracious to me. I was worried when she first wanted to speak with me, but she just thanked me for helping you."

"My mom is not a grudge keeper," I smiled.

"She loves you very much," Dalley said almost wistfully.

"I love her too."

"Make sure you let her know that the next time you speak with her."

Dalley's pensive response led me to believe that maybe my mother shared more with her than I thought.

While I was still thinking about the telephone call between Dalley and my mom I heard Ravn speaking curtly to someone on his phone.

"What do you mean for now? Thanks a lot. This is not going to go well and you expect me to tell her?" Ravn snapped.

I could only assume Ravn was talking about me, and the only person he could be talking to was Pierre. He hung up the phone and threw it into his bag.

"Cristiano is safe. I don't know the details, but for *now*, he's safe," Ravn offered up reluctantly.

"What does that mean 'for now?' I whispered under my breath.

No one said another word as we boarded our flight.

I pulled out my journal before anyone even put away their bags, knowing writing was the only way to stave off the anxiety attack that lay in wait beneath my new hair and clothes.

"Maya? Do you need anything?" Dalley asked, practicing her newfound friendship skills.

"Thank you. Just a cup of tea if they have something decent to offer."

"What is decent?" she said, laughing a little. "Lord knows, I know nothing about tea except what you've taught me."

"Just ask if they have some earl grey and a little cream."

"I'll see what I can do," she said, watching me carefully.

I opened Christopher and began.

> *Hello Friend,*
>
> *I have no idea what day it is. I think…oh it doesn't matter.*
>
> *The next leg of my journey is taking me to Cairo. He promised me an adventure, but I had hoped we'd be doing this kind of thing together. My nerves are on fire and as much as I want to say I know what I am doing; I don't … I am not sure if I am mad or sad right now. I guess I won't know until I see him.*

I continued to write until my hand ached and my anxiety was put back in its box. When I looked down, a full cup of lukewarm tea sat waiting for me patiently and Dalley was resting her head on Ravn's shoulder looking peaceful.

Ravn had jumped back into her life no questions asked and was ready to do anything for her. For a moment, I felt a pang of jealousy. Ravn had run towards Dalley when she needed him, so why had Cristiano run from me? I wouldn't really know why until I heard the words from his own lips. I needed to find him and the truth. I had to trust that I would figure out what to do when I saw him. If it meant leaving without him and accepting that he didn't want me, then I had to be prepared for that truth too, but I was not going to give up until I looked into his eyes and saw it for myself.

A shift in the air pressure alerted me to the fact that we were close to landing. I started to breathe more heavily and the hair on the back of my neck bristled. I grabbed my things and was ready to jump as soon as we stopped moving.

Ravn leaned over and patted my shoulder. "Maya, you need to relax. We are tourists, remember? Happy go lucky, not a care in the world. Pierre has arranged a driver. His friend Ammon will be picking us up in his taxi. Don't make eye contact with anyone in the airport; just look at each other and I will guide the two of you through." Ravn was so firm he left no room for us to question him.

When the plane stopped, we did just as he said. We made our way through the throngs of people towards the airport exit pretending to be the happy tourists. Dalley had to pinch me a few times to remind me to smile.

The heat was stifling when we walked out of the airport. I could taste the dust instantly as if Egypt had landed on my lips. Next came the yells and shouts of people trying to get us to take their taxis into the city. At that point, Ravn reminded us to keep our heads down. He was taller than most and was scouring the crowds, looking for our driver.

"Come with me," he said loudly, pulling us along.

"Get in, get in," I heard a man say.

I was pushed from behind and flew into the front seat of a taxi. By the time I was organized and looking for a seat belt, we were on the move. My heart raced and my senses became heightened. At first, I thought the source of my adrenaline was from fear, but I quickly realized it was not; it was Cristiano. I had caught a scent of him, and my instincts went into overdrive.

"Dalley!" I turned around and whispered with heightened enthusiasm. "He's been here. In this taxi."

"Maya, don't let your imagination get the better of you."

"This is not my imagination. I know! Cristiano has been in this taxi," I yelled, pounding my hand on the seat.

The car went silent.

"You are right, he has been here," Ammon said, confirming my suspicions.

I didn't know what to say at first, then the words came flooding out.

"Where is he? Is he safe? Can you take me to him? I must see him. Does he know I am coming?"

"Slow down, Maya. Yes, he is safe. No, he does not know you are here yet. Pierre asked me to wait. He thought we should leave him to take care of his business first. I'll bring him to you later."

"Why can't I see him? I need to see him right now! Take me to him or I'll drive there myself." I went to grab for the steering wheel, but Ravn reached over the seat and caught my arm.

"Maya, you need to stop." Ravn tried to settle me down but it wasn't working. Dalley attempted to rub my back, but that didn't go well either.

"I will take you to your hotel then bring him around to you later," Ammon said gently again, trying to appease me.

I was so angry and frustrated. No one was listening to me. "Ammon just tell me where he is," I pleaded in low tones. My heart ached. "He needs me," I said, collapsing back into the seat.

"Maya, you need to listen to Ammon right now. He will bring Cristiano to see you later," Ravn reiterated Ammon's words.

"Why? Why are you keeping him from me? Dalley, what do you guys know that I don't?"

"Don't put this on me. I have no idea what is going on right now. Ravn?" She looked at him with annoyance.

"Why can't we just go see him right now?" I shouted like a spoiled child and slammed my hand on the dashboard.

Ravn made eye contact with Ammon and made one last attempt at changing my mind. "You have been up for hours, Maya. You should get some rest and freshen up before you see him."

"Tell me what is going on!" I yelled back at him. "What don't you understand? I need to see him now," I screeched in full articulation.

Ammon's phone buzzed twice. He picked it up and read the text then made a hard right, stopped the taxi and got out. The silence between Ravn and I was deafening. Ammon was only gone a minute, then jumped back in the taxi with a new sense of urgency and took off down the street.

"Change of plans," Ammon said nervously.

"Which plans?" Ravn asked him.

"All of them."

He turned down one road and then another. As we moved farther out of town, all I could see was sand and a few palm trees. Ravn tried phoning Pierre, but there was no cell service.

"Don't worry." Ammon turned quickly to look at me and smiled. "Soon," was all he said.

"Ravn, are we in danger?" Dalley whispered but I could still hear her.

"Honestly, I don't know. But I think Ammon now knows something I don't," Ravn shared reluctantly.

"Now?" Dalley sneered at Ravn. "We'll talk about this later."

Ammon looked over at me again. He smiled, nodded, and patted my arm.

I resigned myself to the fact that I had no idea where I was going and that I had to trust a stranger to get me there. As I leaned my head against the window, I had an urge to feel the wind on my face. My hand moved over to the window switch and a collective "NO!!" rang out of everyone's mouths just as a gust of sand blasted through the small opening.

"Roll it up, roll it up, Maya!" Dalley yelled.

Ammon closed my window from his side before I could even touch the button. He started to laugh.

"Oh, I forgot to tell you not to open the windows today. There is a sandstorm coming."

I turned around to see Dalley and Ravn covered in a fine layer of sand and not looking too pleased with me.

Dalley shook her head. "Okay, are we even *yet*?"

"Getting closer," I said without any humor.

"Let me know if I need to get some protective wear for the next round," she rallied back.

The hair on my arms suddenly raised up and a shiver ran through my body. "Dalley, we're getting close."

"Yes, I know, that's what you just said."

"No, not about us," I shot back at her.

"Close to what then?"

"To him."

"Who?"

"Cristiano. We're close. I can feel him," I barked at her with desperation.

"Maya, I know you want to find him, but right now, we just have to figure out where Ammon is taking us."

"Dalley, it doesn't matter where we're going. He's near."

"Ravn, can you please help me out here," Dalley asked for some support.

"I don't know Dalley. From everything you've told me about these two, maybe she can sense he is close. I've seen some pretty remarkable things over the years."

"You're not helping, Ravn."

"You're being too practical, Dalley," he teased lightly. "You've got to believe in the power of love … and the mystery that it holds."

"Power of love? Mystery? Honestly Ravn, what are you talking about? The only things out here are sand dunes."

"When did you get so jaded?" Ravn asked with a crooked smile.

"This isn't about me. I'm worried about Maya."

"Miss Price, no need to worry, Maya is correct. He is near," Ammon stated firmly while looking in the rear-view mirror at Dalley.

Dalley had told me about her fire-breathing butterflies and it appeared they had traveled to Egypt with us and taken up residence in my stomach. I could hear their wings fluttering, smashing against my chest with every hot breath. I inched closer to the edge of the seat and pressed my face up to the glass. I was not sure what I was looking for but was certain that when I saw it, I would know.

Dune after dune whipped by us. "I'm close. Where are you? I'm here," I whispered through the window. "Can you hear me?"

Ammon slammed on his brakes, then yelled to me, "Get out!"

"Good Lord, not again," Dalley screeched, referring to that first day in Lisbon when the taxi driver drove us out to the country market and left us standing on the side of the road.

"Not you," he said curtly to Dalley as she made a motion to follow me.

"You, Maya. He needs you."

I wanted to move, but I was frozen. Ammon got out of the taxi and ran around to open my door.

"Maya, he's waiting for you. He may not know it yet, but he is."

I ran up the hill, each step sinking deep into the virgin sand. I could hear Dalley yelling after me, but her voice quickly disappeared when I crested the dune and saw him collapsed over a piece of burned-out airplane wing.

Cristiano

I held on to the broken and rusted wing of my parents' downed plane, hoping it would reveal the answers I had been looking for all my life. But all I heard was the sound of the desert, gently nudging me to let go, to say goodbye.

When Ammon said he would take me to the crash site, I hesitated at first but knew I had to come. I had held the sadness in my heart for such a long time I wasn't sure I wanted to let it go, or even if I could.

In the morning, we drove to the site in silence, but when we arrived Ammon offered me a few thoughts.

"Your parents loved you very much. Cristiano. It is time to say goodbye and open your heart up to the love you deserve."

He gestured for me to walk up the sand dune indicating that what I was looking for was on the other side. I wasn't sure what to expect, but when I reached the top, it was different, beautiful. Somehow, I had imagined the crash site to be a barren, horrible place but as I made my way down the other side of the dune, an oasis was revealed. It was just a few trees and a water hole, but it was simply flawless. I slid down the dune, stopped only by a large piece of metal protruding from the sand—a wing, an airplane wing. It was so odd and perfect all at the same time. I wasn't sure what to do. They were buried somewhere under twenty years of sand and life, yet the wing revealed itself to me that day.

I leaned up against the nearest palm, feeling the heat radiating off the metal like it was alive. I'm not sure how long I stood there but the desert palm shaded me, keeping me safe.

Then I heard it—the snap of the metal wing contracting. It broke my spell and I collapsed forward. I hung off the metal, no longer able to stand on my own.

I heard a breath behind me, but I could not look. I was fearful that the ghosts of my past had now started haunting me during the day.

Maya

I slid down the back of the dune and breathed in the dry dusty air, swallowing in a history of courage and pain that hung in the desert sand from centuries before. I never thought I could be strong in a moment like that, but with each step I took in the hot sinking sand, I found the motivation to move toward him. What I didn't realize until I got close enough to touch him was that it was not just courage or strength that got me there, but a mixture of love and anger. I was mad. A part of me wanted to yell, to hit, and to ask him how he could have just left me standing there in the dark as he drove away. The emotions flooded my heart and mind, leaving me confused and ashamed and not sure what to do next.

As I took one step closer, his frame shook and reeled, and my body responded in kind. The myriad of emotions that radiated from his body soon incinerated my anger, leaving only a sense of clarity and my love. Nothing else mattered in that moment but he and I.

Reaching out, I placed my hand on the back of his head, offering him all that I had. He flinched like my touch had disconnected him, then turned and stared.

Our eyes met and we both fell into one another's hearts like there had been no photographs, no blogs, no Jade, no Steven. I placed my fingers over his lips and then touched them to mine. Tears sprung from his eyes like the stones breaking free in an old dam. We slid to the ground, our weight supported by a rusty piece of metal. I held him as he excised a lifetime of sadness and regret, allowing him the time and space to speak only when he was ready.

"Maya?" he whispered, his eyes still telling me the story that he could not believe I was sitting in the desert with him.

"Yes, I'm here." I smiled, stroking his tear stained cheeks.

"I thought …?"

I leaned in and touched his dry lips to mine. He kissed me softly at first. Then something shifted, and I could feel an urgency in his touch. He pushed me back against the wing; his body pressing close to mine. I resisted at first, but soon gave in. I wanted him. I wanted his touch, his lips. The wind was hot, and his body bent under my fingertips. We were both crazed, but he was not going to get off that easy. I tore myself from him, pulling back and panting.

"Yes. What were you thinking? How could you just leave me?"

He cast his eyes down and sighed. "I don't know … I saw you in his arms and … it looked like …"

"Like what?"

"I don't know, like you believed I would cheat on you. That I wasn't good enough for you. He was there to catch you when you fell. That was him, wasn't it?"

"Doesn't matter. He's gone and I am here with you," I snapped back.

He pushed his hands through his hair. "Deep down I never thought I deserved your love. I never thought I deserved you. I couldn't imagine why you would want to be with someone as broken as me." His eyes filled again and then he looked away. "I am so ashamed. I should have known better, trusted you more. I love you, Maya. I cannot lose you. Please don't be angry with me anymore. Please, I need you."

"There is no one else Cristiano. There will never be anyone else." I touched his heart. "I'm sorry that you even doubted that."

"I am broken, Maya—look at me," he said half-laughing.

"I am looking, and I am seeing you. I love you, all of you."

"Why?" he asked simply.

"What a crazy question. You're sitting in the desert, under the shade of a palm tree, saying goodbye to two of the most important people in your life. Where else would I be? Yes, you are a little broken. But good God, so am I. I'm only now just starting to understand who I want to become but I don't want to do it alone. Do you?"

He traced my cheek with his finger as I continued to talk.

"When we met, you promised me an adventure."

"This isn't quite what I had in mind for you, for us."

"I don't know, I think it's a pretty good place to start, don't you?"

He smiled and held my hand to his heart. "You need to know, having you here with me has changed everything. I love you Maya Wells. I will *never* leave you again and we will face life together no matter what it brings …"

"Cristiano! Maya!" We heard our names, and both looked up to see Ammon. "The storm is coming. We have to leave now."

"I don't care. Just give us a few more minutes," Cristiano responded rebelliously.

"Cristiano, is that really the best idea?" Dalley asked, stepping out from behind Ravn and Ammon.

When Cristiano looked up and saw Dalley, he broke away from me and started running up the dune at an extraordinary pace. He was headed straight for her and it was not to give her a hug. Ravn stepped in front of Dalley, holding his hand out to block Cristiano's approach.

"Woah, Cristiano. Stop right there!" Ravn commanded.

Cristiano ran into Ravn's hand. "What the hell are you doing here, Dalley? You have some nerve showing up. You ruined everything you selfish, lying bitch!"

I scurried up after him. "Cristiano, stop. Let me explain," I uttered breathlessly.

"That would be nice," Cristiano said. "Because sandstorm or no, I'm not getting into a car with her without a damn good reason," he barked with an unfamiliar acidic tone.

I placed my hand on his vibrating arm, trying to steady him. "Cristiano look at me; look at where we are. I would not be here if it wasn't for Dalley and Ravn. She made a mistake, Cristiano, and is trying to make things right. She knows what she did was wrong and when she offered to help me find you, I was hesitant at first, but honestly I just couldn't do it on my own."

His arm relaxed just enough that I felt I was getting through to him.

Dalley interjected, "I promise you, once we get your parents' luggage and get you guys out of the country, you can yell at me all you want." She was trying to be funny but her attempts at humor did not go over well with Cristiano.

"What do you know about the luggage?" He looked at Dalley and then me, the muscles in his arm tensing again.

"Cristiano, you've been through a lot today, this week, this month. I just need you to trust me right now," I said, trying to soothe him and hoping Dalley would not open her mouth again.

He looked over to Ammon. "If this is about finding the relic, the Ptolemites can have it. I don't care."

"This is not about the relic Cristiano. It's about claiming the last of their belongings. You know that. You came here to close a door on this chapter of your life, not to leave with unfinished business." Ammon ushered everyone towards the taxi. "We can discuss it on our way to the storage unit."

Cristiano lagged for a moment, took in a deep breath, and released it slowly. He exhaled until there was nothing left, then he tossed his dark curls back with his hands and patted his white button-down shirt like he was giving it a press. When he was finished, he offered me his hand.

Ravn walked up to Cristiano. "Let's try this again. I'm Dagmar Ravn, but everyone calls me Ravn. And we had better get moving."

Cristiano nodded his head. He took one last look down at the wing and squeezed my hand tightly. "I am never letting go of you again, Maya Wells."

⋯

"Cristiano you might want to loosen your grip on Maya. She may need her hand again one day," Dalley teased as Ammon sped down the road trying to outrun the sandstorm.

Cristiano laughed a little but only pulled me closer.

As we drove, I kept touching his chest, feeling his heartbeat.

Cristiano stared back at me. "Maya, how did you find me here in Cairo?"

"Well, that is a long story, but the simple answer is—Pierre."

"Ammon, when did you know that Maya was coming to Cairo?"

Ammon was silent.

"This morning when you talked to Pierre, he told you didn't he? And he told you not to tell me."

"Cristiano, I'm sorry, I …"

"Oh Ammon, it is not your fault. All you have ever done is to try to help my family. This is on Pierre. He could have told me the whole story at any time, but he didn't. He sent my mother into harm's way and then twenty years later, the woman I love." He grabbed my shoulders. "If anything happens to you, I don't know what …"

"Cristiano! Don't talk like that. Nothing is going to happen," I responded, trying to calm him down.

Just then Ammon slammed on the brakes, throwing us up against the front seat, barely stopping in time for a herd of goats as they lazily crossed the road. "At least not tonight," Ammon said, breaking the tension.

I added, "Yes, that would be ludicrous if I was able to escape a herd of crazy goats in Portugal, but a band of Egyptian kids were able to complete the job." Dalley burst into laughter and even Cristiano was able to let out a chuckle.

"I've missed you, Maya. No more secrets, ever again," Cristiano said, touching my cheek.

"This may not be the time, but there is one more thing I need to tell you," I said, breathing in.

Ammon's phone rang and he picked it up with some skill.

"There has been a break in at the storage unit and the auction has been canceled. The Ptolemites, they know you are here. We have to get off the roads right now."

33

Heart Gifts

Maya

IT WAS A HARROWING DRIVE as Ammon attempted to find somewhere safe for us to stop. We had no idea what was really going on but thought it best to let Ammon deal with the situation. As we got closer into the city, he had us scoot down in the seats to hide as best as we could. My heart beat like the wings of a hummingbird.

Suddenly we turned a corner and I fell towards Cristiano, my wrap-around skirt opening slightly and my body pushing up against his. I quivered as his fingertips accidentally brushed along my thigh. It was a relief to feel the surge of electricity again. I hadn't realized how much I missed his touch until that moment. When he left, a part of me had worried that maybe I was wrong about us, but I wasn't. I moved closer towards him as we crouched in the car, our bodies no longer touching unintentionally.

He stared at me for the longest time, then started to laugh, "I have missed you more than you could imagine," he said, leaning in to kiss me. My lips melted like milk chocolate in the sun.

"Are you guys serious?" Dalley asked. "You're going to do this now? Can you just wait until we get out of the car? Please? I never really believed it before, but you've erased all my doubts."

"You never believed what?" Ravn asked, jumping into the conversation from the front seat.

I knew what she was talking about and started to explain. "Dalley and the ladies back at Netuno made a bet about my sex life," I answered openly.

"Seriously?" Ravn asked, with a chuckle. "Why?"

"Because we decided to 'wait'," Cristiano responded bluntly.

"Wait for what?" Ravn asked, not putting the pieces together.

"*Wait* ... Ravn," Cristiano said slowly, with a smile.

"Oh ... OH!! Are you two serious? Why?"

"Oh Ravn, leave them alone. They made some sort of pact with one another when they met," Dalley said, almost defending me.

"That doesn't include sex? That's crazy," Ravn said, shaking his head vigorously.

"Yes, I know. You are a free spirit and the idea of not having sex is a foreign one to you, and I am thankful for that. But some people do things differently," Dalley said, being the surprising voice of reason.

"Thanks for defending my sex life, Dalley," I said, starting to feel a little uncomfortable.

"Sure, why not? I'll try anything once."

We all broke into laughter, but that soon ended when Ammon suddenly slammed on the brakes. He told us to get out of the taxi and make our way into the abandoned building.

"I'll be back in an hour or two and whatever you do, don't go outside," he pleaded with us.

As we looked for the entrance, Dalley and Cristiano began round two.

"Nice place," Dalley said sarcastically.

"He doesn't live here," Cristiano retorted.

"Well that's encouraging. Can we trust this guy?" Dalley asked suspiciously.

"You're asking me about who we can trust? Really?" Cristiano looked at her with dismay.

"Cristiano," I snapped a little.

We tried the door of the building and with a little effort, were able to get it open.

"Cristiano," I said, touching his sleeve.

"What? I haven't had as much time as you to embrace Dalley being back in our lives. You do remember what she did to you right? You need to be patient with me."

"Look, you don't need to *embrace* me, Cristiano," Dalley postured a few feet away. "I know what I did was wrong. I screwed up and created a platform for Jade to make things worse. I should have come forward before she went crazy, but I truly had no idea that her family was trying to take control of Netuno."

"What?" Cristiano staggered backwards.

I had forgotten that Cristiano had no idea about the attempted hostile takeover.

"Maya? What the hell is she talking about? Is everyone okay? Netuno? Puro?" His anger quickly turned to remorse. "I should have been there. The brothers … Carmo, Bento. They are my family and I should never have run off." He held his head in his hands.

"You couldn't have known, Cristiano," I said as I tried to settle him down.

"Yah, well, I should have known better. I'm not eighteen anymore. I can't just run off and abandon the people I care about." He walked into the bathroom and slammed the door.

I turned to follow him, but Dalley held my arm. "Let him go, he is right. He shouldn't have run away."

My anger sparked. "Let me go. What do you know anyway? You ran too."

"Yes, but …" Dalley tried to come up with some excuse.

"But what? What does it matter? He ran away when he got scared. You ran away when you couldn't face what you had done. I ran to find him. What about you Ravn? You ever run?" The tension in the room was very thick.

"Interesting question. I stopped running away from my life the day Dalley ran from me."

The look on Dalley's face rested somewhere between pain and shock.

"Really Dalley? You're surprised?" Ravn added. "You've been running away your whole life. Give Cristiano a break."

Dalley's face turned crimson and I swore I saw a puff of steam come out of her ears. She turned without saying a word and walked into a second room, smashing the door closed. Ravn and I sat down on two wooden crates and stared at one another.

"So, what do we do now?" I asked, genuinely mystified.

"About those two or this situation we are in?"

"I guess both."

"Well, they will eventually come out of their caves and we will still be here."

"And where is here exactly? What are we doing, Ravn?

"I'm not quite sure, but I get the feeling we may need to make a quick exit. My instincts are on high alert. This isn't my first game of hide-and-seek, but this one is a little different. I've never really had to worry about anyone else beside myself before."

"Are you worried about Dalley?

"Yes, but don't tell her that. She is already mad at me."

"You love her."

"Yes, from the first time we met. I never stopped."

"Even after all those years. There was no one else?"

"No one that mattered. She landed in my heart and I just couldn't let her go."

"So, you just waited for her?"

"Yes, ten long years. Maya, you are much braver than I ever was. You knew you needed to find Cristiano and you did whatever you had to do to make that happen, including forgiving a friend who hurt you. I just sat back and waited for her to come to me. Some may say it was patience, but truthfully it was more about the fear of rejection. Thankfully, she called. Now, I better go smooth things over with her or this could be a really long night."

I shook my head, thinking about myself as brave. Then I started to nod instead, realizing that maybe I had changed, and I could get to like this new me.

I dove into my bag, passing up the tablet and grabbing Christopher.

In a room somewhere in Cairo,

I found him. I can't believe I found him. He was standing in the middle of a desert oasis. You wouldn't believe me if I told you. Hell, I don't believe me .

I briefly thought about writing my next blog, but then realized maybe it's time to put my privacy settings back on my life. The blog served its purpose, but I think I'll just hand it back to Dalley, with a few new rules.

It is dark in the room and only a few shafts of light are breaking through the windows. It looks quite beautiful.

We will get through this. Whatever this is. I love him more than my heart can express. When I saw him today, I felt the pieces inside me shift. I feel lighter, like things in my body fit better. Years ago, I wrote a poem that never seemed to fit into my life, but today it seems perfect:

Where are We?

Where are we when the sun is shining, and the skies are so blue that we can reach up and feel the newness of life?

Where are we when the flowers begin to open, and the smells of spring are so vivid that we taste the fresh-ness of life?

We have arrived in a land of happiness.

The simplicity of arriving and the complexity of traveling.

A land where you only want to smile.

A land where only tears of happiness are shed.

I read my poem out loud several times. Then I quickly wrote down:

I wish Cristiano would just come out of the bath-room already.

Maya

I heard a shuffle behind me and there he was leaning up against the wall, smirk on his face, curls hanging in his eyes, listening to me. I was stupid in love with this man.

"You are a woman of many talents. I thought I was the only poet in this relationship," he said.

"Well I can't let you have all the fun."

He placed his finger on my lips and moved in swiftly so that our bodies could touch, then gently removed my sweater revealing my naked quivering arms and goose-bumped skin.

"You're cold."

"No. I'm not."

"Should I keep going?"

"You better not stop."

Cristiano's fingers traced along the inside of my arm until he reached my palm. Taking my hand, he placed it against his chest where I could feel his solid body and warming skin. As I reached for the top button of his pants, he laughed and then broke away. My eyes flashed open and I found him kneeling in front of me.

"Maya Wells, I have been a fool. I knew from the beginning that having you in my life was the only path. I was stupid though, frightened of my feelings. I ran away when I should have run forward, but I'm not afraid anymore. I want to spend the rest of my life living out this adventure with you. I will always love you."

"Wait …" I uttered trying to catch my breath. I couldn't say yes, not without him knowing the last piece of the puzzle. "I met them, all of them. They know everything," I blurted out.

He paused for a moment. "Who? What are you talking about?"

I adjusted myself and tried to think how best to tell him. But before I could say anything, he answered his own question.

"My birth parents, my brother, my sister." He slid back onto his heels, landing on the floor with a thump. Silence occupied our space at first, but soon words and questions tumbled out.

There was no anger or frustration, just his curiosity peeking through. "I saw her, you know," Cristiano said. "Standing on the balcony of her home. I wanted to ring the doorbell, but I lost my nerve and drove away. I think she saw me."

"She did." I said, placing my hand on his cheek.

"What are they like? She looked sad from where I sat. Were they kind to you? Did they believe you?" he asked with a childlike eagerness.

I smiled and took a quick breath. "Yes, they were kind, gentle, funny, emotional, passionate, just like you, but a little confused at first. Your mother is smart. I tried to explain how and why I had landed on her door-step, but gave up and handed her Avo's letter—everything but the last two pages, as I know you haven't read them yet."

"The letter, the last two pages," he commented pensively.

"Yes, I went to your apartment looking for you and no, I didn't read them, they belong to you."

"Thank you. Oh … how is Jack?" he asked, looking a little embarrassed.

"Yes, about Jack. Well, he finally agreed to help me and gave me your parents' address. He really is difficult sometimes."

Cristiano laughed. "Yes, he can be. But he is also very loyal, maybe to a fault."

"I know. Anyway, Euphemia quickly put all the pieces together about who you were, and how you and Jack and Marcos fit together." I paused. "When she found out about your parents and the plane crash … well, if she had known, she would have found you."

I waited for him to say something as he paced back and forth.

"Tell me more about them. My brother and sister? I'm guessing they didn't know I even existed. What about Marcos, my …"

He tried to say the word, but couldn't. He went on like that for several minutes asking and answering his own questions, then stopped suddenly.

"Does Avo know? About any of this? I don't want to hurt her anymore."

"Yes, she knows everything." I bit my lip and took another breath. "A lot happened during the first forty-eight hours after you left." I stood up and started moving around the room. I didn't know what I was looking for except maybe a way not to relive those first few days, but he needed to know.

"After you left, I wasn't doing very well and went to stay with Avo. I needed to be at the cottage with her. When I arrived, she knew something was very wrong and took me out to your tree. We sat quietly together, and when we returned to the garden, the bread in the oven was burning. I ran to take it out, but she held me back. She made me sit and watch it …"

"Turn to ash?" he said in a reminiscent tone.

"Yes, exactly. Turn to ash."

"And did she make you throw the pans away in her bread pan graveyard?"

"Yes, she did." I laughed lightly.

He shook his head. "Yes, she can be quite dramatic when she wants to make a point," he said lovingly.

I smiled. "She is gifted, that's for sure. She also gave me my voice back."

"You lost it?"

"Long story." He reached out and grabbed my arm. "Yes, but she …"

"No need to explain Avo to me," Cristiano added. "She has been offering up little miracles my whole life."

"No, it wasn't just that. After burning the bread and finding my voice, something changed inside of her. She became frail and wanted to be alone."

I could feel his sadness and guilt surfacing, but I couldn't stop. He needed to hear what I had to say. All we had was the truth, and if we were going to move forward we had to be open about everything.

"The next day when Puro found out how she was doing, he insisted she come back with me. He set her up in one of the suites, but as unwell as she was, she refused and insisted on a simple room at the back of the inn." Cristiano shook his head, knowing how stubborn she was.

"I miss her," he said, smiling briefly. "Have you spoken to anyone back home about how she is doing?"

"I spoke with my mom before leaving Paris. Avo insisted on going back to the cottage but my mother is going to check in on her. I know Avo is in good hands, as my mother has been helping to take care of her since she arrived."

"Your mother? She is in Portugal?"

"Yes, like I told you, a lot has happened. She flew out to be with me when all the craziness happened with the blog."

"I assumed your mom couldn't travel."

"Well apparently, my mother's doing much better than I thought, and it's me who hasn't been doing so great. A very humbling experience."

He gently took my face in his hands, tears trailing down his cheeks as he held me.

"Maya, can you ever forgive me? I hurt you so much."

"Cristiano, a part of me wishes it *had* been all about you, all my tears and sadness, but I can't give you all the credit. I had not been dealing with my own fears long before I met you. Then I jumped on an airplane to a beautiful country and was determined to leave it all behind. Build a new life, blah blah blah. Well it doesn't really work like that, does it? When you left, all the feelings, and I mean *all* of them, came back. I think that is what stole my voice. As I told you though, Avo helped me get it back. But it was my mom who encouraged me to find a way to keep it, to search for you and seek out my best self along the way."

"So, have you found her?" he asked, raising an eyebrow.

I laughed. "Yes, I think I started sprouting my own wings when I went shopping at the train station after visiting Mrs. Dutra."

"Mrs. Dutra. Is she mad at me?"

"Only for letting Jack stay at the apartment. She is finding him a little loud. You are going to have to bring her a special gift when you go home."

"And you, do I need to get you a special gift too?"

"Let's not worry about gifts right now. We just have to get out of Egypt."

"Yes. I'm sick about having put you in this kind of danger."

"Cristiano, you didn't put me anywhere. I chose to come here. I chose to find you and I choose to love you. That includes your past and present."

"Does that present include throwing you in the middle of my new family? I am so sorry."

"What are you sorry about? They are great. Your sister, Jacinta, is so excited about meeting you. Your brother, Zef, may need a little more time but he was coming around when I left. It's funny though, he almost seemed relieved in some way once he got over the shock of knowing you exist. He said it explained a lot about Euphemia." I paused, watching him carefully, wondering if he needed me to stop.

"Please tell me more, tell me everything." he asked eagerly.

I smiled, squeezing his arm, then continued. "She told me that at the time of the adoption her parents made her stop seeing Marcos. But as I wrote in my letter to you, they saw each other secretly until she turned eighteen. Then they ran off and got married. But before they left, she drove out to Avo's cottage. She saw you in the garden playing with your parents. Avo was baking bread and you were just learning to walk. Saying goodbye to you again was the hardest thing she ever had to do."

I paused again briefly as I saw the sadness show around his eyes. "She told Marcos they had to move far away so she could let you live your life.

She never told Marcos about that last visit, she never told anyone until me. She loved you always. Loves you. Your mom and dad love you very much."

Cristiano, looked startled, like he had been shocked. "Maya?"

"What's wrong? What did I say?"

"You called them my mom and dad. It just caught me off guard."

"Oh—I am so sorry; I wasn't thinking."

"No, it's okay. I'm just not sure how I should feel. I want to meet them, but I need to finish what's going on here first."

Just then, Ammon came crashing through the door. "We have to leave, right now!" he yelled.

34

Get Down

Cristiano

MY FIRST RESPONSE WAS TO protect her, to shield her from whatever might be coming through the door. When we knew the danger had passed, she peeked out from under the protection of my chest and started to laugh.

But there was nothing humorous about the situation.

"Gather your things, we must leave right now," Ammon yelled to us.

"What is going on?" I asked, filled with adrenaline.

"I'll explain everything once we are on our way. It's no longer safe for any of you."

I had lived my whole life in fear of truly feeling something, and then, all at once, I could feel everything: a sense of duty, love, passion, anger, and instinct. My instinct told me I needed to protect her. Maya had followed me down to Egypt and now I needed to get her out.

"Maya, get Dalley and Ravn. I will gather the bags. Ammon, what about the luggage, the relic?"

"I'll tell you everything once we are on our way." Ammon had moved from panic to calm too quickly, but I could feel the urgency just under the surface.

Maya knocked forcefully on the door letting Ravn and Dalley know we needed to go.

No stranger to stressful situations, they came out of the room disheveled, but ready to run. We left the safe house and jumped into the taxi like our lives depended on it, and truthfully, in that moment they did.

Ammon began slowly driving down the back lane, creeping along in the dark, trying to stay invisible. Then came a flash of light as a set of high beams shone into the vehicle, lighting us up like we were on stage. There was no room to turn around, so Ammon threw the taxi into reverse and started to drive.

"Everyone get down!" Ammon barked.

"Ammon, what is going on?" I thought my head was going to burst.

"Cristiano, I think Ammon is a little busy right now," Dalley quipped.

Maya interrupted me before I unleashed my frustration on Dalley.

"Ammon, please do whatever you have to do to get us out of here," she said with a surprisingly calm tone.

I grabbed her hand and gave it a squeeze as the vehicle sped backwards. Then came the first pop and shattered glass. In the movies, when people are being shot at, it is always so loud, so much yelling and music, but it was so quiet in the car.

I felt sick. It didn't sound real.

"They're shooting at us!" Dalley screamed. Then all chaos broke loose. "Hurry up!" she shrieked, hitting the back of Ammon's head.

"I thought I had left this all behind years ago," Ravn uttered, looking grey and being thrown back into a bad memory.

Another pop and ping on the car.

"Maya, get down on the floor!" I shouted.

"And what, leave you in the seat to get shot?" she answered rebelliously.

"Please listen to me. I have to help Ammon get out of the alley." I pushed her to the floor, feeling her resistance at first, but she finally relented.

"Ammon, we're just about out, turn around now! Now!" Ammon made a hard turn and swerved onto the road. For a moment, we were part of the chaotic flow of regular Cairo traffic. Then Ammon spotted our pursuers in the mirror, jumped the curb, and drove like a crazy man.

"Ammon where are we going?" I yelled, not holding my fear back.

"Pierre has a plane waiting for you at a private air strip."

"What happened while you were out? Where were you?" I grilled him.

Ammon suddenly zigged back into traffic and slowed down a bit.

"Looks like we lost them temporarily," Ravn offered.

Ammon had beads of sweat rolling off his temples and soaking his shirt.

"When I left you, I went to the storage unit in hopes of finding the luggage myself, but by the time I had arrived, someone had beaten me there. They had broken into the unit and found your parents' suitcases. Their clothes were torn, and their possessions tossed all over the ground."

My heart stung with anger at the thought of my parents' belongings being touched and destroyed by thugs.

"What about the relic?" My thoughts jumped to that stupid hair piece, hoping they had found it, hoping this was all over.

"That's the problem, Cristiano. I don't think it was in the luggage."

"What makes you think that?"

"The sheer destruction they left behind and the fact that they are shooting at us. They did not find what they were looking for and won't stop until they do."

I was filled with an irrational urge. "I need to go to the storage unit," I yelled. I knew it was foolish, but I couldn't just leave pieces of their lives strewn on the ground like garbage.

"We have to get to the airstrip," Ammon said, trying to reason with me.

"No, no, no! I need to go and collect their things," I cried out like a child.

"Cristiano, there is no time. We have to get to the airplane right now," Dalley screeched. "I know how you feel, but really …"

My irritation with Dalley exploded.

"Don't ever tell me you know how I feel!" I screamed shutting her down.

Maya unfurled from her position on the floor and crawled back up on to the seat beside me.

"Ammon how far to the storage unit and then to the airstrip?"

"Not far," he said, answering Maya's question. "We can do it if I hurry," he said with certainty.

"Okay, go! I don't want to hear another word from anyone in this car. We are going to the facility and then to the airport," Maya snapped.

The car was silent. Ammon did just as Maya instructed, and when we arrived at the storage unit, the gate was open. He rolled in and drove to where I saw clothes and shoes strewn about on the pavement.

"Everyone get out and help!" Maya ordered.

"Maya, this is crazy!" Dalley resisted.

"Crazy or not, you owe me," Maya said shooting a look at her.

"I don't owe you my life, do I?" Dalley quipped.

"Dalley, just get out of the car and help," Ravn pleaded with gritted teeth.

In silence, we gathered all that we could and threw the items into the least broken suitcase and jumped back into the car.

"So, is anyone hungry? Should we stop for a bite to eat before we leave?" Dalley spat with sarcasm, but at the same time I could hear the fear in her voice. My anger relented. She was right, my need to close this chapter in my life had put them all at risk, but Maya understood that.

Then I felt it, the increase in speed and the evasive turns: it wasn't over.

Maya looked at me and squeezed my hand. She was so calm it almost frightened me. "They found us," Maya whispered into my ear.

We weaved in and out of traffic, fear gripping the vehicle as Ammon worked to evade them.

"Down, everyone down," Ammon yelled.

Just as I pushed Maya down, a bullet cracked through another window. I was not going to move until she was safe. My heart crashed against my ribs and the thought of losing her made me nauseous.

That's when I took Maya's hand. Turning towards her I saw that her eyes were squinted like she was concentrating. She was neither crying nor breathing hard. I wanted to let her know I would never leave her again, that we were bound together in life and death.

"Marry me," I whispered into her ear.

Then it happened. A smile formed on her lips and in her eyes.

"Yes," was all she said.

The world stopped for just a moment; I leaned in and kissed her like my life depended on it. Then our reverie came to a screeching halt as Ammon slammed on the brakes.

"Get out, grab your things, and run!"

35

A Little Distance

Cristiano

AMMON HAD MANAGED TO PUT some distance between ourselves and the Ptolemites, but we knew we only had a few moments. I jumped from the taxi, pulling Maya out behind me.

It was then I saw a look of horror on her face.

"You're bleeding," she screamed.

"It's nothing, we have to keep going," I yelled back at her over the engines of the plane, then pulled the suitcase from the trunk.

Ammon stood quietly by his open door, engine running.

"How can I ever thank you, Ammon?"

"Just stay alive my friend, and let Pierre know he owes me a personal tour in Paris."

"Cristiano, we have to go." Maya pulled at my arm.

"Ammon, come with us," I pleaded.

"No, I will be okay. This is my home, but I had better leave now. I may need to find a new profession in the morning, as I can't drive a taxi with bullet holes in it. Tourists don't like it," he laughed a little. "Now go, the plane is ready."

I turned around and could see Dalley waving her arms, jumping up and down, but could not hear her over the engines. She was pointing. We all turned and saw three sets of headlights coming our way.

By the time we reached the plane and I closed the door, I looked out on to the tarmac. Ammon had disappeared and the cars were dangerously close.

Before I could yell to the pilot, he was already taxiing down the strip and preparing to take off.

We looked out the window and saw the distance growing between ourselves and the Ptolemites.

"Those bastards are shooting at us again," Dalley screeched as she shook her fist and gave them the middle finger.

As the airplane began to climb into the sky, Ravn and Dalley started to laugh. It appeared an adventure of this nature suited them quite well. Maya on the other hand settled into a seat away from everyone. Her brow was furrowed, and my worry began to grow.

My thoughts were only of her as I stepped into the aisle. The next thing I knew I was in a heap on the floor after tripping over my parents' suitcase.

Maya ran over to join me on the carpet. "Cristiano are you okay?" she asked, checking me over with more concern than the fall warranted.

"Yes, of course."

"I wasn't talking about the fall. Take off your shirt!"

"Really, Maya, now?"

"Don't be dumb, you're bleeding."

"Yeah, it happened when we were in the car."

I undid the buttons on my shirt with a little struggle. Once the shirt was off, the trickle of blood increased to a steady flow. Maya turned green.

"You've been shot," she choked out while holding my bloodied shirt.

"Maya, put pressure on the wound while I grab the first aid box," Ravn instructed.

While Maya pressed the shirt into my shoulder, her hands began to shake, and her green complexion turned white. Still holding the bloody garment in her hand, she ran to the bathroom.

Ravn started cleaning up the blood, assessing the damage.

"Good news, he wasn't shot. Bad news, I have to clean it and get some glass out. Dalley, please go look in on Maya. I'll finish up here with Cristiano while you help settle her down. Please let her know it isn't a bullet wound, just a nasty cut. It must have happened when the bullet shattered the taxi window. He is going to be fine, but maybe keep her back there until I get all the pieces out."

"Well I can't stand the sight of blood, so I'm glad you're here to deal with it, Ravn," Dalley said, covering her eyes. She added, "Cristiano, I'm glad you're okay."

"Thank you, Dalley, so am I." As Ravn dug around in my shoulder, the pain was minimal compared to the worry I had for what Maya was going through.

⁓

"Ravn, thank you for helping," I said, wincing slightly as he finished dressing the cut. "It looks like you've done this before."

"Yeah, maybe a couple of times. When I was your age, I took a few extra risks. It's an easy thing to do in my line of work."

"You're a journalist, right?"

"Yeah, I am."

"Have you ever been shot?"

"Just once," he whispered. "But don't tell Dalley. It happened just after she left me. I took an assignment in a dangerous place to distract myself. The bullet that hit me went straight through. I was sore for a long time, but no lasting damage. Oh, here they come. Now that I am done we need to find you a new shirt," he laughed as he checked the dressing around my shoulder.

Ravn went back to his seat and Dalley jumped over me, laughing.

"I say keep the shirt off. The wound needs to settle," she chuckled, looking at Ravn, who went into his bag, pulled out a t-shirt, and threw it to me.

"How's Maya?" I asked Dalley.

"Thankfully, she didn't have very much to throw up. I don't think the girl has eaten properly since she left Porto."

I looked up at her, not being able to hide my distress.

"You did know about her going to Porto right? I don't want to make any more mistakes tonight," Dalley said with a hint of embarrassment masked in sarcasm.

I smiled. "Yes, she has told be everything about my family."

Then I saw Maya making her way towards me with my dirty shirt in her hands.

"Maya, it is just a shirt. Why don't you give it to me? I'll throw it away."

Maya looked past me. "Ravn, you're sure he wasn't shot?"

"Yes, Maya. He is fine, just a few cuts. No bullet holes in your superman."

Maya ignored Ravn's lame joke. "Are you okay? Does it hurt?" she asked, looking worried again and poking at the shoulder.

"Not as much as I deserve."

"What are you talking about?"

"Let's be honest here, Maya. Leaving you, coming to Cairo, my parents, the relic—choose one. I'm sorry I came here, sorry I insisted on going to get their things." I placed my hands over my eyes trying to hide from the decision that almost got us killed.

"Nonsense," she said, sitting up straight again. "You did what you needed to do and so did I. Besides, we are all in one piece, right?" She smiled and swallowed hard. "More or less. Now what about that suitcase? Maybe we should open it."

"Not before you put my shirt on," Ravn said, rolling his eyes. "Dalley is drooling over here and there is only so much a man can take."

I slipped the shirt over my head and Maya helped me maneuver it around my shoulder. Then she opened the case.

As we started going through the dirty and ripped clothes, I saw a little bulge inside a small, zippered compartment. My heart leapt.

"What did you find?" Maya asked with anticipation.

I unzipped the pocket and found a small article wrapped in brown paper.

"No, Maya, it is not the relic, but I believe it's something far more valuable, at least to me. Hold out your hands."

I placed the paper in her shaking fingers.

"What is it?" Maya asked in anticipation.

"Just open it already," Dalley squealed impatiently.

"Relax, Dalley," Ravn said, giving her a poke. Then he whispered something in her ear, and she settled down.

Maya pulled the paper apart. Inside was a small beautiful charm of the pyramids.

Her voice began to shake. "Your father, he bought this for her."

"Yes, yes he did," I smiled. A warmth cascaded over my body, like a familiar touch on my shoulder.

She offered her wrist to me. I unclasped the bracelet, listening to it sing, then placed the charm in between all the others.

"What's going on in that beautiful brain of yours?" I asked gently.

She ran her fingers over the bracelet, holding each charm with such reverence that it made my heart stop.

"I took it off for a few days, vowing I wouldn't put it back on until I found you. But then I gave in and thought maybe it might help me to have you close." She paused. "Beautiful brain? I'm not so sure about that."

While we were chatting, she had picked up a sweater of my mother's; it had been her favorite. I gently took it from her hands and held it to my face.

"I can still smell her, after all these years." I held the sweater close for a minute, remembering everything about her, about them. Tears fell but I was happy. "It's time," I said as I handed the sweater back to Maya. She neatly folded it up and placed it back into the case. "Just one more thing," I added, hoping those bastards had not stolen it. I rooted around until I found it tangled up in all their things. "My dad's watch," I said, picking it up and placing it on my wrist.

"Yes," she said quietly. "It's time to say goodbye." She paused. "When we land, what should we do with the suitcase and the rest of their things?"

"We will take it back to Avo."

⤙⤚

We settled back into our seats, holding hands and taking a moment to breathe, but it was not long before I saw her mind start to move and whirl.

"I am assuming we are going back to Paris. How much longer before we land?" Maya asked.

"I'll check with the pilot. I think you are right though, as Paris is the only place that makes sense. Pierre will want us back there," I said, gritting my teeth at his name.

I got up and walked past Ravn who was raiding the mini bar.

"You okay, Ravn?" I asked, noticing his shaking hands.

"Sure, it's been a few years since I've been shot at and the adrenaline just wore off." He winked at me. "I forgot how it can set the nerves off. Invigorating and a little rattling." Then he leaned in and whispered, "A little more stressful when you have someone beside yourself to keep alive." He tilted his head towards Dalley.

"She is quite the someone," I responded.

Ravn laughed. "Yes, that is one way to describe her, but I love her."

"I can see that. Good luck." I shook my head.

"Yes, I think I'm going to need all the luck I can get," he teased.

"Are you two talking about me?" Dalley smirked, then motioned for me to come closer to her.

"Cristiano, I'm sorry for giving you such a hard time on the ground in Cairo. I am new at being nice and having friends."

I could not help but laugh. Maya was right. Dalley really was trying to turn things around. So, I decided to make peace with her. "Dalley, I want to thank you for stepping up and helping Maya. I still don't understand everything that has happened, but I'm sure Maya will explain."

"Yes, I'm sure she will be happy to tell you all the details but for now, like I said, please believe me when I say I know I was a bad friend and I'm working on changing that."

I pointed to the open computer. "What are you doing there?"

"Don't worry, I won't be publishing a thing unless Maya says yes to it."

"Yes to what?"

"I want to come clean, say sorry to my readers. I want to take my blog back and write it in my own words."

"Take it back?" I responded with surprise.

"Oh, that's right, you didn't know. Maya tried her hand at blogging on my site for a couple of days. It was how I tracked her down. She put way too much personal information in there, but I think she was really hoping you were going to read it."

I flinched with regret at all the distress I had caused Maya.

Dalley clapped her hands, shifting the mood. "Can you imagine, we are on our way back to Paris again," she yelped.

"Yes, Paris. Pierre would want me back on his turf with their luggage in hand wouldn't he? Won't he be disappointed to find out the relic is still missing."

"Well that's not very nice," Dalley scolded.

"When it comes to Pierre, I don't think I feel like being nice right now."

"Well I'm just thankful he was able to get us out of that sandpit in time."

I fell into the empty seat across from her. "I guess I could thank him for that."

She looked like she was going to add something else, then smiled and changed the subject.

"So, did she say yes?" Dalley asked teasingly.

"To what? Who?"

"Maya! You asked her to marry you," she stated bluntly.

I must have looked shocked as Dalley started to laugh.

"Don't be so surprised. You two are so easy to read. In the car? When we were being run down by gunmen?"

I laughed. "You can be very observant when you want to be, but yes, she said yes," I answered happily, not feeling the need to hold it back.

"Is it going to be a double wedding back at Netuno then?"

"Double wedding? Who else is getting married?" I stopped and rubbed my forehead, realizing that I needed to find out everything that had happened since I left. "Can the two of you please fill me in on everything that I've missed."

"Everything?" Dalley said, making the one word long and drawn out.

Maya looked up from writing in her journal and I noticed she was not holding Athena.

"Everything," I remarked. I was determined to set things right and that was not going to happen if I did not hear what they had to say.

"Oh, where to begin?" Dalley teased.

"Maybe with who else is getting married," I asked.

"Carmo and Bento," she said, sounding pleased.

"What? Really?" I looked over at Maya and she was smiling. "What are you talking about?"

"Maybe Maya should tell this part of the story. She was the one who was actually there," Dalley said, motioning to Maya.

"Yes, that is true," Maya said, putting her journal down along with the pencil she was holding. "When Jade's family tried to take over Netuno, there was a chance that Bento could have lost everything. He decided he didn't want to face that situation without Carmo. So, he asked her to marry him. It was very romantic."

"Don't forget about the moonlight and the ring on the olive branch," Dalley interrupted.

"Yes, he did that too as part of his proposal," Maya said with a smile. "Carmo was thrilled and said yes right away. At first they were going to have the wedding after the harvest, but she changed her mind and wants to have it while everyone from the contest is still there. The wedding will take place in just a few days. In addition to the wedding, Puro went to Vancouver to see Maggie, as you know. He was supposed to stay there for a week, but Maggie insisted on returning to the vineyard immediately with Tim.

"I think being at Netuno will give Tim at least a chance to heal," I said, reflecting back on that night in the hospital and remembering Tim curled up in a ball on the chairs after watching his twin brother die.

"I hope some of the wedding excitement also puts people in a forgiving mood," Dalley interrupted. "Ravn and I are heading down there—I have some groveling to do, but may need to bring a little something extra to help with the forgetting part."

"Yes, I think I have a few apologies of my own to make when I return home," I said, making eye contact with Maya again.

✧

When I returned to my seat Maya was holding her journal and an old HB pencil.

"Where is Athena?" I asked with confusion.

She hesitated and looked over at Dalley.

"He said he wanted to know everything; it's your turn," Dalley quipped.

"A lot happened that Friday night after you left Netuno." She swallowed hard, like the words were stuck in her throat. Then she unclenched her hands and began. "When Puro handed me the box you gave him, I opened it right away. On seeing the pen, I knew the truth. I didn't know the details of how or why, but I knew that somehow you had gotten Athena back for me. No one could convince me you had done anything wrong because you hadn't. Next, I punched Dalley in the face and knocked her out," she said covering her mouth in embarrassment.

"You did what?" I stared at her, hardly able to believe it, then turned to Dalley, who rubbed her jaw and laughed.

"I deserved it. I didn't know she had it in her. But I deserved it." Ravn shook his head and pretended to take a punch and pass out. "Hey that's not funny, only I can laugh at myself." He shrugged and went back to reading a magazine.

"So, what happened to the pen then?" I asked, still confused.

"Yes, Athena. The next day as my head was spinning, I needed to write things out, so I grabbed Athena out of the box. She felt light. When I unscrewed the lid, I discovered why. She was empty, her ink was gone, and she was broken inside."

"Broken? How?"

"Jade," was all she needed to say.

"Why would she do something like that?"

"Oh, I don't know, but I think she is an incredibly sad person. Maybe mentally unstable? Ravn can concur with that. He spoke with her two days ago in a faux 'interview' for some made up paper. From what we understand, after she screwed up with the blog stuff, her father fired her. I thought when she left Netuno that was the last I would ever see of her but Ravn said she's on her way to Europe right now. She blames me for ruining her life. Kind of ironic, don't you think? Anyways I can't write with Athena again, so I just keep her near me."

Maya went into her bag and pulled out the two broken pieces. I took them from her, hoping that somehow I could fix it, but she was right. Jade had ruined Athena's ability to write, but she could still shine.

"It's okay, I'll keep my eyes open and one day I'll find you another pen that will sparkle just like Athena."

"I don't think I could ever replace her," Maya said, putting Athena away.

"Well maybe not replace her, but I promise you I'll find something else that is just as special."

I wrapped my arms around her, inviting her to settle into my chest.

"I'm so tired. I need to rest my eyes," she whispered.

As she danced on the edge of sleep, I held her tightly, enjoying the softness of her skin and the warmth of her hand. I started thinking about the heroic drive to the airport and the timing of my proposal. *Did she really mean to say yes? Or was it just a knee jerk reaction to the danger we were in? Bento's proposal was romantic, mine was frantic. Not every girls' dream.* Then my nerves started to roll through my body, and she squeezed my hand and opened her eyes.

"What is it?" she asked.

I looked nervously at her, "Yes."

"Yes, what?" she asked, now fully awake and looking concerned.

"You said yes, I just wanted to make sure …"

She laughed. "That I meant it?" she said, sitting up in her seat. "I have had two men ask me to marry them. The first time I said yes, it took me two weeks to answer. I should have said no. And the second, well there was only one word, one thought. I've never felt clearer about anything in my life. The truth is, I want to get married to you as soon as possible."

"Really?" I responded with anticipation and relief.

"Yes," she answered resolutely.

"How soon?"

"Tomorrow."

I could not tell if she was teasing or serious. "Maya. We can't get married tomorrow. This isn't Vegas. And as much as you think you want to get married right away, I think you would regret it."

"Nope," she said stubbornly.

"You are being childish now."

"Yes, I am. But you're right. We can't do it tomorrow, but we can next week," she said, sparkling. "My parents will both be here."

"Both?"

"Oh, yah, I forgot that part. My dad is flying in for Carmo and Bento's wedding. I'm sure he would stick around for ours. Don't worry, my mom will set him straight before you have to meet him."

"Set him straight? Oh, okay," I said, suddenly feeling nervous, but the anticipation on her face of us possibly being able to marry next week pushed the nerves of meeting her parents to the back of my mind—almost. "Tell me what you want, and I'll make it happen."

"The chapel at Netuno. I want it there, with a priest and only a few people."

"Hmm, sounds like the right people will already be there but it may take a little while to get the priest in place."

"Are you telling me I may have to *wait*?" she scowled at me while placing her hand high on my thigh.

I laughed. "Yes, my love, you may have to *wait* a little longer for everything," I said, removing her hand.

"*You* started this back in the desert and then again at the safe house," she said, shaking her finger at me.

Dalley sighed with exasperation. "Oh my God you guys, just make it official and join the mile-high club already. Ravn and I will put on some headphones and then you can have the wedding any time."

"Getting married isn't about *that* for me," Maya rebutted.

"You are such a liar. The two of you have been on edge ever since you found him crumpled over that airplane wing."

"Dalley, that is enough," Ravn intervened as the whiskey that Dalley had been enjoying was starting to show through in her conversation.

I had to give Dalley some credit though. She was right about one thing: I was tempted to give my heart and body over to Maya, but I could not give in. It meant too much to both of us.

"What are you thinking about?" Maya asked spryly, "Mile high? Perhaps?"

"Don't you start too. I'm not sure I am that strong." I gave her a little push away.

"Maybe we are crazy, maybe we should throw caution to the wind and just …" she said, leaving her words hanging.

"No, I am standing firm on this one, for both of us," I said, folding my arms across my chest.

"Are you, now?" she batted her eyes.

"Yes, I am," I said resolutely.

"Well, as firm as you are, that doesn't mean I can't have a little fun. Does it?"

She leaned in and kissed me with such gentle and persistent passion that my hands started to shake. I could feel a flurry of goosebumps rise all over my body. I was hot and cold at the same time. It told me so much. How much she loved me, that she was ready to move forward, to build a life, no matter where it took us. I pulled back and stared at her for a moment, then dove back in, leaving behind any thoughts of Dalley, Ravn, or the world that we needed to deal with once the wheels touched down in Paris. When our lips met again, I could feel the ragged edges of my heart smoothing over and coming back together. In that instant, all the pain, everything I had gone through, it was all worth it as it had led me to her and to the life we were going to build together.

36

nice

Jade

"Stop touching me and get your hand off my armrest."

"What is your problem lady? This is economy, not first class."

"Lady? I'm not old," I spat back at him.

"Whatever, *lady*," he said, prodding me as he spread out his arms, flopping farther into my space. I think he was laughing.

"I hate people," I said loud enough for him to hear.

"Well, I'm pretty sure people hate you too." After that he put on his headphones, closed his eyes, and went to sleep.

We were now just thirty minutes into the flight to Lisbon and I was in hell. "*She* put me here. *She* created this whole mess."

In that moment I wasn't sure who I hated more: Maya or the bastard who was stealing my armrest. "Maya, definitely Maya, I just want to kill her, but you come a close second," I said scowling at my neighbor. "She could have saved me all this trouble if she had just stepped out of my way on that day in Montreal and let me have Cristiano. None of this would have happened and I would still be sitting in first class."

I attempted to push the man's arm away from me, but it was dead weight. So, I was left to squirm in my seat, sandwiched between some geek playing video games and Mr. Flabby Arm, who I was sure must have eaten an entire onion before he got on the plane.

"Hey," the gamer grunted.

"What do you want?" I bit back at him.

"What is your problem?" he asked, laughing at me.

"You shouldn't talk like that, it's rude."

"I'm not rude, you're rude. You bumped me and made me lose my game."

"Oh, shut up," I snarled.

"You can't tell me to shut up."

"What kind of parents raised you?"

"What kind of parents raised *you?*" he laughed.

"My dad is a multi-millionaire asshole and my mother is dead."

The fellow's eyes widened. He shut his mouth and went back to his game. Mission accomplished, or so I thought.

"How old were you when your mom died?"

"Little. I was actually the one who found her." I wasn't sure why I answered his question.

He placed his game console in the back of the seat and started to talk.

"That's horrible. Someone I loved very much died last year. I was really sad; I'm still sad." He touched my hand but pulled back quickly when I flinched. "I don't know what I would do if my mom died," he said reflectively.

I thought back to the day I found her. "I remember seeing her on the floor. She was grey and cold. She didn't look like herself. She almost looked flat," I said, wincing a little at the memory. "I tried to wake her up but didn't understand what was happening, so I called 911 and opened the door for the paramedics. They called my dad, but he was already at the office working. He never came home. He just told the ambulance driver to drop me at school. The driver told me it was okay to cry, but I knew that if my dad found out I had cried, I would be in big trouble."

"Your dad left you by yourself? After you found your mom dead on the floor?" He looked horrified. I had always liked telling that story to shock people, but this guy actually felt sad for me.

"Yeah, no father of the year awards. When he got home that night he told me that people die, and people disappoint you all the time. He said the only person you can count on is yourself."

"Seriously, that's the only advice you got from your dad after finding your mother dead on the floor?"

"That, and three days later when he moved his mistress into the house he told me to 'embrace the change,' and to be nice to her and call her mom."

"Your dad really is an asshole."

"Yes, no doubts there."

"He sounds like the exact opposite to my mom. She is nice to everyone, and generally really happy." the gamer shared.

"Well, she sounds weak," I said, wanting to get a hold of the conversation as it had gotten too personal.

"Wow, are you always so mean? And no," he said, defending her, "she is not weak. She is the strongest and most courageous woman I know."

I froze for a moment as he crossed his arms.

"Maybe you can pretend to be nice for a minute? I see my mom coming down the aisle."

"Hi dear, how are you doing? Settling into the flight?" the middle-aged lady asked her son.

"Oh, I'm alright mom. You know me, making friends already." He motioned toward me.

"Hello," she said gently, putting her hand out towards me. I took it cautiously and she wrapped both of hers over mine. "I'm Hazel."

I rolled my eyes.

She smiled and let out a little chuckle. "I know it's an old-fashioned name. My mom was just like that. Oh, you have the loveliest complexion, and your outfit is so stylish. You look like a model."

I was speechless for a moment. The gamer was right. She was the exact opposite of my dad—nice."

"Hi, I'm Jade Axeline," I answered with caution.

"Oh, Jade, what a lovely name. I had better make my way to my seat. George, if the young lady wants anything, make sure you take care of that for her."

"Yes, mom. I'll come see you in a few hours," he said, sounding embarrassed.

After Hazel returned to her seat, I felt undone. Or maybe unnerved. I couldn't tell which.

"George, is it?"

"Yes,' he said with a shrug.

"You're right. Your mom is kind. Maybe there is one nice person in the world—maybe even two," I said as I smiled slightly at him.

"Hm, you're not completely horrible like some people are saying."

I felt a wave of shock roll through my body. "So, you know who I am?" I asked, feeling my walls shooting back up.

"Yah, I figured it out a few minutes ago. At first, I could not place your face, but the name, well ..." He shrugged his shoulders. "My mom only follows a few knitting bloggers, she has no idea who you are."

I huffed a little. "Don't go telling anyone about me having a moment of weakness or you may ruin my reputation. I prefer to be mean; it takes less energy than being nice."

I woke somewhere over the Atlantic and touched my hand where Hazel had held it. I thought about the interaction I had had with the gamer and decided I had better channel my inner Axel and move to a different seat while he slept. Once settled in my new seat, and after ticking off two flight attendants, I pulled a hand wipe out of my bag and wiped Hazel's niceness off, then threw it on the ground. And thankfully fifteen minutes later I was feeling more myself and plotting a full-scale revenge scenario against Maya. I ultimately removed murder from the list but was prepared to do pretty much anything else—I wanted her to suffer and to know that I was part of that.

37

Healing Hearts

Maya

"ARE YOU GOING TO INCLUDE me in your conversation?" Cristiano asked as we waited for the airplane door to open.

"Sorry, I didn't think I was talking out loud."

"You weren't. But your face is very expressive and easy to read. Besides, I don't need to hear the words to know that you're a little curious about where we go from here."

"Yes, literally and figuratively. But I wasn't really having a conversation with myself, it was more like an argument."

"Did you win?"

"Yes, I did."

"Well then, that's all that counts," he said, giving me a squeeze and not asking what the argument was about.

Ravn and Dalley pushed passed us, wanting to be the first ones off the plane.

"Well I don't know about you two, but Ravn and I are heading down to Netuno as soon as possible. He said I had to arrive a few days before the wedding to set things right. Let's hope Josie and Petra will forgive me, not to mention everyone else. At least Maggie and I had a chance to chat before we left. Maybe she will soften them up for me. Any last-minute advice Maya?"

I smiled. "Bring a couple bottles of French wine."

"I think we might need to buy a case," Ravn smirked, but clearly was not kidding.

Dalley sighed, then her eyes sparkled with mischief. "I guess that means maybe one or two more days in Paris?" she smiled at Ravn.

"No, we fly out to Lisbon tonight. I am taking you back to the scene of the crime before you chicken out."

Dalley shoved him lovingly, but before stepping off the plane she turned back to me, "Maya, I want to thank you."

"Thank me? For what?"

"For trusting me when you had no reason to, and for punching me."

"You're thanking me for punching you?" I laughed and shook my head.

"Yes, your punch actually woke me up and helped me to find Ravn and myself again—well maybe myself for the first time. I feel like I want to start over. I know we haven't spoken about it yet, but I was wondering if I could take back Price's Portugal?"

"Oh, it's like you read my mind. I'm done with being in the public eye. Yes, you can have the blog back just as long as …"

She interrupted me, "No, you don't need to say it. Every word will be my own and if I tell someone else's story, I will do it through my own lens, the way it should be. I don't know if anyone will ever read my stuff again, but I don't care. At least I know it will be mine."

"Maybe it's time to write your own story. From what you told me I think you have a lot to say."

Dalley breathed out slowly and smiled.

Ravn kissed her forehead and the two of them stepped off the plane. She yelled back as she walked down the stairs, "See you at the wedding!"

"So, where to? London? Madrid?" Cristiano asked, holding out his hand.

"That sounds tempting, but I made a promise a few days ago that we need to keep."

"And what promise would that be?"

"Porto, we are going to Porto. I promised your family that when I found you, I would bring you home."

"Home? I'm not sure what that means yet. Besides …" he said, changing the subject. "I thought you might want to get back to Netuno right away, to see your mom, to get ready for our wedding."

"Cristiano, as silly as I was on the plane, I know we can't get married yet, but we can go and meet your family. Then we can head down for Carmo and Bento's wedding and you can meet my parents. My mom can live without me for a few more days. Your mom, on the other hand, has been waiting to see you again for twenty-eight years."

I saw the tears form in his eyes, but he held them firmly in place. Gathering our things, we headed out into the cool French air. As we walked onto the tarmac, an airport representative approached us.

"Monsieur, you are Cristiano Lazaro?"

"Yes, I am."

"Monsieur La Nou dropped your car off earlier and had it detailed. It is in the private lot."

We stared at one another. Cristiano had not mentioned Pierre's name after we narrowly escaped from Cairo. I had overheard his conversation with Dalley on the plane and knew he was still terribly angry.

"Do you want to see him?" I asked hesitantly.

"No," he blurted out with agitation. "I'll fly back after Carmo and Bento's wedding and deal with him then."

"Should we call him?"

"No, if he wanted to see me, he would be here right now. Besides, I don't know what I would say to him." He stood for a long minute, swinging his keys in his hand. "I just wish he had told me the whole story and had not left it up to me to put the pieces together. He put you in danger. If anything had happened to you, I don't know what I would have done."

"You can't blame Pierre for me going to Cairo. I knew it could be dangerous, but I didn't care. It only made me more determined to find you. There was no stopping me. I figure my first rescue mission went not too badly."

He shook his head and took a breath. "First?"

"Yes, it feels like my inner adventurer has broken out of the box, and she's not going back anytime soon."

"So, where does that leave us now? Dalley might need some rescuing from the people at Netuno." he said playfully.

"Or maybe an adventure with a hot shower?"

"Well how about I leave that up to you. Tonight I am up for just about anything that ends with some food, a shower, and a comfy bed … but I do have a thought that might get us started."

His boyish smile sent an inviting thrill up my spine. When I reached out to trace his lips. He kissed my fingertips, causing a shock to cascade over my skin. He didn't say a word but stepped in closer to me. My hands began moving along the lines of his body, following each curve and muscle. There was a wanting within me I had never felt before. He felt it too, but he held back just enough for me to know the rules had not changed. I was not going to let that stop me though from testing his resolve. I started with the small of his back, then found the perfect spot just below his belt where his body started to curve at the tip of his tailbone. My fingers lingered, gently stroking his warming skin. He looked at me, appearing flushed.

"Maya," he said weakly melting under my touch.

I pulled him in closer, slowly edging my hand back up to his waist.

"What am I going to do with you?" he asked.

"I've changed my mind. Marry me and we can solve this conundrum," I answered simply.

"I thought you said you were in no rush."

"That is not what I said. I said I understood it might be difficult to make something like that happen in a week's time, not that I wouldn't jump at the chance if I could."

Clearly my touch had transported him somewhere else and it was taking every ounce of concentration for him not to just take me on the tarmac.

But we needed to focus. "How long will it take us to drive to Porto?"

"Porto. Yes, I almost forgot," he said, blaming me for his memory loss.

"Oh, there is no forgetting. I promised your sister I would bring you back before she started school. She was afraid that something bad might happen to you and she would never get a chance to meet you, but your mom was lovely and knew just what to say to help her."

"My mom. It feels strange to call someone else that. To know I have a mother again after all these years, but a different one."

☙

When Cristiano saw his car, he took a breath and sighed like when you see an old friend.

He stepped back and stared intensely at me with his eyes glistening as he spoke his next words.

"I love you, Maya."

"I love you, Cristiano."

Our declarations were interrupted by the sound of laughter as a group of people walked by, heading towards their own car.

"I think we had better get on the road if we are going to make our first stop."

"And where would that be?" I asked, feeling a spark of anticipation.

"Do you want me to tell you?"

"No, make it a surprise. How long until we get there?"

"We haven't even started driving yet, Maya."

"I just want to know if we need to stop for snacks."

He laughed. "Five hours in good traffic."

"So, you mean three hours the way you drive?"

"Maybe three and a half. We are in France and I don't want to break any laws." He chuckled, then threw our bags and his parents' suitcase behind the seats and opened the door for me.

"Last chance," he said, casting his eyes to the ground before coyly looking up.

"Last chance for what? Me to drive?" I jumped into the car and pretended to climb into his seat. He threw his keys to me calling my bluff.

"Sure, whatever you want, I trust you," he said, breaking into a snicker.

I rolled my eyes and threw the keys back at him. "Not unless you want to end up in Romania."

"Romania is very nice this time of year," he said with a shrug.

"Yes, but opposite to where we are trying to get to," I reminded him.

"If we hurry, we can make our destination by about 2:00 a.m. I think. Fancy or rustic?" he asked.

"Fancy," I responded, feeling a little whimsical and having no real idea what he was talking about.

"Can I have your phone?"

I searched through my bag and handed it over to him. Our fingers touched innocently, and our bodies connected in warmth. He felt it too as his hand lingered near mine.

He made a call and booked us into a hotel. When he handed the phone back to me, I went to put it away, but a loud thought popped into my head and I figured I had better listen.

"Who are you calling?" he asked with interest.

"My mother."

"Are we in trouble?"

I shrugged my shoulders.

"I don't know. She and I are just getting to know one another. We only spoke briefly before I left for Egypt."

⁓

"Mom, its Maya. I know you're there; I can hear you breathing." Next, I heard her exhale, so I jumped in. "We've landed in Paris. I'm safe." I paused. "You didn't worry too much, did you?"

"No, my dear, of course not. I am fine now. Pierre called again a little while ago, letting us know you both arrived safely."

"Again?" I asked her while looking at Cristiano.

She paused. "You *are* safe? Right?" she whispered into the phone.

"Yes. I'm with Cristiano. I'll see you in a couple days when I get back to Netuno."

"A couple of days?" She sounded disappointed by my news. "You're not coming back right now?"

"No, Cristiano and I must go to Porto. I promised his family that I would bring him home when I found him, Mom."

"Of course, Maya, I understand." I heard a sigh, and then a small laugh. "I'm proud of you. Oh, I just heard from your dad. He'll be arriving in a few days."

"Mom, how is he doing with all of this?"

"Well, truthfully he does not quite sound like himself. I am sure he will be fine when he sees that you are all right. There was a pause. "Maya, may I speak to Cristiano please?" I cringed and then passed him the phone. "My mom wants to talk to you."

He looked panicked at first but pulled himself together.

"Hello?" His face was serious to start, then I saw something change. While concentrating on her every word, he ran his hand through his hair and nodded his head as if she could see him. "I understand. You're sure? If not, we can come right now." He burst into laughter. After a few quiet moments, several tears rolled down his cheeks. "Goodbye Judith. Please send her my love and let her know I will be home soon." He hung up.

"What did she say?"

"She told me to tell you that she loves you."

"No, I know that. What did she say to you?"

"She let me know that Avo is doing better and is waiting for us to come home." He leaned in and kissed me again.

"What did she say that made you laugh?"

"Ah, that's between the two of us."

"You're already keeping secrets from me?"

"Yes, just this one."

"Well, as long as you don't make a habit out of it."

"Secrets don't have to be a bad thing. She was lovely by the way."

"Well, one down, one to go," I said trying to smile.

"One to go?"

"Your mom is next."

He paused and looked at the phone like he wanted to drop it.

"I am sure by now she knows we arrived." He looked at me asking how. "When we landed I texted your sister to let her know we were safe and in Paris," I paused. "I told her we were coming there as promised."

"Oh, so you confirmed with her before you checked with me? Are you sure we're not married yet?"

I rolled my eyes and took the phone out of his hand, scrolled through my short list of numbers, then pressed call. I offered the phone back to him, but he couldn't take it.

"Maya? Is that you?" Her voice was so warm and inviting.

"Hello, Euphemia."

"Is he there?" Her voice trembled.

"Yes, you're on speakerphone if that is okay."

"Whatever he wants."

"He's not quite ready to talk, but he is listening."

Cristiano looked at me, not sure what to say. He mouthed to me, 'I can't do this.'

"Euphemia, just start talking," I said, trying to encourage her.

"Oh, of course. Hi Cristiano, it is me, Euphemia, your mother. You can call me whatever you like though." She paused. "I saw you in your car the other day. I had this strange feeling, but I was not sure why. I even ran downstairs, but you had already left." She stopped again. "I loved you, love you." Cristiano took the phone and leaned back into his seat.

"When I found out I was pregnant with you I loved you like you had always existed. You were part of me, and I did not want to let you go. When my family told me I was not allowed to keep you, I almost died. The only thing that kept me alive was knowing that you were loved by Rosa and Michel and Avo." She paused. "On the days when my heart ached, and I thought I would break apart, I would imagine holding you in my arms. I came to see you one day, when you were little. You were at Avo's and just learning to walk. I wanted to run to you and steal you away, but you were not mine anymore. So, I had to go. Saying goodbye the second time tore me in half, and it took months for me to start breathing again, but Marcos and I helped each other find a path without you. I left home that day with your father so we could be together and start our life, but we never forgot about you."

There was no holding back my tears as I heard the story of a mother having to walk away from a piece of her heart, leaving it in the care of another woman. I could not imagine the strength and courage that would take. I knew I could never do it.

"I was loved …" he whispered back into the phone, his tears now rolling too. "They gave me everything they could in the seven years I had with them. And Avo, well, she gave me everything else … Mom?"

I heard a gasp through the phone line that made me tremble.

"Mom?" Cristiano tried again.

"I …" was all we heard, then she burst into tears.

"Please don't cry. I don't have to call you that if you don't want."

"Oh, Cristiano, it's not that at all. I've never wanted anything more in my life. I just never thought I would ever hear you say it. Please say it again," Euphemia asked between her sobs.

"Hi, Mom," he said awkwardly.

More tears flowed from both sides of the phone.

"We are on our way there right now," he said with some urgency.

"Are you okay? How did Maya find you? She loves you very much. Did you know your father flew her out to Paris? Your brother and sister are waiting to meet you. Your father well, he kind of met you, didn't he? Do you know about that? Of course you do, but we can talk about that when we see each other. Oh goodness, I'm rambling now."

"Listen to me. We have lots of time to get to know one another—the rest of our lives actually."

A male voice came on to the phone. "Cristiano, I think your mother needs a few minutes."

Cristiano's face went pale.

"Cristiano? Are you there?" Marcos asked gently.

I jumped into the conversation. "Marcos, it's Maya; maybe we should save the rest of the hellos for when we arrive. Cristiano and I will be there in two days."

"Two days?" His voice cracked. "You're in Paris. Just fly home, please. I'll buy the tickets," he said, sounding desperate.

"Marcos … I hope you understand but Cristiano and I really need some time together." The phone went silent on the other end.

"Hi Maya, it's me Jacinta. Sorry about the two of them. They're crying on the couch right now. Did I hear my dad correctly? Two days?" Jacinta asked impatiently.

"Yes, two days."

"Well, hurry up. I am so excited. Can I talk to him?"

I looked over and Cristiano was smiling.

"Yes, he's right here."

"Hi Jacinta," he said. "I'm really looking forward to meeting you."

"Cristiano, I feel like I know you already with everything that Maya has told me; I can't wait. Hey, I was wondering, with you being a flight attendant and us being family now, does that mean I get a discount on my flights?"

I heard a tussle on the phone and the other male voice of the family took over.

"Cristiano, it's Zef. You must think we are all crazy. My sister, ah, our sister doesn't really have a filter and, well, the other two are a little broken right now."

"And you?" Cristiano asked. "What are you right now?"

"I have a brother. I just want to get to know you. See you soon." The call ended, and he handed me the phone.

"Should we fly?" he asked with uncertainty.

"No, we should drive. We need to be together. We need to drive." I squeezed his hand.

He nodded his head, turned the key, and revved the engine. As we left the lot I heard him mumbling something to himself about his brother and home.

❧

During the first two hours of the drive, I tried to engage Cristiano in conversation, but he was deep in thought. So, I just closed my eyes and enjoyed the night air as the wind kept me company. At one point, Cristiano took a hard corner and by accident my hand gently brushed his leg. Startled by my touch, he swerved slightly into the lane of oncoming traffic but quickly recovered. I drew my hand back, not sure what to say. As my heart rate returned to normal, it appeared his had not. He looked tired and agitated and I noticed there were a few spots of blood leaking through the bandage that Ravn had taped to his shoulder.

"You're bleeding again," I said with concern.

"We should stop and eat," he said ignoring my comment.

"Yes, whatever you think. Does it hurt?" I asked quietly.

He shrugged, acknowledging me but not answering.

He took the next exit and we stopped at a little French tavern. I wasn't sure what was going through his mind, but from what I saw, he didn't really know either.

The tavern was quite lively, and it was clear he wanted none of it.

"Do you have something quieter?" he asked the hostess.

The girl smiled then led us out back. As Cristiano walked ahead, she noticed the blood on his shirt and looked at me with alarm.

"Do you have some bandages? He had a fall," I lied.

She smiled warily, and after seating us scooted off only to return a few minutes later with a few gauze pads and tape. She discreetly gave me the supplies and I placed them in my bag, as he was still not talking to me.

After ordering our food the silence at the table became almost too much for me. I was about ready to launch into an 'I'm worried' speech when he suddenly asked for my phone. It was in that moment I remembered a conversation Grandma Stella had with me a few days before I was supposed to marry Steven. She was talking about moments in a marriage when you just need to be quiet and let him be. After acknowledging that I was inside one of those moments I pulled out my journal and dropped into my own quiet world.

> *Doesn't matter what day it is...*
>
> *We are sitting right now at a tavern somewhere in France. We made it out of Egypt, and he asked me to marry him. I said yes, and then I said yes again. I told him I would marry him tomorrow if we could.*
>
> *He is quiet right now, looking things up on the phone and picking at his food. I'm not sure what or how he is doing...I want to ask him, but I don't think I should.*
>
> *Are you kidding me? Sorry Grandma Stella he has been silent long enough. You also said there may be*

a time when you need to knock them upside the head. Maybe it's time for that.

"Cristiano. Cristiano!" I said, raising my voice slightly. "What is going on?"

He looked startled. "Nothing. I just wanted to take care of a few things that were on my mind."

I decided it was not the time for head knocking as he looked close to tears.

"Anything I can do to help?"

"No, thank you, you go ahead and write.

He reached over and touched my hand. "I'll be fine."

He says he's fine but I'm not buying it. I'm giving him until the end of our meal and then let the head knocking begin.
Maya

He continued to work busily on the phone. I don't think he could even tell me what he ate. When he was done, he paid the bill and we left.

"We should arrive in Bordeaux very soon," he said abruptly.

I nodded my head waiting for the right moment. We drove for another hour or so, his silence still dominating the conversation. When I was just about ready to lose my mind, he pulled off the highway and headed down a dirt road.

"We're here," he said almost sheepishly.

"Where's here?" I asked, feeling annoyed now.

"Just wait, two more turns," he said excitedly. Suddenly he was acting like the last two hours hadn't just happened.

Then I saw it. "What is this place?"

He laughed. "This, my love, is our hotel."

Calling me his love was all I needed, and I threw my feelings of worry and annoyance into the glove box.

"That is not a hotel!" I said, laughing and looking at its palatial columns.

"Yes, it is. You said fancy, and it is my job now to answer your call."

"Your job?"

"Yes, I am your almost-husband. It is my duty to listen to you and answer your needs."

"Your duty? We'll have to talk about that later, but for now, I am going to throw caution to the wind and say yes."

"Good. I was afraid you were going to say it was too much and make us sleep in the car or something."

"I can be spontaneous, I thought I proved that to you already. Besides, I haven't slept properly for days and I don't think either of us has had a shower recently." I grimaced.

Then we both laughed.

"Oh, I wanted to give you a heads up before we get to our room. The suite I booked only has a king-size bed."

"Suite? Only a king size bed? I guess we'll have to improvise. I do have some self-restraint."

He pulled up to the palatial entry and left the car running. Three young men ran towards us, all vying for the honor to park his car. The man who won beamed as he slipped into the driver's seat and rubbed his hands on the wheel. I knew exactly how he felt. The other two gentlemen took our bags minus the broken suitcase at Cristiano's request.

The concierge approached. "Good evening, Mr. Lazaro, the suite has been prepared just as you asked."

My stomach jumped and my body ached at the thought of a good night's sleep.

The concierge walked us to an elevator. "Mr. Lazaro, your shoulder, it's bleeding!"

"Oh, it's nothing. I had a little accident."

I jumped in. "I have everything we need, thank you."

"Very well. Here is your elevator code. Please enjoy your stay and let us know if there is anything else we can do."

We walked into the elevator and the doors closed silently behind us. He took my hands, his look of distress returning from before.

"I'm sorry," he blurted out. "That was reckless of me. I can't believe I already broke one of my promises to her."

"What are you talking about? What promise? To who?"

"Your mom. I promised her I would keep you safe and I couldn't even do that for two hours. I swerved into traffic, Maya."

"I startled you, Cristiano."

"I should have been paying more attention."

"We both should have been paying more attention."

"You could have been killed."

"But I wasn't."

"I could barely hold things together long enough to get you here in one piece. I'm bleeding all over the place …"

I paused for a moment. "You need to stop." I hoped my assumption was right.

"Stop what?" He looked very confused.

"Wishing you would have made a different decision on Friday night—

"But …"

"But nothing. If you had stayed, confronted Steven, we would not be here, right now. You would not have had the chance to say goodbye to your parents or find the charm." I pulled my hand away from him and jingled my bracelet. "And I, well I would not have jumped on a train to Porto, flown to Paris, and almost got arrested at the Louvre."

"Arrested at the Louvre?" he said, looking baffled.

"Almost … I'll tell you later. I found your family and then you."

He lifted his head. "Maybe you're right, but maybe we could have done without the dramatic car chase and escape from the Ptolemites?"

"Really? I thought that was the best part of our adventure so far. Isn't that when you asked me to marry you? That's going to be the best story to tell our kids one day."

"Kids?"

"Yes, I want them, don't you?" The elevator stopped, and we both froze.

"I could not imagine anything more perfect," he said as the doors of the elevator opened to our room.

Before I had a chance to think, he grabbed me in his arms and carried me into the suite. The lights were low and gentle. Jazz music filled the space. There was a bottle of wine open and ready on a table along with a plate of cheese, bread, chocolate, and fruit.

"I love the French," I sighed. Then he kissed me.

38

Coming Clean

Dalley

AFTER MAKING A QUICK AND humiliating call to ask Joe for my job back, I picked up my peace offering of beautiful French wines. The sommelier we met at the airport wine store was more than helpful and put together an exquisite assortment of bottles that I hoped would soften the ground before my arrival at Netuno. I had the case shipped there and according to my plan, it would arrive just before I trundled down the dirt road and stepped through the door, asking for forgiveness and hoping for a second chance.

It had been a long time since I had hoped for anything, but I was willing to try. Having real friends for the first time, well, it was not something I was going to give up without a fight. I sent the case off with a wish and a prayer. Although I wasn't a believer in magic nor particularly religious, I was willing to try anything once.

"So, what did Joe say?" Ravn asked with some speculation.

"Not a lot, something sarcastic. I told him I wanted to change the name of the blog, but that's where he drew the line. So, I agreed to keep it Price's Portugal for now if he let me post whatever I wanted. He complained that there hadn't been a decent post in days and the traffic was down. At that point, I hung up and texted him I would have something written by morning."

"You will?"

"Yes, I didn't say which morning, just morning."

"We board our flight to Lisbon in about an hour," Ravn offered, changing the subject.

"That's perfect, just enough time." I smiled coyly.

"Time for what?" he asked knowingly.

"Time for anything we want," I said, leaning in closer to him.

He laughed at my not so subtle suggestion, shrugged, and agreed.

"What are we going to do with the other forty-five minutes?" he asked, smirking.

"Eat. I'm starving. What about you?"

"Oh, I could eat," he said, pulling me in for a deep and passionate kiss. When he let me go, we both laughed and went in search of a perfect spot for an airport rendezvous that would satisfy all our needs.

⁌⁍

We had to run to catch our flight, and once on the plane, we collapsed into our seats. It didn't take long, though, before my nerves began to seep into a perfectly lovely moment.

"How could you possibly look worried right now?" Ravn asked, seeing my face. "Over the last seventy-two hours, you found me, set things right with Maya, survived being shot at, got your job back, and we are on our way to a wedding. What more could a girl ask for?" Ravn teased lightly, trying to lift my spirits.

"Ravn, I'm not in the mood. You didn't see them that night, standing there, backs turned to me. They wouldn't listen."

"And why should they have? What you did to Maya was awful."

"You're not being very nice," I said, feeling hurt, wanting him to be on my side.

Ravn took my hand. "Are you with me because I am nice or truthful?"

I sighed and punched him in the arm.

"I thought so," he said, satisfied that he had won that round of our discussion.

Once the plane took off, I pulled out my computer, put on my head-phones, and started. The blog title was:

Coming Clean By Dalley Price

Have you ever woken up with a bruise on your face, looked in the mirror and thought, how the hell did I get that? Well I never wondered. I knew exactly why my cheek was swollen, and I was holding an empty liquor bottle in one hand and three chocolate bar wrappers in another; I deserved it.

I remember the moment when her fist hit my face. I heard a crack and then it went dark. The next thing I remember was me crawling up the stairs. When I arrived in our room, I tore it apart. I was so ashamed. I had broken a trust, a bond of newly forged friendships.

For the first time in my life I had real friends and I threw it away, for what?

The truth is, I didn't believe in myself. For all the confidence that I pretended to have it only took one person's opinion for me to step into an alternative world of deceit and thievery. The most horrible part was that it was exciting, I felt like a spy or a pirate at first, and then when I wanted to stop, when my conscience started to tear at me and wine stopped tasting good, it was too late.

It sounds like an excuse, but somehow I justified taking my friend's journal writings and crafting a series of blogs that told her story as if it were mine to tell. And by revealing her raw truth, I exposed all her vulnerabilities. I scaled and gutted people's lives for a story, for you and for me. My actions created a cascading series of events that almost stole the lives and the livelihoods of people I care about but … it didn't; in the end it brought them together. Their strength and belief in one another allowed them to find a way through the mess I left behind. As for my friend and her journal, well I made it my mission to find her and I did. And she forgave me. I know it is hard to believe, but it's true. Maya then became the superhero, and I her trusty sidekick as we knocked down doors and found the love of her life. Mind you we can't take all the credit. When Maya's mom discovered her daughter was in trouble, she hopped on a plane and flew half-way around the world to help her. She loves her so much. If I had a mother that cared about me half as much as hers, I am sure I would have turned out to be a better person. But when family disappoints us, we have to turn to our friends.

I am hoping that for each apology I make in these next few days, my honesty will allow the wine to start tasting better and maybe one day the women at Netuno will call me friend again, because it is worth it. I am worth it.

Dalley

I read and re-read the blog until Ravn finally took the computer from my lap.

"Did you mean it?" he asked me with a serious tone.

"Mean what?" I answered, staring out the window.

"The apology I am assuming you made to your readers and your friends."

"Yes," I whispered quietly.

He took his finger and moved my face towards him.

"But …"

"But what?" he said forcefully.

"Maybe they won't forgive me."

"Who? Your readers or your friends?" His tone softened.

I smiled. "I can always find more readers."

"We won't know until we get there, will we. Post it when we land, and I am sure it won't be long before we find out who will and won't forgive you."

I had never had anyone walk me through a problem before. My mother always believed I should solve everything on my own, except of course when she convinced me to solve the one problem that wasn't even a problem all those years ago.

A sadness welled within me I had never felt before. When Ravn saw it, he didn't ask why. He just put his arm around me and whispered in my ear.

"Dalley, tomorrow I'll take you shopping for a new pair of shoes."

As shallow as that sounded, it wasn't. He knew me; somehow he knew just what to say. I smiled, and the sadness shifted into another part of my body. I knew it was still there, but in that moment, he gave me just what I needed. It was then I recognized what love was. For the first time in my life, I was loved.

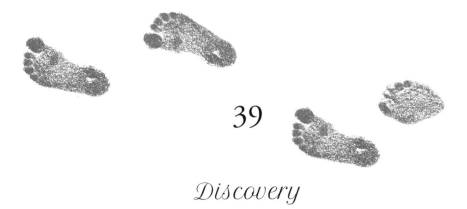

39

Discovery

Cristiano

THE ROOM WAS PERFECT. I set her down and watched her carefully as she walked around, touching the drapes and the furniture and finally resting her hand on the velvet couch. She sat down and patted the space beside her.

"Too bad it's not purple," she chuckled.

I cracked a smile, thinking back to that day in Paris at the Louvre when she and I created mayhem in the private viewing room. I looked coyly at her and sat down.

"You are not going to break me," I stated firmly.

"Why would I even try?" she said, nuzzling in closer to me.

I wanted her so badly; I wanted to take her in my arms and make love to her on that couch or wherever she would have me. As I saw her sitting there, I knew I would love her forever and would never doubt her love for me again. She had saved me twice—the first time when she spilled her cup of tea, and the second when I turned around and saw her at the crash site in Cairo.

Maya appeared to pick up on my wandering thoughts and stood up.

"I really need to take a shower. It's been a long couple of days," she offered, giving me a chance to be alone.

I sat thinking about our future, wondering what was next for us and imagining what kind of life we were going to have. It wasn't until I heard the gentle rain shower replaced with the thunderous sound of tub water that my curiosity was piqued.

There was a scuffle of feet and a few expletives that floated from under the bathroom door, which prompted me to get up and knock.

"Is everything okay in there?" I asked hesitantly.

'Oh yes, I'm so sorry," she said laughing.

"For what?"

"I was trying to be quiet, but I slipped and then couldn't find what I was looking for at first …"

"Maya, what are you doing?"

"Come in and see."

"I already told you," I said, exasperation blanketing my words.

"Oh relax, I know the rules. I kind of like them right now. Come in and see."

I walked gingerly into the bathroom and saw her lounging in the tub with bubbles covering every inch of her.

"Come, sit and talk to me," she said poking a toe out from beneath the bubbles.

She had taken every bath towel in the room and put them on the floor for me to sit on.

"Maya Wells, you are impossible."

"Yes, I know, but would you want it any other way?"

I could feel happiness radiating from all around her. She loved me. I could feel it when she looked at me and when she touched my hand.

She sat in the tub for almost an hour and while the bubbles popped, she told me more stories about her childhood. She finally told me what happened with her 'almost' arrest at the Louvre and how Pierre and Dalley helped her out of that difficult situation. When the bubbles had shrunk to a thin layer, I saw a brief reveal of the future that soon would be mine.

Maya lifted her arm out of the tub. "Can you pass me one of the towels please? As fun as this has been, my fingers have started to prune, and I am feeling a little cold."

I grabbed a towel for her and winced as I twisted my arm the wrong way while holding it up for her. I felt a spray of water and heard the slosh of her getting out of the tub. My heart smiled as she grabbed the warm fluffy fabric from me.

"Do you remember the first time you saw me in a towel?" she asked with sparkling eyes.

"How could I forget? I think that's when I knew …" I laughed, feeling my body flush with the memory.

She sighed with my answer and stepped forward, staring intently at me. I took a smaller towel and started wiping the water droplets and bubbles out of her hair. Then something shifted. It was slow at first, then the tears fell faster, and her breath started to hitch.

"Maya? What's the matter? Did I say something wrong?" She fell to the ground holding her knees and crying harder than I had ever seen anyone cry in my life. All I could do was hold her.

As the tears fell, she tried to talk but words continued to fail her.

Sometime later, when the tears stopped, she began talking. The words were slow and fragmented at first, "I thought I lost you," she uttered, shaking her hands at me. Then her hands became one pointed finger that she poked into my chest again and again. "Promise me, promise me you

330

will never leave me again. I love you Cristiano, I love all of you." Her body was shaking as she insisted that I promise.

It was I who was shaking now. "Maya Wells, I promise, I will never leave you again. I will love you with all my heart, for all my days. No more running." I pointed to my shoulder, "And about this, well, more stories for our children," I said smirking.

I wiped her tears and helped her stand, then placed a warm robe around her. We walked out to the living room.

"Rest, my love." She settled down in front of the fire and watched it carefully as the flames danced and swayed rhythmically. "Can I leave you for a few minutes to have a shower myself?"

"Yes, of course. Oh Cristiano, I feel so silly. I'm not even sure what that was all about."

"It needed to happen. By the way, can you redress my wound after I get out of the shower?"

When I stepped into the bathroom, her towel was still on the floor soaking up the last of the bubbles and tears she had shed. I picked up the towel, started to fold it, but ended up holding it close to me as I could still smell the remnants of fear and pain she had left behind.

I undressed slowly and removed the bloodied bandage from my shoulder while working through all the thoughts that whirled in my mind. As I stepped into the shower, the hot water acted like a switch. My tears fell fast and hard, and the sobs left me holding on to the shower wall. It was painful but in a strange way, it felt good.

As I dried off, I heard a small knock on the door.

"Cristiano?"

"I'll be out in a minute."

"You were in there for a long time."

"Yes, I know."

"Do you want to talk about it?" she offered.

"If you want," I said hesitantly.

She opened the door and walked in with bandages in her hand.

Her smile held me as she moved across the room, offering me her love, and her silence provided the privacy to pull myself back together as she tended to my shoulder.

೭ᛉᏅ

"You mean everything to me. I wish there were another way I could say it," I finally whispered, breaking the stillness.

"There is," she smirked. "We just decided to wait … right?"

"Yes, about that, I may have a solution to our dilemma." I took her hand and walked her back out to the couch. We cuddled under the blanket, letting some parts of our skin touch. My heart was almost beating out of my chest as she took every opportunity to press herself close to me.

"Do you have to do that?" I asked, feeling my body temperature rise.

"Yes," she said with no hint of apology. "What is your possible solution?"

I took a deep breath. "I may have a way for us to marry tomorrow."

"Tomorrow?" she said, jumping up. "That's impossible."

"No, not impossible, if you know the right people."

"And you know the right people?" She cast off the blanket and started pacing back and forth. The tie on her robe began to loosen and I sucked in a quick breath before she cinched it tight with a knot.

"I might," I said, breathing out deeply, but then she stopped. "Or not," I added. "We don't have to do anything you don't want to."

Taking me by surprise Maya jumped on me, sending us backwards into the couch "No, I don't want to wait!" she said fiercely pinning me down. "When will we know?"

"I am waiting for a call." We silently waited, excitement growing with every minute.

When the hotel line rang, we both jumped. "Are you ready?" I asked in anticipation.

"Yes, we'll either marry tomorrow or another day, right?" she declared, clearly hoping for the former. Then I saw a look of worry flash across her face.

"Maya what is it?"

"I'm just wondering how mad Beth will be if everything does work out and we can marry tomorrow."

"As soon as we know, you should call her."

The phone rang. "*Oui?*" I held the line close to my ear and listened as my new-found friends at the nunnery let me know what they were able to do.

The call only lasted for a few minutes.

"So?" she asked, shaking her hands in the air.

"Well, Maya Wells, if you still want me, tomorrow you can say yes and become Mrs. Cristiano Lazaro." I paused. "That sounds a little old fashioned."

"No, I think it's just right," she peeped in a little voice.

"Really?"

"Yes, I just have one question, well maybe two. How and where?"

"I'm not sure about the how, I left that to the nuns, but the where will be at a nunnery in El Escorial, Spain."

"Tomorrow is going to be our wedding day," she sang while twirling.

"Yes, it is."

She stopped suddenly. "I had better call Beth."

"Are you sure you don't want to talk with your parents first?" I asked, not sure if I really wanted the answer.

"No, I don't. What about you? Do you need to call anyone?"

"I do want Avo to know."

"But she doesn't have a phone," Maya looked confused.

"Yes, she does, she just doesn't tell anyone. I had it installed for her just in case I needed to call her. I am the only one who has her number. I think this counts as a need-to-call situation."

"Yes, I would agree with that."

Maya went into the bedroom to call Beth and I dialed Avo.

She picked up on the second ring.

"Avo." I heard a sigh on the other end of the phone.

"You are good," she said.

"Yes, I had to go to Cairo, just to see where it happened. Maya found me with Pierre La Nou's help. I'm so …" She didn't let me get the words out before setting into her own speech.

"I should have told you sooner. I should have told you when you were a boy; it is me who is sorry."

"You should have told me what?"

"About the adoption."

I had never heard her speak in should haves or apologies, it just wasn't part of who she was.

"Well if you can say sorry, I should be allowed to say it also. I've done enough stupid things to upset you to last a lifetime."

The silence I heard on the other end of the phone was one of contemplation.

"Yes, you're right. Did you say sorry to Maya?"

"Yes."

"Did you tell her you love her?"

"Yes."

"Did you ask her to marry you?"

At that point, I started to laugh, as I knew she knew the answer; she always knew.

"Yes, I did, and you know she said yes, too."

"Mmhh," she hummed with satisfaction.

"When?"

"Tomorrow."

"Where?"

"El Escorial."

"I'll have your room at the cottage ready for the two of you when you get home."

"Thank you," was all I could say.

"Cristiano?"

"Yes, Avo?"

"You saw where they died, touched the ground where their hearts lay."

"Yes, I did."

"They are at peace now. I can feel it. They knew you were there. I'm going to bake bread …" There was a pause. "Cristiano?"

"Yes, Avo?"

"Just a minute."

I heard some shuffling in the background and then a big crash and a bang.

"Avo? Are you okay?" I yelled into the receiver.

"Yes, yes, yes," I heard her saying as she got closer to the phone. "Pierre La Nou? That's the name you mentioned. I can't believe I forgot about it for all these years."

"Forgot about what?"

"Three weeks after your parents' death, I received a package for Pierre."

"A package? What kind of package?" I shifted, my heart rate quickening.

"It's small. It was from your parents. They sent it to the cottage before they left Egypt. I placed it in a cupboard for him, but I forgot all about it until you mentioned *his* name. Cristiano, I'm going to bake. Goodbye." And she hung up.

I was going to call her back, but my beautiful bride-to-be stepped out of the bedroom, her robe loosened just enough so I could see flashes of her glowing skin. As she stepped towards me, thoughts of Avo, Pierre, and the package were abandoned when her soft, magical lips met mine.

40

Forever and a Day

Maya

WE WOKE EARLY IN THE morning to hear a bell coming from the elevator. He smiled and wandered over as if he had been expecting someone. Cristiano entered a code and the doors slid open.

"*Bonjour* Monsieur, we have brought everything you requested. Anything you do not want, please leave on the rack." The porter smiled and stepped back into the elevator.

"What is all this?"

"We can't get married in our robes today, can we?" he asked slyly.

"No, I suppose not. The nuns may be a little offended."

"Oh, I'm not so worried about the nuns, but we are getting married without either of our mothers present. The least we can do is give them a nice photo."

I laughed a little, then sighed,. "You don't think we should wait, do you?" I asked with hesitation, hoping he would say no.

"No, we are getting married. Today is about you and me. It's as simple as that."

My heart settled, and I reached up to tug on the edge of his robe. The knot came loose, and the robe fell open.

"Oh, Cristiano," I cried out, covering my face instinctively. "I am so sorry. I was only teasing, I didn't ..."

He laughed and laughed as he pulled the robe back together and moved over to the rack. He shook his head and then motioned for me to come closer. "I didn't know you were so tricky."

"Honestly, I didn't mean ..."

"I know, I'm just teasing you. But enough of this. You have some work to do."

Somehow he had arranged for a selection of wedding clothes to be delivered to us.

I went through the rack and once again, just like that night in Paris, all his choices were flawless.

For himself he had chosen a pair of ecru-colored pants and a fitted white linen shirt. Both were perfect.

For myself, I decided to break all tradition and let *him* pick out my wedding dress. I thought he might object, but instead he turned it into a game. He had me try on each dress and model it for him. His only rule in the game was that I was not allowed to look in the mirror until he decided on the one. He hummed and hawed, taking *his* part of the game very seriously. He made me try on several dresses twice and at one point, I lost my patience and made a break for the bathroom to see my reflection. He beat me to the door and pulled me back, letting me know he was close.

Then I tried on the last gown at the end of the rack. A smile came across his face as I stood in front of him and he immediately walked me over to the full-size mirror. He had chosen well. It was the color of champagne and flowed elegantly over my body, falling just below my shins in the front and dipping slightly longer in the back with a small flare floating around me when I turned. The bodice was tight and low in the front with a simple two-piece lattice that lay across my collar bone, highlighting my tear of bravery with perfection.

"I never asked you last night how things went with Beth?"

"She was good; a little surprised, but good. She just wants me to be happy."

"And are you?"

"Happy? Yes. Forever and a day. And what about you? Are you happy?"

"I'm not sure happy really describes what I am feeling right now, but it is a good start."

"You asked about Beth. What about Avo? How did she feel about our news?" I asked with a hint of trepidation.

"One of the first questions she asked was if I had apologized to you. Once we cleared that up and had a chat about Cairo …"

I shot a look at him.

"No, I didn't tell her anything about the Ptolemites. She just wanted to know if I had made it to the site where my parents died. Then she let me know our room will be ready for us when we get home."

"Home. I like the sound of that."

"We'll have both the apartment in Lisbon and the cottage. Or I can buy us our own house if you want?"

I chuckled. "No, I think two homes are enough, don't you?"

He stroked my cheek gently. "Truth is, you're my home no matter where we are."

"Thank goodness I haven't done my makeup yet," I said, letting a few happy tears slip out.

"Well, we had better get on the road if we are going to make it to our wedding on time." We gathered our things, then stood for a moment in the beautiful suite. He looked at the velvet couch and shook his head.

"We have some unfinished business here. We are coming back one day, and soon."

I smiled, then dragged him into the elevator.

✌

The seven-hour drive became five and even those seemed to melt away as we talked through every mile. When we arrived in El Escorial, my thoughts came alive. It was like that first day in Lisbon and Paris: fresh and exciting.

"What's on your mind, Maya?" he asked, catching hold of my spike in emotion.

"The possibilities," I answered with enthusiasm.

"I like the way that sounds."

As he drove, he took one hand from the wheel and aptly pulled something from his pocket. It was a flat little piece of paper neatly folded into a square. He gave it to me while smiling.

"Think of it as your first wedding present."

I unfolded the parchment carefully and when I got to the center, there lay a charm of a gondola.

"It's beautiful, but I don't understand," I paused. "Did you find this amongst your mother's things?"

"No, it's not my mother's; it's for you. Let me explain. When I left Jack in Setubal, I headed straight for Porto. On my way, I had to stop for gas in a little town called Aveiro. I had always heard that it was like a smaller version of Venice but had never been. While I was getting fuel, it was the strangest thing, the station had a little charm bar and when I saw the gondola, I instinctively bought it for you. I didn't know if I would ever see you again, but a part of me needed to believe I would."

"Well then I guess at some point you and I are heading off to Aveiro, but I thought your dad only bought your mom a charm once they had visited a place together."

"Well, that was them and this is us. Maybe it's time for me to step away and figure out who I want to be without them. I didn't know what Cairo would mean to me before I left, but I do now. It gave me the push I needed to realize that I had become comfortable in my sadness and had allowed it to become my fallback emotion when something went wrong. No one should live that way. Do you remember that first time when our fingers touched at the airport?"

"We sparked," I said, remembering the moment.

"Yes, exactly, it was like you started my heart again. A heart that needed to heal."

"And …"

"My heart is whole now, Maya. I am whole now."

I breathed deeply, knowing I loved him, and he loved me. I carefully placed the charm on my bracelet and clasped it back on to my wrist, then I heard the faint ringing of my phone.

"Don't answer it," he insisted. "This moment is about us. We deserve a few hours to ourselves, don't we?"

I nodded, found the phone and without looking, flicked the switch over to silent.

I hesitated for a moment.

"Whatever it is, it can wait," he said leaving no room for discussion.

⁂

Cristiano parked the car in a quaint, unassuming neighborhood under a series of shade trees which protected us from the heat of the afternoon.

"We can walk from here."

He jumped out of the car and ran around to open my door.

"You don't have to do that."

"Yes, I do. This moment needs to be perfect."

"Well then, who am I to stand in the way of perfection?" I said, smiling and accepting all his love.

He took my hand and I could feel the electricity building between us; it was magical.

"What's it like?"

"What?"

"The nunnery."

"It's like being in another world or traveling back in time."

He almost glimmered as he spoke. Then he stopped and led me up a couple of stairs towards a simple stone building and knocked gently on the old wooden door; so gently in fact, I could not imagine anyone hearing it. But to my surprise, not only one set of ears were waiting but three.

The door opened and three cheerful, habit-wearing ladies took our bags and shooed us farther into their humble home. I smiled with hesitation on my lips as they separated Cristiano and I, but he just laughed and nodded.

Two of the sisters took me to a room where they pulled my wedding dress out of the garment bag and hung it in the open window, letting the afternoon sun and wind give it a natural press. They looked at my hair, then at each other; next, one of the sisters yelped in excitement and ran out of the room. On her return, she came back with branches of a plant I was not familiar with. The stock was flexible and had tiny green leaves. She carefully trimmed the branches and began weaving them together into the most beautiful and delicate wreath, then placed it on my head. I dressed, and while I did so, they cleverly attached a plethora of white silk ribbons to the back of the greenery. They had made me a veil.

Cristiano had been right: being at the nunnery was like stepping into a different time and place. It offered me a level of peace that I could wrap around my shoulders like a new cloak.

As I stood waiting for them to pin the veil into my hair, they looked down at my sandals and shook their heads, then asked me to remove them.

"Much better," one of them said. "Closer to the ground."

Although I had not noticed it before, all the nuns were barefoot.

"Closer to God," the other sister added.

It appeared I was to be married in my bare feet.

I was ready. They walked me through a series of passageways out into a beautiful fairy-like garden and like floating angels, there were twelve nuns walking on intricately woven paths, gliding by one another chanting their cannons in perfect harmony.

Then I saw him standing at the end of a path. He looked so handsome; he took my breath away. I looked down at his feet and smiled; he too was barefoot, along with the priest. I started to laugh as I could not imagine my parents' priest walking into church barefoot, let alone marrying someone with no shoes on. The moment *was* perfect, which proved to me that the world was filled with all different kinds of perfection. I looked around for the entrance to the path, to Cristiano, but found none.

"Jump," one of the sisters said with a smile. I frowned and then she made an over exaggerated leap onto one of the paths.

"Jump," she said again.

So, I hoisted my dress up and jumped as far as I could, landing solidly on the second ring. She clapped and Cristiano laughed. The chant increased in volume as I walked closer to him, and with every step I gained a strength and confidence I had never felt before.

I had no doubt about me or him and knew that no matter what was going to happen once we left our little haven, we would face it together.

When my path finally intersected with his, we stood together and the priest asked us just one question in broken English: "Are you ready to marry one another with clear hearts before God?"

We looked at each other. "Yes," we both answered.

The nuns stopped singing as the priest began the ceremony, but the song lingered in the stone walls.

One of the nuns who was standing as my witness translated the service for me quietly into my ear. She was like a little fairy, whispering a magical Spanish recipe to me.

When the priest got to the part about the rings, I froze, realizing we had forgotten. But my fairy friend pulled two rings from her pocket and handed them to us. Somehow, Cristiano had managed to procure two simple rings and have them ready for the ceremony. I sighed happily and a smile landed on his lips as he could feel my contentment.

We placed the rings on each other's hands and in an ancient part of the wedding ceremony which I had only heard about, the priest took a white linen cloth and tied our hands together. The nuns began to chant again, and we walked the paths, bound together with God. When the chanting stopped, the priest made his way over to us and untied our hands then carefully folded the cloth and handed it to me. He leaned in and whispered something into Cristiano's ear. Cristiano blushed, smiled, and nodded, then kissed me for the first time as his wife. The nuns started to titter and we both laughed.

It was time for us to leave, so we picked up our belongings, which lay on the stone bench near the exit. Our new friends walked with us to the gate and waved goodbye.

My mind was buzzing, trying to comprehend the idea that we were really married. "What do we do now?" I asked with a freshness in my tone.

"Oh, I have a few ideas," he said with shining eyes and a mischievous grin.

41

Next Exit Please

Cristiano

I HAD NEVER BEEN so nervous and excited in all my life. It wasn't as if it were my first time, but it truly felt like it.

After we said goodbye to the nuns and jumped into the car, my skin was buzzing. I felt like a teenager on his first date.

But I wasn't a teenager anymore and I wasn't on a date. I was driving in the car with my beautiful new bride. She was glowing like a star and we were both more than ready to end our game of touch and wait.

"Maya, I know this is bold but …"

"But nothing," she interrupted me.

"Oh, thank goodness," I exhaled with laughter. "I was hoping you'd say that. I honestly wasn't sure how much longer I could …"

"… wait? Well the wait is over," she whispered in my ear.

"I saw a place not far from here when we entered the city."

"Oh, so you were planning a quick exit from the nunnery before I even said I do?"

"Avo always taught me to keep my eyes open, just in case," I laughed.

"Well then remind me to thank Avo for yet another of her lessons that you listened to."

We drove in silence for several miles as we backtracked through the streets of El Escorial. Her silk ribbons were floating around her head, caught in the wind like the leaves on a fall day. When we arrived at the hotel, she waited for me to open her door.

As I held my hand out to her, I leaned over and quite innocently caught sight of the edge of her lace bra. My heart slammed against my chest.

Maya

He guided me to the registration desk and threw his credit card on the counter.

"How many nights?" The young man asked.

We both laughed. "One."

"Just married?" he asked pointing to my veil.

"Yes, thank you," he responded smiling.

"Then let me finish here quickly," he said, chuckling at Cristiano.

We stood waiting for the elevator with several other patrons, but impatience took over and I started looking for an alternative route to our room. My gaze landed on the emergency exit stairs.

"I'm game if you are," he whispered.

He sprinted past me at first.

"Whatever you do, don't fall," he shouted to me.

"I only fell down the stairs that day at Netuno because you distracted me."

He laughed, then stopped mid-stair. "Well I had better take your hand then; we don't need any mishaps."

We ran hand in hand down the hallway to our room. When he saw our door, he grabbed me and gently pushed me up against the frame. I could feel the heat of his mouth on mine, but before I even had a chance to respond, he aptly opened the lock with the other hand and pulled me inside.

His hands moved quickly and before I knew it, my champagne wedding dress became a decoration on the floor along with my lingerie. When he was done, I stood in the room wearing only my veil with its silk ribbons cascading over my shoulders. I reached to take it off, but he stopped me.

"No, leave it on. It is our wedding day."

My body flushed and quivered as he pushed himself up against me, then ran pieces of ribbon over my skin. I felt a subtle vulnerability as I stood naked in front of my new husband, but he countered my shift by taking my hands and placing them on his shirt, inviting me to start undressing him.

I slowly undid two of his buttons, trying to make the moment last but as soon as his perfectly crafted chest was exposed, an instinct kicked in that surprised both of us.

I tore open his shirt, the last four buttons flying off in every direction.

"Hey, I liked that shirt," he said, smiling.

But I couldn't respond. I was driven to see him, to touch him. With a little scuffle and shuffle, the two of us stood in front of one another wearing only our wedding rings and a few stray pieces of silk which dangled behind my back.

"Do you want me?"

I nodded my head.

"I need you to say it. I need you to tell me you want me."

"I want you. I want you to make love to me," I responded almost breathlessly. I reached out and took his hand and placed it over my heart.

"Do you feel that?"

He held one hand in place, while the other slid down my back and then swiftly made a detour around to my inner thigh. His fingers moved gently until he found what he was looking for. I gasped and he smiled.

"Yes, I would say we are both ready."

He walked me backwards to the bed and playfully pushed me down. My skin responded to every stroke and kiss until my body was shaking and burning at the same time.

"I need you!" I breathed out with urgency.

Cristiano complied swiftly.

Our pace became frenetic as our bodies connected. I dug my nails deep into his skin. As he cried out, I pulled back slightly.

"No, don't stop," he whispered into my ear.

I'm not sure how long we flipped and moved and sweated but our bodies were in complete sync. I didn't know it could be like that … every touch, every kiss, every moment.

It wasn't until the room was submerged in darkness that we realized how late it was.

"Hey, I think we missed supper," I giggled.

"I think you're right; I'm starving, and as much as I hate to say it, I think we need to get on the road and at least get across the border into Portugal tonight," he said, looking disappointed.

"Yes, your family is kind of expecting us tomorrow. I paused. "Mind you, I did say a few days didn't I? And it has only been two. How do you feel about staying incognito for another day? We have just been through two life-altering experiences and I don't think taking an extra twenty-four hours on our own is going to send up too many red flags, do you?"

"Well, if you put it that way, the only thing I really need to think about is feeding you and getting you back into bed. Room service?" he asked coyly.

"Perfect." I slipped my lingerie back on, as it was the only thing I had to wear while looking over the menu.

"Are you trying to kill me here?"

"Tease maybe, but not kill."

"Well then let's hope the food comes quickly once we order because I am starting to think that food is overrated right now."

I shook my head as he walked up behind me and started to explore the edges of my lace.

"Food, remember?"

"Oh, I'm putting you in charge of the food. Order me anything. I'm going to take a cold shower while you make me wait."

Cristiano stepped into the bathroom leaving me alone with the menu and my thoughts. For a moment I was lost in the reverie of our afternoon, then my stomach growled again.

"I heard that!" he yelled through the door. "You better order that food now."

I decided to order supper and pre-order breakfast and lunch for the next day, too. Just in case. The young man tried to stifle his laugh on the phone, but we both gave up. There was no hiding my intentions for the next twenty-four hours.

"Oh, and can you send me up a pot of tea, please?"

"Right away," the young man complied.

Cristiano came out of the bathroom just in time, as there were three quiet knocks on the door.

"You go freshen up. I'm not sure opening the door in *that* is exactly the impression we want to make on the wait staff."

"And you looking like some Adonis wearing a towel is any better?"

"Yes, it is for me anyway. I want to keep you all to myself. Is that too much for a husband to ask?"

I shook my head and went into the bathroom. When he opened the door, I heard a young lady's voice stuttering as she wheeled the cart inside.

I started to laugh, thinking about the first time I saw him, and he was completely clothed. That poor girl was getting the best show ever. At least she would have a story to tell her friends. I heard the door close and stepped outside into our room.

"Well that must have been interesting," I teased.

"Oh, it was. Hey, I signed off on a bill that included breakfast and lunch for tomorrow too. Is that correct?"

"Yes, I was thinking ahead."

"Really," he said slipping free of his towel.

"I just wanted to make the most of our bonus day."

"Hm, can you eat and make love at the same time?"

I ran from the bathroom and launched myself at him sending him backwards onto the bed.

"I'm not sure, but I'm willing to try."

❧

The night rolled into the morning and then into the afternoon. When the sun dipped below the horizon, the two of us lay quietly in bed: exhausted and completely and utterly happy. Our twenty-four hours of honeymoon bliss was over, and it was time to go meet his family.

The two of us rolled out of bed and started gathering our wedding attire. I easily slipped back into my dress but when Cristiano reached for his shirt, I cringed a bit.

"I think I may need to sew a few buttons back on."

"You think, Mrs. Lazaro?"

"Well, it could be worse. I could not know how to sew, and we would have to ask the bellman," I smirked.

"Oh, that wouldn't be so bad, I feel like I could shout from the roof-tops right now."

"I think you've already done that."

"No, I think that was you."

We found two of the missing buttons and then replaced the other two with a red one and a blue one from the bathroom sewing kit. I was not a seamstress, but they would hold until we could get him changed.

❧

"That would be two nights and *all* your room service," said the young man who had checked us in the day before.

Cristiano nodded and settled the bill, but not before I caught the unspoken exchange of acknowledgement that occurred between the two men.

I shook my head, laughing at them. "Well that wasn't awkward at all.," I said to Cristiano as I tapped on his chest.

"What? He was just congratulating me … I mean us."

"Alright, enough. We had better get on the road."

❧

Soon after we crossed into Portugal and several hours into the drive, fatigue began to show on Cristiano's face.

"It's been a long couple of days—lots of driving for you. We are about two hours outside of Porto now. Let's stop for the night."

"You want to get me back in bed, do you?"

"Yes, but this time just so you can sleep."

"Sure, that's what they all say," he gently teased.

We turned off the highway and found a little unassuming lodge.

"It's no palace, but I think you're right. I need some rest."

"I don't need anything fancy. Just a shower and a change of clothes. I think we've gotten our money's worth out of our wedding attire. Don't you?" I laughed, feeling free of worry.

He smiled. "I'll agree to retire the wedding clothes if you agree to keep that lingerie."

"I think I can manage those terms," I smirked.

"Can you grab our bags while I check in? I don't think they have a bellman here."

"Oh, that's just not acceptable," I teased.

For a brief second, he checked my face to make sure I was joking, but it did remind me that we still had a lot to learn about one another.

"I'll meet you inside," he said, gently stroking my cheek.

As I grabbed our things, I thought about checking my phone for messages but easily convinced myself that we deserved one more uninterrupted night.

42

Just as Cunning

Jade

"WEAK! I CAN'T BELIEVE DALLEY apologized for any of it. How embarrassing."

"Excuse me, Miss? Could you please lower your voice a bit?" the server asked, interrupting me.

"What the hell do you want? Just bring me my food. What is taking so long? And no, I can be as loud as I want," I shrieked.

The woman next to me stared rudely as I waited for my meal.

"Is that really necessary?" The woman asked with a strong Irish accent.

"What business is it of yours?" I hissed back at her.

"You're right dear, she really is a nasty thing," she commented to the man who sat across from her.

He smiled and stared at my cleavage, then I undid another button on my shirt just to make a point.

"If you're trying to shock me, you'll have to do better than that little girl," the man said, laughing at me.

The woman smirked. "We've been married a long time. He's allowed to look, but he knows better than to touch. Anyway, he likes them real," she said with an unpleasant smile.

I paused for a moment, looking down at the best birthday present my dad ever bought me, then scowled back at the couple.

When the waiter arrived, he dropped my food in front of me.

"Bring that to my room. I can't stand to be around any more stupid people. And make sure it is still hot when it arrives," I said, storming off.

While waiting for my food, I couldn't help but start thinking about Dalley again. Why did she apologize? Why would she want to be friends with all those women? With Maya? I pulled out my tablet.

"Let's stir things up a bit. Ruby, that's what I'll call myself."

Ruby: *Coming clean did you say, Dalley? What a load of crap. You treated them all horribly. A lame sorry on your little blog just isn't good enough for what you did to all those women, and especially Maya. And now you've included her fragile mom into the mix. It breaks my heart. Did you really say sorry in person? You said she forgave you? Are you sure? Really sure? Maybe she was just using you to find him? What are you going to do to make sure?*

"Well that should do it. I know that will irritate her. As nice as she wants to be, Dalley's ego is just about as big as mine."

There was a knock on the door and when I opened it, the young waiter from the restaurant was holding my food. He pretended to smile. I grimaced back at him, took the plate, and slammed the door in his face. I paused for a second, thinking what Hazel would do. She would be nice to everyone. But I wasn't Hazel and being mean was way more fun.

"I hate you, hate you, hate you Maya Wells!!"

During the declaration of hate, I sent my lunch flying. The plate shattered and the food splattered. It was a spectacular mess.

After taking a breath, I decided I would stay in Portugal for as long as it took to get back at Maya. I needed to show Axel how smart and ruthless I could be, and what better way to show him than to bring down the girl at the root of all my problems. He eventually would have to give me my job back, so I thought it best to move things along a bit; deciding that a well-timed text was just what my dad needed to get him started.

I can be as cunning as you. Just wait and see.

When I reopened the link to Price's Portugal, Dalley was screwed and I was so happy to be part of that. The comments were nasty, and I loved it.

Picking up the phone I demanded more room service in celebration of my little victory. "Bring me an ice-cream sundae, and it better not be melted when it gets here!"

I looked down at the blog again and found what I was hoping for. Dalley had commented back.

Dalley: *Ruby, and to the rest of you, we all make mistakes. But yes, I have taken measures to fix this situation and Maya has accepted my apology. And no, she is not plotting any revenge, that is for people like Jade. And yes, I am on my way to set things right with everyone else too, so just back off.*

Ruby: *Oh, that is so good to hear Dalley. I am sorry if I sounded harsh. I was just routing for Maya and Cristiano. I had hoped with all my heart she would find him ... Oh, and everyone else stop being so mean to Dalley. She's right. Everyone makes mistakes. So, what about Maya?*

Dalley: *I promised her I wouldn't write anything about her directly, but I am sure she wouldn't mind me letting everyone know that we found Cristiano in Egypt of all places.*

Ruby: *Sounds intriguing. I'm sure if Maya has forgiven you, she wouldn't mind you telling us more about what happened when she found him. I'm just so curious.*

Dalley: *All I can say, is that the whole thing was quite an adventure. Thank you Ruby and to all my readers. I'll make another post in a couple of days. I'm heading to Netuno for a wedding. Ciao for now.*

"Wedding? They're getting married. That's why her mom is here. Well, I wouldn't miss that event for the world. September seems like such a bad month for a wedding. So many things could go wrong. Where the hell is my ice cream?"

❧

There was a little knock on the door and when I opened it, my sundae was on the ground.

"Coward!" I yelled as I saw my waiter sprinting down the hallway.

"Enjoy!" he barked back and then laughed as he disappeared around the corner.

I climbed into bed and dove into my meal of ice cream, chocolate sauce and whipping cream. I hadn't ordered the chocolates that were sprinkled over the sundae but when I bit down on them, they popped in my mouth. It was only after I finished the sundae that I noticed a strange after taste and pulled out an insect leg that was stuck between my teeth.

"I'm going to kill that little jerk."

43

Pick up the Phone

Dalley

FLYING INTO LISBON BROUGHT BACK memories of those first few days in Portugal when I thought I knew who I was and what I was doing. By the time we landed, Ravn had stopped telling me to relax and let me spin on my own like a top.

When we arrived at the hotel, he went straight to bed. For me, however, it took some time before I could stop pacing, but when I did, I crawled in beside him. He reached over in his sleepy state and touched his fingers to mine, letting me know he was there for me. His touch was all I needed to allow my eyes and thoughts to rest at least for a little while.

When I woke, the sun was up and Ravn was dressed and having coffee at the table.

"Good afternoon sleepy head. It's 1:00 pm. I ate breakfast hours ago and am hungry for lunch. You ready to get up?"

"Yes, Ravn. I'm sorry about last night. I had too many things on my mind and could not turn it off.

He chuckled. "I know. Why don't you take a shower and put yourself together; you'll feel better."

I paused at the door. "Are you sure we can't wait until Maya and Cristiano come back from Porto before heading out to the vineyard?

"No, we can't," he said with certainty.

"Have you heard from either of them since we said goodbye at the airport?"

"Dalley, after everything they have been through, they may need a couple of days to themselves."

"I know. I just thought Maya would send me a text on how everything is going."

"Really?" he said, looking humored.

"Well, that's what friends do, isn't it?"

He laughed. "Yes, when you're fifteen. Clearly, we need to review friendship rules when you're over thirty. I'm sure she would send a note to Netuno if there were any problems. Please just take your shower, worry doesn't look good on you."

While standing in the hot water, I ignored Ravn's suggestion and allowed myself to indulge in some good old-fashioned catastrophic thinking.

"What if the Ptolemites followed us back? What if Maya and Cristiano are in trouble?"

"Ravn!" I yelled at the top of my lungs.

"What is it, Dalley?" He ran into the bathroom. "What's wrong?"

"I don't know. But could you please send Maya and Cristiano a text? I have a funny feeling."

"Well who am I to doubt one of your funny feelings," he chuckled slightly but stopped when he did not hear me laughing along.

"I'm sure everything is fine with them, but I will send them a message right now if it makes you feel better."

Ravn tried changing the subject with minimal success.

"Hey Dalley, I had a thought. Maybe we could spend the day in the city just poking around. How does that sound? We'll head out to Netuno tomorrow. That should give the ladies plenty of time to break open the case of wine and read your apology note. What do you say?"

"I say I am a little suspicious, as you are the one who was trying to get me there as soon as possible."

"Hm, maybe I was wrong, maybe it is okay to give them a little more time."

Ravn's attempt to extinguish my worry about Maya worked beautifully as he seamlessly shifted all my concerns back over to my upcoming visit at Netuno.

"What if they won't even let me in?" I yelled through the shower door, thankful that the water was masking my anxiety.

"Look Dalley, you gave them the file on Jade, you helped Maya find Pierre, and Pierre helped us find Cristiano. You are like a hero," he said with encouragement.

I smiled. "Yes, I did do all those things, but I don't think I would consider myself a hero."

"Well, you are in my book. Just finish up and we can talk more in a few minutes."

"I'm done." I turned off the water and opened the shower door.

He stared at me. "Are you okay? Why are you looking at me like that?"

"You really love me," I stated, standing dripping on the bathroom floor.

A look of relief crossed his face.

"Yes, I do. I'm delighted that you finally believe me."

"Well, miracles do happen."

"Oh, I know that, but I never thought I would see one swirling around you."

"Don't be such a jerk. Hand me a towel."

"Ah, a jerk who loves you." He wrapped the towel around me, and I followed him out of the bathroom. "Talking about jerks, have you heard back from Joe? Or from anyone about your grand blog apology?"

"You could say that." I smiled and rolled my eyes. "One reader hit a nerve last night but changed her tune really quickly. It was a bit strange," I said, biting on my nail.

"Dalley, what did you do?"

"Nothing really, I think."

He shook his head and opened the site on his tablet. He read for a minute then ran his hand through his hair.

"Well it could be worse, but *my* instincts tell me there's something off about Ruby. Please don't let her goad you into writing something you shouldn't. That is the last thing you and Maya need."

I rolled my eyes at him, knowing he was right. "Did Maya text you back yet?" I asked, changing the subject.

"No, it hasn't been that long."

"Can you please just call her?" I asked with annoyance.

"And say what? No Dalley, if you want to talk to her, you call her yourself."

"You're being mean." I stomped back into the bathroom, hair still dripping.

"Dalley, at least finish drying off. You're distracting me from being mad at you."

I spun around. "You're mad at me?" I shrieked.

"Yes, you are being very rude, and you hurt my feelings," he said, concealing a smile behind his eyes.

"Can't you see I am upset here?" I softened my position ever so slightly.

"Yes, I'm awful. You're standing in front of me dripping wet and madder than hell. I'm sorry but you are very sexy when you're mad."

Before I gave in, I pulled out my phone and dialed Maya's number, but it went straight to voicemail.

"Hi Maya, I know you are probably playing checkers somewhere in a French cottage with Cristiano, drinking wine and eating good cheese, but could you please give me a call and let me know when you will be arriving at Netuno. I could use a little moral support."

"Do you feel better now?" Ravn asked while rubbing my shoulders.

"Do you really think she's okay?" I questioned Ravn again hoping he could say something to help get rid of the feeling I was having.

"Well, I think they'll get back to us when they are free. Maybe they decided not to wait anymore. I am not sure how Cristiano managed this long."

"I don't believe it," I said, shaking my head.

"Well, believe me when I tell you. *I'm* not waiting any more. Come here right now Miss Price."

⟿

"Okay, I am officially starving now. Why don't we go out for something to eat? I've had enough room service." Ravn suggested as the two of us got dressed.

"Are you asking me out on a date?"

"Sure, Dalley, let's call it a date."

"You must really like me."

"Yes, I would say I like you very much." He laughed. "Go get ready before I leave without you."

I walked into the bathroom and looked at my dark, sleek hair, then yelled back to him, "I miss my fuchsia streaks."

"You had fuchsia streaks?" he hollered back to me. "Your hair is perfect just the way it is."

"I don't like it."

He stepped into the bathroom. "Okay, then let's go do something about it."

⁕

"So, you now have a pair of new shoes and an extremely expensive pair of boots and this is the third salon we've stepped into. Please tell me this is the one or I am going to eat one of your shoes as an appetizer," he said, scowling while reaching into my bag for a shoe.

"I'm a reasonable woman, Ravn. Why don't you leave my shoes here and go and find us some food? This place will be fine. I shouldn't be too long."

Ravn kissed my forehead and stepped out into the street. When he returned with the takeout he sat down beside me and opened up his supper. I stared at him, asking for the tenth time without words.

"Stop looking at me like that, I will check my phone in a second." He gave in and took a quick peek while slurping up a noodle.

"No, nothing yet, but that doesn't mean anything," he said with a flash of worry slipping between the words.

"What do you mean by that?" I asked, looking at him from the corner of my eye.

"Nothing, I didn't say anything," he answered hurriedly.

"It's what you didn't say that makes me nervous."

"Dalley, just finish up here. Let's eat and then we'll figure something out. Oh, by the way have you checked *your* phone?

"I didn't hear anything."

"Is your ringer on?"

"I think so," I answered hesitantly.

He grabbed my phone from my purse looking a bit perturbed. "No, it's not. You have two texts, but neither are from Maya—they're from Pierre."

"Pierre? What would he want?"

"I don't know," Ravn answered.

"Can you please call him?" I asked, starting to feel a dash of fear.

Ravn stepped outside with my phone. When he came back in, it was the first time I could see glimmers of his age as the wrinkles around his eyes looked deep with worry.

"What did Pierre say?" I asked as the fear quickly turned to nausea.

"Like us, he has texted and called them, but there has been no response for two days."

Ravn paused, looking like he was trying to find the right words to continue.

"What was he worried about, Ravn? Just tell me."

He took a deep breath. "I think he is reaching but he's concerned that maybe the …" He paused, looked around, and began to whisper, "that the Ptolemites might have followed us back."

I swallowed hard, knowing that the thought had crossed my mind too, but I had been too afraid to say it out loud.

"What was that? Right then what were you thinking about?" He jumped at me grabbing my shoulder.

Startled by his touch my thoughts fell from my lips. "Pierre might be right. Maybe the Ptolemites did follow us back, but I don't understand why. If the relic wasn't in the luggage then Cristiano's parents must have had it on the plane with them. It's as simple as that," I said, trying to convince both of us.

"There is nothing simple about any of this. The truth is, they don't know we don't have it. They might think the reason we left Egypt in such a hurry was *because* we actually found it." Ravn's tone was filled with speculation and concern.

"But we didn't …" I said, suddenly feeling uncomfortably warm.

"Dalley, that's the point. They don't know that. They knew we were in Egypt. They have resources, and I can guarantee you that right now they are searching for every piece of information they can find on all of us. I want you to think back. In your last blog did you mention anything about Netuno or Cairo?"

I became flustered. "I might have, you read it!" I started to feel sick again. "In the comments, I told Ruby that I helped Maya find Cristiano and we all got out of Egypt safely...and that I was going to Netuno for a wedding. Ravn, do you think they could be here? On their way to Netuno?"

"I don't know that, but I do know we are driving out to Netuno first thing in the morning."

"Ravn, what if it's true?"

"Then we are going to need some help," he offered with a weak and worried smile.

Ravn convinced me to try and get some rest, but at about 3 a.m. I gave up. That's when I found him on the couch researching Pierre's theory and breaking down every electronic door to find Maya and Cristiano.

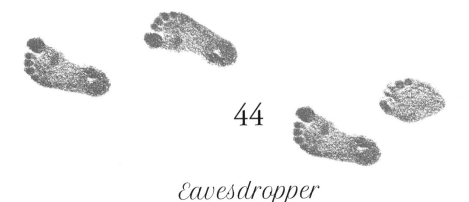

44

Eavesdropper

Jade

IT HAD BEEN SEVERAL DAYS since I'd arrived in Lisbon and my only source of entertainment was pretending to be Ruby. I couldn't afford to move hotels, so poking Dalley became my source of fun. But when she stopped responding, I wondered if she had figured out who I was.

"Well, what am I supposed to do now?" I asked myself as the sun came up again. It was time to start focusing on Maya and what I was going to do next. I needed to eat though, as my dad always told me never create a revenge plan on an empty stomach. So, I put myself together and headed downstairs to consume another subpar hotel meal.

While I was arguing with my waiter about my order, I turned around when I heard a familiar laugh. The voice was the same, but she looked so different. Her hair was dark, but the fuchsia streak gave her away. It was Dalley, and she was standing at the front desk with a very rugged looking older man. He had his hand resting on the small of her back.

"What are you doing here?" I whispered in her direction.

"I am trying to take your order?" My waiter responded with annoyance.

"I am not talking to you. Just bring me three waffles, not two, and I want *four* pieces of bacon and hot chocolate with whipping cream."

"Sure, Miss Axeline, whatever you want. We do have a fit meal if you prefer?"

"Leave me alone." *Was he calling me fat?* Then I heard the laugh again: familiar, forced. I casually got up from my table and snuck behind a plant.

"Ravn, did you find them? Are they safe? Any news about the Ptolemites? I can't believe that they could have actually followed us back."

"No news on our Egyptian friends and not much on Maya and Cristiano either. I called in a favor and tracked them down to a hotel in France and then in Spain. But after that—nothing. My Spanish is a little rusty, but the fellow at the hotel in Spain said something about them being in costume? And hiding away I think? It was quite confusing."

"Hiding? Why would they be hiding?" Dalley asked, looking panicked.

"Don't get ahead of yourself. I don't know what's going on but I'm sure they just took a couple extra days while on their way to Porto."

"I don't know, none of this feels right," Dalley said with concern.

My waiter tapped me on the shoulder, startling me. "Miss Axeline, your food is on the table."

"Shh!" I said as I whipped around. "I am never going to give you a tip."

"Oh, don't worry," he responded sarcastically. "I'm not expecting one. All the other guests are paying me extra to get you out of the café as soon as possible. I can put your food into piggy bag if you want."

"A piggy bag? That's it! Are you calling me fat?"

"Oh, I wouldn't say fat, but those pants might not be able to hold the extra bacon and whipping cream," he said as he walked away laughing.

"Leave me alone!" I shouted at him as I heard my stepmother's voice reminding me what I needed to do to stay a size zero.

My heart pounded as I fought to forget and forced my thoughts back to Dalley. "Porto?" I asked myself. "Why are they on their way to Porto? What about their wedding?" As I tried to work through what I had heard, something was bothering me; the man's voice, it was so familiar. I slowed down and filtered through my drunken memories. Then it hit me. "The journalist on the phone, it was him. You're more cunning than I gave you credit for, Dalley, but now I know they're not at Netuno. Hiding from a group of Egyptians? The Ptolemites? Who the hell are they?"

When I turned back around, Dalley and the man were gone.

"*Merde!*" I snarled to myself and then walked over to the front desk. I put on my best fake worried look. "Oh no, I hope you can help me. My friend Dalley Price was just here with the tall gentleman. Last night when we were having drinks, she lent me some money and I need to pay her back. Where are they going? Maybe I could catch up and surprise her."

"You'll need to hurry. They just checked out and rented a car. They mentioned they were on their way to Netuno. Are you familiar with the winery? It has become quite popular in the last few days. I could call and book you a room at the inn if you want?"

"No!" I screeched at him, breaking my concerned friend face and feeling more like myself.

"No, I wouldn't stay overnight at Netuno if it was the last place on Earth, but a little visit wouldn't hurt. I need to check out. I'll be back down with my bags in one hour. Have a car and driver ready for me."

The phone rang three times before I heard his voice.

"Why, hello Jade. I'm surprised to hear from you. I thought we decided it was best if we didn't speak anymore outside of the office."

"Why? Am I not allowed to phone a friend in my time of need?"

"Are we friends now? Is that what we are calling it?"

"Of course we're friends, why wouldn't we be?" I said, pouring on the sarcasm.

"Stop it, Jade. I thought we decided it was in both our interests to forget about that weekend at the lake house."

"Oh, you mean my dad's lake house?"

"Jade, you know exactly what I'm talking about."

"Yes, I do. What do you take me for? I'm not an idiot. He may have fired me, but I am still his daughter. What do you think he would do if he found out his most trusted employee of thirty years was screwing his vulnerable daughter?"

"Daughter yes, vulnerable no. Truthfully Jade, I'd say we both have a 50/50 chance of coming out on top. But since he is already pissed at you for ruining the Netuno deal, and with his mood today, maybe it's tipping 70/30 in my favor. So, what do you want because blackmail isn't going to work this time; your father needs me more than he needs you right now."

I paused for a moment to recalibrate.

"I forgot why I agreed to screw you in the first place. Oh yeah, that's right. I needed to make sure I had a favor banked for when I needed it," I spat back at him, pulling out all the stops.

"What did I just say about your dad?"

"Oh, I'm not worried about him. You are right, business always comes first, but your wife on the other hand might be curious to find out where you were last Valentine's Day."

There was a long pause on the end of the line, and it appeared I was getting through to my dad's old friend Richard.

"Jade what do you want? I had to step out of a meeting with your dad. He's waiting."

"Oh, let him wait. You can tell him it was your girlfriend. I need a favor. I need an introduction with some Egyptians. They call themselves the Ptolemites?"

"No," he answered crisply.

"No, you can't? Or no you won't?" I said, raising my voice.

"No, I won't. It's one thing having sex with the boss's daughter, but getting you killed would surely get me fired. It's best if you just leave them alone."

"So, you do know who they are?"

"Only by reputation. Your father and I ran into a business associate of theirs a few years ago. Let's just say, it didn't turn out so well for him. Jade, your dad would not want you doing business with them. If you really need something, I am sure he will help you find it."

"I don't need his help, I need yours."

"What is this about?"

"I have something I think they want—or someone, to be more specific."

"Jade, for the record, I don't think this is a good idea. Maybe we should run it by your dad?"

"Richard, just do what I say, and you may still have a marriage to go back to."

"God, you are more like your dad than he realizes."

"Call me when you have the introduction set up. Let them know I am in Lisbon."

"I'm warning you Jade; these guys are dangerous."

"Don't try and scare me. I know how to handle myself. I'm Jade Axeline."

"Yeah, not sure that's going to help you this time. I'll text you with the time and place."

45

One Red Button

Maya

IT MUST HAVE BEEN CLOSE to 4:30 in the morning when I opened my eyes and saw him sleeping peacefully beside me. The dawn was just starting to take over the evening darkness, and in that moment all I could feel was joy. I stared at my ring finger and could hardly believe that somehow I was forever connected to the man who slept just inches away from me. I placed my hand on his bare chest and could feel his heart beating under my fingertips. His body fluttered under my touch and my heart raced just to see him move.

I remember stepping into the lobby the night before, holding our bags. He was at the front desk trying to check in, but the young woman standing behind the counter appeared to be tongue-tied. She just kept nodding her head every time he spoke.

I dropped the bags and the girl's eyes shifted from staring at him over to me. His gaze followed hers and he broke into the largest smile. He was beaming. I had never seen anyone so happy to see me before. The girl handed him the key and watched him dreamily as he walked over, picked up our bags, and kissed me on the cheek. I smiled at the young lady and she blushed.

Once inside our room, he placed his finger over my lips motioning for me not to speak. He then stepped behind me and slowly unfastened my dress and scanty silks, leaving me naked and waiting.

My body shook with anticipation as I waited for his next move. When he finally let me turn around, I found him standing one step away from me, bare and vulnerable; I took the hand he held out for me and followed him into the bathroom.

Turning on the water he tested it until satisfied with the temperature. "I have dreamt about this moment since that night in Paris. I had to use every ounce of my restraint not to join you then. But now, it's all coming true. This is the most wonderful day of my life."

I was speechless. I was joyful. We stepped into the shower and let the water fall over the two of us as he held me tightly. He caressed my skin so softly I wasn't sure if it was the water or his fingertips that gave me the goosebumps. As his lips touched my neck and gently traveled down my collar bone, my nerve endings came alive and I knew it was all him. We played a game of kiss and touch and it was not until I felt a splash of cold-water rain down over our heads that I said my first word of the night.

"Cold!" I shrieked.

He laughed then turned off the water.

We jumped out of the shower and climbed into bed. I saw the look of love in his eyes and then a little yawn betrayed him.

"Cristiano, you are exhausted."

"No, I'm good."

"I know you are good, but you've been traveling non-stop for days. Maybe we should just get some sleep."

"No, no, no," he fought me. "I'm ..." and he yawned again.

"You're done for the day," I answered with a certainty he could not refute.

"Really? You don't mind?" he said, giving in more easily.

"No, I don't," I whispered back to him, moving his curls out of his eyes.

He pulled me in, our warm damp bodies touching under the sheets. It only took a few more moments until I heard his breath change, and he was fast asleep.

I fell into a light slumber myself, letting the perfection of the evening envelope me. I drifted in and out for hours, deep sleep never quite taking hold.

When I woke and saw the light shifting ever so slightly outside, I peeled our bodies apart and unwound his fingers from my hair. As I rolled skillfully out of bed, I went in search of Christopher, a sharp pencil, and Cristiano's wedding shirt from the floor. Doing up the buttons, I laughed as my fingers lingered on the red one. The linen held his scent as if he were standing beside me and I breathed in memories of our barefooted garden wedding. Sneaking back into the bedroom I curled up on the chair that sat opposite to where he slept.

Day three as Mrs. Lazaro

I love watching him sleep. Something so simple but it is everything. Right now, the light of the early dawn is arguing with the moon, each one offering me a splash of light over my page. I'm not sure which one I want more; to hold on to our night or to step bravely into the new day. Maybe a little bit of both?

As much as I want all my thoughts to be about him right now though, I am wondering how my parents are going to react when I tell them about the wedding.

Maybe we should not tell them right away? Oh, that is stupid. We already told Beth and Avo.

I have nothing to be worried about. It is my life. I stopped one marriage that wasn't supposed to happen and stepped eyes wide open into another that was meant to be. I have experienced more love, life, and passion with Cristiano in the last month than I ... well Steven and I had none of that.

But here I am...

Sitting half naked in a chair watching my husband sleep. He is so handsome I can hardly believe some days that he wanted me. I can feel something shifting inside me right now. The other night when we made love for the first time, it was frenetic, followed by 24 hours of crazy passion. I just want to slow things down, but how do I ask for that.

I feel so silly

"Tell me what you're thinking about that has caused that crinkle in your forehead?" he asked, interrupting my argument.

"You're awake!" My nerves bristled and embarrassment trickled out of my tone as if he knew what I was thinking.

"Yes, I'm awake. I turned over and didn't feel you next to me, and then there you were, sitting in the chair, wearing nothing but my shirt and a frown. I cannot imagine what has you looking so distressed. A secret perhaps?" He chuckled.

I sighed. "No, no more secrets."

"Tell me," he said sitting up.

"It's early, you should get more rest," I suggested.

"No, I've slept enough, tell me," he said coyly.

I half covered my face and very quietly whispered, "Slowly."

"Slowly, what?" he asked.

I felt the heat in my face rise, as I had never asked for anything like that before in my life. I put my shaking hands down and took a breath. "This morning can we make love more slowly, take our time?"

"Oh, Maya," he laughed. "Come here. You look too good in my shirt to be sitting there all by yourself. And yes of course, as of this moment, time doesn't exist," he said lifting the sheets.

I made my way over to the bed, crawled in, and buried my face into his chest.

"That's much better. If I had known that was all it was going to take to get rid of that frown, I would have offered sooner," he said, running his finger over my now unwrinkled forehead.

I leaned in and brushed my lips over his. "I love you."

"I love you," he whispered back.

In one stealth movement, he sat me up and slowly started unbuttoning his shirt, but at button three he looked at me and smiled, "What the hell!" He laughed and ripped the shirt open. The buttons once again went flying around another room. "No hotel sewing kit will ever fix this shirt again," he said, shrugging his shoulders.

"That was slow?"

"Well maybe not, but … you are so beautiful," he whispered as he ran his fingers gently against my skin. "Better?"

I nodded. At first, I felt breathless under his touch and wanted to change my mind. I wanted him to take me, but then something shifted. His eyes became shy and he hesitated just long enough for me to take control.

"Don't move," I directed. His eyes smiled and danced, as I moved around him on the bed laying gentle kisses on his quivering body. His frame was still but his heart was beating so fast I could see his chest tremble just at the thought of where I might touch him next. He tried to speak, but I placed one finger on *his* lips and the other on his thigh, edging slowly upwards.

I had never taken charge before. I felt so alive. I knew our moments of touch and kiss were just about over though, as I felt a restlessness growing within him.

"Now," was the only word he needed to hear.

He pulled me in and started with a kiss that left me gasping for air and craving for more. It was then I released myself from any notion that I might be able to control *any* of what was about to happen next.

I offered myself over to him and he took me without hesitation, honoring every curve and crevice he could find. He paused briefly, staring deep into my eyes, stroking my skin with an open invitation.

"Yes," was all I could gasp.

"Yes, what?" he said as he smiled, and his fingers slowly moved up my thigh following one direct path.

"Yes, take me," I said with a little more urgency.

"Take you where?" Now he was playing.

"Anywhere, as long as we go together," I puffed breathlessly.

He smirked. "That's the plan." His fingers continued to climb.

He was incredible, every look, every touch.

Our bodies connected like the last two pieces of a puzzle; everything made sense. Making love to him was as natural as breathing.

"I love you, Maya."

In response, my fingers dug into his back. We made love until the room was engulfed in sunlight and our happiness had been elevated to pure bliss.

☙

"I, I wasn't expecting that," he gasped, trying to catch his breath. "You continue to surprise me, Mrs. Lazaro."

I blushed, feeling excited that somehow I had given him something he wasn't expecting.

We lay peacefully beside one another for several minutes, until he abruptly hauled himself up in bed.

"What is it?" I asked.

"Maya, it's been three days since we spoke with anyone. It might be time to break our silence and reconnect with the world."

"Really? Can't we have just one more day?" I whined.

"No, I'm thinking we've probably maxed out our alone time, for now."

"I am worried what our families are going to do when they find out about the wedding," I said. "Maybe we should call Jacinta first. She could break the news to all our parents."

"Maya do you really think they are going to be angry?" he asked, scrunching up his face and biting his bottom lip.

"Maybe not yours, but mine might be a little perturbed. My dad was already acting strange on the phone the last time we spoke."

We both took a deep breath.

"Well at least one good thing has come out of this conversation. Now I know what your worried face looks like," I said with a shrug of my shoulders.

"Do you still love me?" he asked, rolling his eyes.

"I love you no matter what you look like, as long as you never lose your charm."

"Well then, I guess I'll just have to win them all over with my charm."

"Not sure that is going to work on my dad. But first things first. Your family *was* expecting us yesterday. They might be a little worried."

"Alright then, here's the plan. Let's get some breakfast, check our messages, and text our families. Can you send a message to my sister? That way she'll let my parents know we are on our way." He paused. "Where do you think I should meet them?"

"The house seems like a good idea, unless you want somewhere more neutral."

"No, I think the house is good," he said, biting his lip again. "That way if anything goes wrong, we can just get up and leave and there'll be no audience."

"Cristiano nothing is going to go wrong. They love you; they just want a chance to meet you."

46

The Text Moment

Cristiano

I WATCHED MY LOVELY WIFE as she puzzled over the menu trying to figure out which item was which.

"You do know that you're going to have to learn Portuguese now, right?"

She looked at me, slightly horrified. "Oh yeah, I guess you're right. I imagine there are lots of things we still have to figure out, but for now, I'll use Google translate so I don't end up with liver for breakfast."

We both laughed as she rifled through her bag looking for her phone and I heard something clink.

"What do you have in there?"

"Oh yeah, I borrowed this from your place," she said, smiling.

She went into her bag and pulled out one of my laughter jars from when I was a child with Avo. "You've been carrying that around all this time? Porto? Paris? Cairo?"

"Yeah, I have. I thought we might need it. Silly, I know."

She handed me the jar and I read the label out loud., "Open in case of a Laughter Emergency." I smiled and added, "No not silly at all."

"The phone is taking forever to boot up, maybe you can order for me just this once?" She asked, batting her eyelashes."

"How could I refuse?" I smiled.

As we waited, I was thinking that I should give Jack a call and get my phone back from him as soon as possible. I heard the ping of a text message come through on her phone, then another and another.

"So, what's that all about?"

"Not sure," she half-laughed, staring at the screen. "Looks like …" Her face went pale and her hands started to shake. "Seventeen text messages and nine phone calls," she managed to get out. "Cristiano, I think we're in trouble." She wasn't laughing anymore.

I tried to keep things light. "What kind of trouble could we have gotten into in three days? We haven't spoken to anyone."

"Yeah, that appears to be the problem. There are messages from everyone. They think something has happened to us."

I paused for a moment, trying to figure out what to do.

"Here," I said, holding out my hand. "Let me go through the messages. I'm the one who told you to turn off your phone."

"Yes, but I'm the one who pushed the button," she said with a deep sigh. I could see a layer of worry come across her face.

"Why don't we get our food to go and we can call everyone back once we are on the road."

Maya went to the bathroom, and as I waited for the food, I quickly scanned the texts and listened to the phone messages. The last three were from Maya's father.

"What is it?" Maya asked as she approached me.

"Well, it all started with Pierre and Dalley. When neither of them heard back from us, they jumped to a few conclusions and began to speculate if the Ptolemites followed us back here and if we were in trouble."

"The Ptolemites?" she gasped. "That's not possible."

"I don't know, Maya. But I do know that everyone thinks something is wrong."

"When you say everyone, who do you mean?"

"Well from what it sounds like, by the time Ravn and Dalley arrived at Netuno they were convinced that something bad had happened to us and set off a series of alarm bells. Next your dad called Beth, Puro went to see Avo, and Jack called my parents."

"So, basically, everyone either thinks we're in trouble or ran off after we eloped. I can only assume they all know what happened in Egypt?"

"I think that would be a safe thing to assume."

Maya's face hardened. "Cristiano, let's just go."

I grabbed the food and we headed out to the car.

"My dad called three times?" she asked, looking at her phone.

"Yes, and it appears there is one more complication that has arisen." She looked at me with annoyance.

"When Dalley and Ravn arrived at Netuno, an old classmate of ours, Luca Palito, was already there to help with Carmo and Bento's wedding."

"Yes, actually I met Luca on the Friday night after you left." She paused. "He was very kind. He helped me ..."

"Helped you how?" I felt a little sting of jealously and embarrassment having to ask.

"Doesn't matter right now. What matters is that I know he's with the police, international crimes if I remember correctly. So, if he was there when Dalley and Ravn arrived, this has truly turned into a *situation*." I saw her hands shake and her face flush.

"Are you okay?" I asked, reaching out to her.

"I don't know," she said, pushing my hand away as we walked to the car.

"Maya, it's going to be okay," I said, trying to reassure her.

She turned around and snapped at me, "Which part? The part where we were almost killed by fanatics three days ago? Or the part where everyone thinks we've disappeared? Or maybe the part where those crazy people could actually have followed us back. Not to mention that this was not the way I wanted our families to find out about us getting married!" She got into the car and slammed her door.

"Maya, I'm already on top of it. I texted Puro and Jacinta to let them know we are safe and asked if they could let everyone know we would call them shortly.

"Oh," was all she said.

"Maya, everything is going to be fine, you'll see; nothing is going to happen to either of us. I promise."

She stared deep into my eyes, looking for reassurance. I would never say it out loud, but a part of me wondered whether the Ptolemites *would* at some point in the future come looking for the relic.

"Maya, there is no way those guys could get into the country. Besides, I think my sister and your dad are the two scariest people we will have to deal with today," I laughed trying to hide my nerves.

As we turned onto a back road that led towards Porto, Maya's phone began to ping.

"Which one is it?" I asked with a little smile.

"My dad. He's insisting I call him right now," she said with annoyance.

"I'm sure he is upset. I would be too if I just found out my daughter had been in a life-threatening situation and then eloped twenty-four hours later."

"Why is he being such a jerk?"

"Maya, he's not being a jerk, he's being a dad. Call him."

As we sped down the road, I was hit with the most uncomfortable feeling. I pushed it off, not wanting to worry Maya any more than she already was but I couldn't shake the sense that something bad was coming.

She dialed her father and waited for him to pick up.

"Dad? It's Maya and before you say a word, Cristiano and I are safe." She was quiet for a long time, and I saw her nodding her head at first. "Yes, I am fine." Then her face wrinkled up and I could see the color in her cheeks popping out. "Mom wanted me to find him. NO! I was not being irresponsible by quitting my job." There was another a long pause. I wished I could hear what he was saying. Then I saw the tears well in her eyes; they were not happy tears. I went to reach for her hand, but she pulled away suddenly, crying out loudly, "NO! No. You're wrong, I did not make a mistake. This was … this is the best decision I have ever made in my life." Then the color drained from her face and she stopped yelling and started whispering, "What are you talking about, Dad? We are too." Silence. "God said so! Well, you're wrong!" she yelled back at him. "And no, I am not going back," she said with ultimate defiance. "I love him, and he *is* my husband and it doesn't matter what you or they say," she screamed into the receiver.

She was shaking so hard I could hardly keep my eye on the road. "Maya, what is it? What's wrong?"

Then it happened, the car came out of nowhere. One shot and the windshield shattered. I swerved but it was too late.

Epilogue

Cristiano

ALL I COULD HEAR WERE unfamiliar voices. I could see her face, but she was covered in blood. When I reached for her, my body screamed in retaliation and I fell back into the darkness.

I wasn't sure if it had been an hour or a week, but when the black turned to grey, I could hear the voices again.

"Cristiano! Where is Maya?" he yelled at me.

"Please don't yell at him like that!" a woman entreated.

"Let's all just calm down. We have been up for days," said another voice. "It might be best for everyone to go. Avo and I will stay with him."

"Days?" I thought. "What was he talking about?"

"When he wakes up, we'll find out more," he said, trying to calm the other male voice. "We'll find her."

Then I smelt it, a scent so familiar it was like coming home. I pushed out of the darkness and with a last effort opened my eyes.

I was in a room, a hospital room. It was filled with people I didn't know except for Avo and Puro. Avo was standing beside me with a loaf of bread resting in her arms. I tried to smile but the pain was staggering. My body pushed back into the mattress and one of the women standing near Avo gasped, then took my hand.

"Hush, my son," she said, squeezing my fingers intensely. I looked at her and my heart lurched forward. I recognized her from the balcony. It was Euphemia, my mother.

"Don't move dear, you've been in an accident."

My eyes darted around the room looking for Maya. All I could remember was the windshield shattering into a thousand glass knives. I had failed her again.

"Cristiano," Euphemia said quietly. "Where is Maya? When the ambulance and police arrived at the accident, they said she was gone, and the passenger seat was covered in blood. Maya's father said he was on the phone with her when it happened."

My heart raced and my thoughts bounced back and forth. I pushed through the pain to answer my mother's question. "She was crying, her father said something to make her cry." I could feel my body start to shake; it was like I was freezing to death. "Bleeding, she was bleeding and in pain. I tried to move, to help her, but I couldn't. They pushed me forward and grabbed my parent's suitcase. I didn't understand what they were saying. They were yelling so loud." My teeth started to chatter. Another flash of memory hit me. "They pulled her out," panic pressed through my veins, "Where is Maya? Where is my wife?" I managed to utter.

The man pushed passed my mother and Avo, yelling at me once again. "Wife? She is *not* your wife."

"Phillip, this is not the time for *that* conversation," another woman interjected.

"Where is Maya, Cristiano? Where is my daughter?" he cried out, raising his fist at me.

I deserved whatever pain he was about to inflict but by the time he landed the second punch my body betrayed me and plunged me back into the darkness, but not before I managed one last whisper, "It was no accident, they're here!"

Acknowledgments

First, I want to thank Karen Deise for reminding me of the power of standing barefoot in the dirt and how that single action can help you find the answers you're looking for to almost any question.

To Liz Warwick, my editor, as she helped shape the book by always asking the hard questions. Nada Orlic, whose gentle heart and great patience created book covers that brought The Vinho Verde Trilogy to life. Ben Kelley, whose keen eye and diligent work ethic helped me with the final proofing and formatting of the manuscript and my beta readers who took the time to highlight and comment on my story, giving me honest feedback and inspiring me to be a better writer.

And for my family: my mother who listened to my story during her last hours, my golden doodle Lily who got me out of bed every day at the crack of dawn to write, my son, who made me take a breath when I needed it most and my husband who loves me, and accepts all the crazy and colorful parts of being married to a writer.

INSIDE THE WIND

The Vinho Verde Trilogy

❧

Book III

Coming 2022

Separated by distance and evil intention Maya and Cristiano are confronted with their greatest obstacle yet. Time is running out as both of them are forced to come face to face with their deepest fears if they have any chance of finding a way back to each other.

Maya awakens in excruciating pain, covered in bandages and feeling an arid heat of a foreign nation. As she struggles to comprehend her circumstances her memory takes her back to the final moments before the windshield shattered. She was yelling at her father, refusing to accept the truth he threw at her. But where is she now? Where is Cristiano? And why can't she see?

Confronted in the hospital by a room filled with strangers Cristiano is forced to deal with the new reality that his wife is missing, his body is broken, and his promise to Maya has been shattered. He must learn to trust his newfound family, friends and especially himself if he has any chance of finding her and saving their future.

⸎

Join Oucharek-Deo in the final book of the Vinho Verde Trilogy as *Inside the Wind* takes you on the next part of Maya's and Cristiano's life journey. This novel not only seeks to discover the true value of defending and fighting for love, but it also means to push back against the self-doubt and fear that stop us from taking the next steps on our own adventures, no matter where it leads us.

Check out Michelle's website and subscribe to her newsletter for special story reveals, contests and live link events, exclusive to her subscriber list www.michelleoucharekdeo.com

Author's Notes

'You're stronger than you think.' That was the inspirational phrase that a friend offered me the other day in addition to likening my personality to that of the roman emperor and stoic philosopher Marcus Aurelius. I laughed at first until I started doing some research and realized that my friend might know me better than I thought. The encounter reminded me of a conversation I had with my father many years ago. He spoke about the importance of choosing the right friends and how if you invite good people into your life, that a good life is sure to follow. During the writing of *Barefoot in the Dirt* I put my father's words into action creating a circle of support that guided me through both calm and bumpy waters and I am forever grateful.

I welcome you to join me on my website www.michelleoucharekdeo.com and subscribe to my mailing list as well as follow me on Instagram @moucharekauthor and Facebook @michelleoucharekdeoauthor and take part in my journey as I write new stories, paint new images, and keep my garden growing.

Until next time,

Michelle

Manufactured by Amazon.ca
Bolton, ON

18110517R00236